GOOD HOUSEKEEPING

COMBINATION *AND* MICROWAVE COOKING

WHSMITH

EXCLUSIVE
·BOOKS·

Published by Ebury Press for WH Smith, Greenbridge Road,
Swindon, Wiltshire, SN3 3LD
Ebury Press is an imprint of the Random Century Group Ltd.,
Random Century House, 20 Vauxhall Bridge Road, London SW1V 2SA

ISBN 0 85223 932 7

Editor: Felicity Jackson
Design: Peartree Design Associates
Typeset in England by SX Composing, Rayleigh
Printed in Hong Kong

CONTENTS

INTRODUCTION

The main advantage of microwave cooking is speed, and many foods are not only cooked more quickly but can also be cooked more healthily than by some conventional means. Fish and vegetables retain their shape, texture and flavour far more when cooked in the microwave.

However, the nature of microwave cooking means that foods do not have the familiar brown and crispy finish we all find so appetising. Many favourite foods, such as pies and pastries, cannot be cooked successfully by microwave alone. The answer to these problems has now arrived – the combination oven.

A combination oven has the advantage that it cooks food in about half the normal time and browns it as well. This is really exciting for those who love good food but want it quickly. With a combination oven you have all the benefits of three different cooking methods at your fingertips – a microwave to cook fish, vegetables and fruit to perfection, as well as to thaw and reheat foods; a convection oven for your own tried and tested recipes; a combination of the two for cooking, roasting, baking and lots more exciting recipes.

This book contains a stunning selection of recipes, everything from starters and main courses to vegetables and desserts, cakes and biscuits – some of which can be cooked simply using the microwave and others that use the convection and combination methods to achieve the best results.

Chicken Fricassée; Okra with Coconut

UNDERSTANDING A COMBINATION OVEN

A combination oven is usually a countertop oven about the same size as a large microwave cooker. It combines several methods of cooking in one unit and these methods can be used on their own or in combination with one another. The difficulty is deciding which method is best for which food. Below, each method is explained in turn, with advice on which foods they are best suited to.

CONVECTION COOKING
(also known as 'turbo' or 'conventional heat')
This method of cooking is the same as cooking in an ordinary electric oven. The convection system in most combination ovens is fan assisted, that is the hot air is circulated in the oven by a fan. This has the effect of speeding up the cooking process, so if you are cooking recipes designed for cooking in an ordinary oven, you will need to reduce the temperature by 10°C. The heat controls on all combination ovens are given in °C, so follow the chart below if you usually cook in Fahrenheit or by gas.

OVEN TEMPERATURE SCALES

°Celsius Scale	Electric Scale °F	Gas Oven Marks
110	225	¼
130	250	½
140	275	1
150	300	2
170	325	3
180	350	4
190	375	5
200	400	6
220	425	7
230	450	8
240	475	9

The capacity of most combination ovens is less than a conventional oven (with the exception of the three full-size combination ovens on the market) and space is limited for cooking batches of biscuits or cakes, for example, to be cooked on convection.

When using the convection setting, better results are obtained if the oven is preheated. Ten minutes is long enough for most ovens, but check your manufacturer's handbook as it may recommend longer preheating. The temperature range on most combination ovens is from 40-250°C, but if your oven has a limited range, choose the temperature nearest the one you need and adjust the cooking time accordingly.

HALOGEN HEAT
Some combination ovens use halogen heat as an alternative to the convection method. Heat is created by halogen gas-filled bulbs in the top and sides of the oven. These emit heat and light.

MICROWAVE COOKING
The microwave system in a combination oven is the same as in a microwave cooker. Microwaves are high-frequency electromagnetic rays. They can either be reflected, transmitted or absorbed by things with which they come into contact. They cannot penetrate metal (so they can't get out of the oven) but they pass straight through glass, wood and ceramics. This is why it is important to remember not to use metal dishes when cooking by microwave.

When the microwaves come into contact with food, they are attracted to the water molecules, causing them to vibrate at an incredibly high speed. This vibration creates friction, which produces heat and cooks food.

Most combination ovens have several microwave settings but some have only DEFROST and HIGH settings. Although the HIGH setting on most combination ovens is 600-650 watts, equivalent to the HIGH setting on most top-of-the-range microwave cookers on the market, some models may take slightly longer to cook (consult your manufacturer's instructions).

Use the microwave setting for moist methods of cooking, such as poaching, or whenever you don't expect a crisp crust or a brown appearance. It is good for fish, vegetables, fruit, soups, rice and pasta as well as for thawing and reheating.

COMBINATION COOKING
(also known as 'Hi-speed' or 'dual cook')
This is a combination of convected heat and microwave energy, thus combining the advantages of both cooking methods; the speed of microwave energy with the browning and crisping effects of hot air. To cook on combination, you must first set the temperature in °C for the convection system, and then set the microwave level. Some books and manufacturers generally recommend cooking on a HIGH microwave setting and at

250°C. This certainly cooks the food quickly but it can dry out and burn on the outside when this combination of settings is used. The combination of 200°C/MEDIUM LOW is preferable. On some ovens, the combination setting is preset. This means that you can change the temperature but not the microwave output, making it harder to cook some foods on combination.

Achieving the correct combination of convected heat and microwave energy is very important and can be quite difficult to understand (see right). Recipes cooked on combination are marked with a ▣ symbol.

GRILLING

Some models of combination oven have a grill element installed in the roof of the oven. On some models, this can be used in conjunction with microwave energy for quick cooking (and browning) of chops and sausages.

SPECIAL FEATURES OF COMBINATION OVENS

Below is a brief summary of the overwhelming range of features offered by some models of combination oven.

AUTO COOK/SENSOR DEVICES

The operation of these devices varies from model to model. They are a more advanced and versatile version of the probe available with some microwave cookers.

Auto cook (called 'sensor cook' on some models) works in one of two ways:
Humidity sensors, located in the oven roof, are triggered when steam is released from the food. Once the steam activates the sensor, the food is cooked for a calculated and preset time – the time the food takes to produce steam will vary according to its quantity. It is essential to cover food closely with a well fitting lid and to avoid opening the door during the initial build up of steam. Once sufficient steam has built up, the lid will lift and the sensor will be activated. If the food is not covered effectively, the lid will lift too early and the food will be undercooked. Since the cooking time is preset, the auto cook facility on most ovens is supplemented with a facility to increase or reduce the time by 10%.

Infra red Sensors, which are also located in the oven roof, work by sensing the surface temperature of the food. With this method you can open the door during cooking without distorting the information being fed to the sensor. Food does not need to be covered as closely but the accuracy of this method is reduced with thicker items of food when the surface temperature remains constant and the sensor cannot tell if the interior is cooked.

These methods of cooking work with varying degrees

HOW TO USE THE RECIPES IN THIS BOOK WITH YOUR COMBINATION OVEN

Combination ovens vary in the way that you select the level of microwave energy and convected heat for combination cooking.

In this book either a HIGH, MEDIUM LOW OR LOW setting is used with temperatures ranging from 180°C to 250°C. To discover the correct setting on your oven, turn to your oven manufacturer's handbook to discover the wattage of your settings.

In this book, HIGH is equivalent to 600-650 watts (100% power);
MEDIUM LOW is equivalent to 195-240 watts (30–35% power);
LOW is equivalent to your lowest microwave setting.
REMEMBER THAT THE MEDIUM LOW AND LOW SETTINGS MARKED ON YOUR OVEN MAY NOT BE THE SAME AS THOSE USED IN THIS BOOK.

If you cannot alter the microwave setting on your oven, always cook for the shortest stated time.

If your oven has a series of programmed combined settings, check your handbook and choose the nearest appropriate setting, adjusting the cooking time accordingly.

Cooking times may vary slightly from the recipes, depending on your oven model. Always make sure food is piping hot and cooked through.

of success, depending on the type of food being cooked. They are really most useful if you can't be bothered to calculate cooking times for large pieces of meat or for cooking convenience foods, but they are not very helpful if you are trying to cook anything more adventurous.

AUTO-DEFROST

Auto-defrost is an automatic function controlled by the weight of the food. On some models, the user programmes in the weight of the food and the control calculates the thawing time per 1 kg (2 lb). It may or may not include standing times. On more sophisticated models there is a crystal beneath the turntable which monitors the deflection produced by the weight of food put on top of it and causes a voltage change which triggers the correct thawing time.

AUTOMATIC COOKING

This is the same as an automatic cooking function on a conventional oven. You can programme in the time you wish cooking to begin, the cooking temperature/power level and the cooking time.

COOKING EQUIPMENT FOR USE IN COMBINATION OVENS

TURNTABLE: Most ovens have a turntable situated in the bottom of the oven that rotates when the oven is switched on to ensure even cooking. It should be kept in position for all cooking operations. If your oven does not have a turntable, it probably has a rotating stirrer instead. This is situated behind the oven wall so you cannot see it and its purpose is to distribute the microwaves evenly in the oven to ensure even cooking.

WIRE RACK: The wire rack is rather like a roasting rack. It stands on the turntable during cooking. Its purpose is to raise the food in the oven, thereby helping it to brown more quickly (rather like putting food on the top shelf in a conventional oven). Some combination ovens come with two wire racks, creating shelves for two-level cooking.

If your oven does not have a wire rack it will have a slide-out shelf instead, which does the same job. Leave the lowest wire rack or shelf in position on the turntable for all modes of cooking. Although the wire rack is made of metal, it is safe to use it when cooking on microwave only because the pattern of microwaves is designed to go between the wire supports.

If you are cooking something in a large, deep dish, or a large joint that will not fit on the rack in the oven, you can achieve satisfactory results without it.

INSULATING MAT: Some ovens come supplied with an insulating mat while others suggest using an ovenproof plate instead. This should be put on the wire rack when cooking something in a metal baking tin on combination. It prevents the two metal surfaces from coming into contact with each other, thus preventing sparking. Since microwave energy cannot pass through metal, it seems pointless to use metal containers on a combination setting, and this piece of equipment was not used when testing the recipes in this book.

SPLASH TRIVET: The splash trivet is put directly on top of the turntable, under the wire rack, when cooking roasts or anything else likely to produce a lot of fat or juice during cooking. The liquid drips through the wire rack and the splash trivet on to the turntable. The purpose of the splash trivet is to shield the liquid from microwave energy, preventing it from splashing and absorbing energy needed to cook the food. Most oven manufacturers recommend the use of the splash trivet with the wire rack and turntable, but it is rather awkward to use and you may prefer to cook a roast standing in a large shallow dish on the wire rack. However, it is not possible to cook very large joints or a turkey in a dish, so use the splash trivet for these.

CONTAINERS: There is a great deal of confusion over which containers can be used for each method of cooking. Some manufacturers say that metal can be used when cooking on combination (with the insulating mat in position) while others say it must be avoided. To prevent any errors, it is best to use ovenproof glass and ceramics for all methods of cooking except convection. When cooking on convection only, use any of your usual metal baking tins. For combination and microwave cooking, stick to dishes made from ovenproof plastics, ceramics and glass.

MULTIPLE SEQUENCE COOKING
This function enables you to programme in a series of power settings and times in advance if you regularly cook a dish requiring more than one setting.

PYROLYTIC CLEANING
Pyrolytic cleaning is a system whereby the oven door is locked automatically while the oven operates at a very high temperature for a specified time. This burns off any heavy soiling so that it can be brushed out when the oven has cooled down. It's a particularly useful feature to have if you do a lot of roasting.

COOKING TECHNIQUES FOR COMBINATION OVENS
If you are familiar with microwave cookery you will understand the importance of certain cooking techniques. If you are new to this method of cooking (or in need of a reminder!) here is a brief summary: follow when using a microwave or a combination setting.

ARRANGING FOOD
Since foods towards the outside of the dish cook or thaw most quickly, arrange with the thicker parts towards the outside and the thinner parts towards the centre.

SHAPE OF FOOD

Food cut into small pieces will cook more quickly than larger pieces. Always cut vegetables and meat into even-sized pieces so that they all cook at the same speed.

PRICKING

Foods with a skin or membrane, such as whole fish, egg yolks and jacket potatoes, should be pricked with a skewer or cocktail stick or slashed with a knife to prevent them bursting during cooking.

SIZE AND SHAPE OF DISHES

Foods arranged in a single layer in a large round shallow dish will cook more quickly and brown more evenly (on combination) than foods cooked in a deep dish. Always check that a dish will fit into the oven before starting a recipe.

STIRRING

For even results when cooking stews and casseroles on a combination setting, stir foods from the outside of the dish towards the centre and stir frequently to prevent the food on the top from drying out.

TIMING

When cooking or thawing on a microwave setting, turn thick foods over once during the cooking time, to ensure even results.

COVERING

When cooking moist foods such as fish, vegetables and fruits on a microwave setting they should be covered. At the time of going to press, it has been recommended by the Ministry of Agriculture, Fisheries and Food that the use of cling film should be avoided in microwave cooking, so cover with an ovenproof glass or ceramic lid or a heavy ovenproof plate.

When cooking on combination, do not cover food if you require a brown, crisp result. Cover only when you wish to retain the moisture and do not want a crisp result. Do not cover with cling film or kitchen foil when cooking on combination. Cover as for microwaving.

STANDING TIME

When using a microwave or combination setting, standing time is important for completion of the cooking process. During standing time, the food continues to cook by heat conducted to the centre. It is useful for delicate mixtures like egg dishes and terrines which can easily be overcooked. Where necessary, instructions for standing have been included in the recipes in this book.

USING THE COMBINATION OVEN

PREHEATING

Although some manufacturers say that ovens get hot very quickly, making it unnecessary to preheat, you will get better results with some foods if the oven is preheated. Small items, such as chops, chicken drumsticks, small pastries, cakes and pies, benefit from going straight into a hot oven. They cook very quickly by microwave energy because they are small or fast cooking, and so do not stay in the oven long enough to be browned by the convected heat. Always preheat on convection only. Usually 5-10 minutes' preheating time is sufficient for most ovens, but follow your own oven manufacturer's recommendations.

THAWING

Thawing should always be done on microwave only. Some ovens have an auto-defrost function (see page 9). If your oven does not have this feature then use a LOW microwave setting.

REHEATING

Most foods are best reheated on a HIGH microwave setting. The time needed will depend on the quantity, density, size and shape of the food. It is best to set the timer for 1 minute, then check to see if the food is hot and if it is, it's ready! If it isn't, then return it to the oven for another minute or two until it is hot. Food taken straight from the refrigerator will take much longer to reheat than food at room temperature. If reheating stews, casseroles or soups, stir frequently to distribute the heat.

One of the advantages of a combination oven is that it is ideal for reheating the things that don't reheat well on microwave alone. Reheated pies, pastries and breads are no longer soggy, but retain their crisp texture. Reheat at a temperature of 200–250°C combined with a MEDIUM LOW microwave setting.

CLEANING THE OVEN

Microwave cooking does not make much mess in the oven interior, since there is no dry heat to stick the food to the sides of the oven or to bake it on. However, with convection or combination cooking the oven will get just as dirty as a conventional oven. Unlike conventional ovens, the interior must not be cleaned with abrasive materials as this will damage the metal lining and distort the pattern of the microwaves. It is best to wipe the oven after each use with a soft cloth dipped in soapy water. For more stubborn dirt, foam and liquid cleaners can be used, but should not be applied directly to the oven interior; put them on a cloth first.

Starters and Snacks

A good starter should be attractive to look at and whet the appetite. This chapter contains a wide selection of dishes which fit the bill perfectly. A whole range of soups and pâtés can be made using the microwave alone. Some starters, such as Filo Cheese Trio, are best prepared in advance, and then popped in a combination oven to cook for just 3-4 minutes before serving. Others, like Barbecued Spareribs, can be cooked in advance and reheated when you are ready to serve them.

An endless variety of quick snacks is possible with the help of a combination oven. Bread-based snacks, such as Croque Monsieur and Hot Brie and Prosciutto Sandwich, are cooked and ready to eat in only 5-10 minutes. Served with a crisp mixed salad, they make a delicious snack. And don't forget the ultimate in combination oven snacks, the baked potato, which not only cooks in a fraction of the time, but has a delicious crisp skin too!

Chilled Courgette Mousse with Saffron Sauce

BARLEY AND CHICK-PEA SOUP
If you don't want to use canned chick-peas for this recipe, soak 225 g (8 oz) chick-peas overnight, then drain and cover with enough boiling water to come about 2.5 cm (1 inch) above the level of the beans. Cover and microwave on HIGH for 50-55 minutes, stirring occasionally. Leave to stand for 5 minutes before draining.

PASTINA AND SUMMER VEGETABLE SOUP
Pastina are very tiny pasta shapes which are used only in soups. Shapes vary from bow-ties (*farfallette*) and wheels (*rotellini*) to the tiny rings (*anellini*) and stars (*stellette*).

Picture opposite: Pastina and Summer Vegetable Soup

BARLEY AND CHICK-PEA SOUP

SERVES 4

15 ml (1 tbsp) olive oil
1 large onion, skinned and chopped
1 garlic clove, skinned and chopped
50 g (2 oz) pot barley
900 ml (1½ pints) boiling vegetable stock
2.5 ml (½ tsp) ground turmeric
2.5 ml (½ tsp) concentrated mint sauce
100 g (4 oz) fresh spinach, washed, trimmed and shredded
397 g (14 oz) can chick-peas, drained and rinsed
salt and pepper
60 ml (4 tbsp) set natural yogurt (optional)
10 ml (2 tsp) sesame seeds, toasted (optional)

/ 1 / Put the oil, onion and garlic in a large bowl. Microwave on HIGH for 2 minutes, stirring once during cooking.

/ 2 / Add the barley, stock, turmeric and concentrated mint sauce. Cover and microwave on HIGH for 20 minutes until the barley is tender, stirring occasionally.

/ 3 / Stir in the spinach and chick-peas and season with salt and pepper to taste. Re-cover and microwave on HIGH for 2-3 minutes or until heated through.

/ 4 / Pour into 4 soup bowls. Top each bowl with a spoonful of yogurt and sprinkle with sesame seeds, if liked. Serve immediately.

LENTIL AND BACON SOUP

SERVES 6

100 g (4 oz) streaky bacon, rinded and chopped
25 g (1 oz) butter or margarine
100 g (4 oz) red lentils
2 medium leeks, trimmed and finely chopped
2 medium carrots, peeled and finely chopped
1 litre (1¾ pints) chicken stock
30 ml (2 tbsp) chopped fresh parsley
salt and pepper
orange shreds, to garnish

/ 1 / Put the bacon and butter or margarine in a large bowl and microwave on HIGH for 2 minutes. Add the lentils and toss to coat them in the fat, then add the chopped leeks, carrots and chicken stock.

/ 2 / Cover and microwave on HIGH for 18 minutes or until the lentils are cooked. Stir 2 or 3 times during the cooking time.

/ 3 / Cool slightly, then liquidise the soup in a blender or food processor until smooth. Add the parsley, season to taste with salt and pepper and microwave on HIGH for 2-3 minutes or until the soup is hot. Garnish with orange shreds and serve.

PASTINA AND SUMMER VEGETABLE SOUP

SERVES 4

15 ml (1 tbsp) olive oil
100 g (4 oz) new carrots, scrubbed and sliced
100 g (4 oz) French beans, trimmed and cut in half
225 g (8 oz) young peas, shelled
50 g (2 oz) pastina
900 ml (1½ pints) boiling vegetable stock
30 ml (2 tbsp) chopped fresh mint
4 lettuce leaves, finely shredded
salt and pepper

/ 1 / Put the oil, carrots, beans and peas in a large bowl. Cover and microwave on HIGH for 2 minutes, stirring once.

/ 2 / Add the pastina and stock. Re-cover and microwave on HIGH for 10 minutes or until the pasta and vegetables are tender.

/ 3 / Stir in the mint and lettuce and season to taste with salt and pepper. Microwave on HIGH for 1 minute or until the lettuce is just wilted. Serve the soup piping hot.

JAPANESE CLEAR SOUP WITH PRAWNS

SERVES 4

15 g (½ oz) dried seaweed, such as kombu, wakame or nori
15 ml (1 tbsp) soy sauce
4 raw jumbo prawns in the shell
2 medium carrots, peeled
5 cm (2 inch) piece of daikon radish, peeled
15 ml (1 tbsp) sake or dry sherry
4 slices of lime

/1/ Put the seaweed, soy sauce and 900 ml (1½ pints) boiling water into a large bowl. Cover and microwave on HIGH for 3 minutes or until the water returns to the boil, then continue cooking for a further 5 minutes.

/2/ Meanwhile, remove the shells from the prawns, leaving the tail intact. Using kitchen scissors or a sharp knife, cut along the curved underside of each prawn from the thick end towards the tail, stopping at the tail and being very careful not to cut any of the prawns through completely.

/3/ Flatten out the prawns and remove and discard the veins. Cut a slit in the middle of the prawn and then curl the tail round and push it through the slit.

/4/ Cut the carrots and daikon radish into thin slices or decorative shapes.

/5/ Remove and discard the seaweed from the stock. Stir the sake or sherry, carrots and daikon radish into the stock. Cover and microwave on HIGH for 3 minutes, then add the prawns and cook for 2 minutes or until cooked.

/6/ Using a slotted spoon, transfer the fish and vegetables to 4 soup bowls, then carefully pour over the stock. Add a slice of lime to each bowl and serve immediately.

WATERZOOI

SERVES 6

15 ml (1 tbsp) vegetable oil
2.5 ml (½ tsp) ground cloves
2 celery sticks, trimmed and chopped
2 medium leeks, trimmed and sliced
2 large carrots, peeled and thinly sliced
1 bouquet garni
2 strips of lemon rind
600 ml (1 pint) boiling fish or vegetable stock
700 g (1½ lb) freshwater fish fillets, such as bream, carp, pike or eel, skinned
salt and pepper
2 egg yolks
150 ml (¼ pint) milk
6 slices of toast
30 ml (2 tbsp) chopped fresh parsley

/1/ Put the oil, cloves, celery, leeks, carrots, bouquet garni, lemon rind and half the stock in a large bowl. Cover and microwave on HIGH for 12-14 minutes or until the vegetables are softened. Meanwhile, cut the fish into bite-sized pieces.

/2/ Add the fish, remaining stock and salt and pepper to taste to the soup. Re-cover and microwave on HIGH for 6-7 minutes until the fish is cooked.

/3/ Meanwhile, blend the egg yolks and milk together. When the fish is cooked, spoon a little of the liquid on to the egg yolk mixture and mix together. Pour back into the soup.

/4/ Re-cover and microwave on MEDIUM for 1-2 minutes or until thickened, stirring once; do not allow the soup to boil or it will curdle. Discard the lemon rind and bouquet garni.

/5/ To serve, place the toast in 6 soup bowls, carefully spoon over the soup and garnish with chopped parsley. Serve immediately.

JAPANESE CLEAR SOUP WITH PRAWNS
Seaweed has been an important food since ancient times, and many types are cultivated and used. Seaweeds are high in nutrients, including the minerals iron, calcium, potassium, sodium and iodine.

Daikon radish (Japanese radish) is the traditional white radish variety, often sold in oriental food shops. It is milder than other types and is often grated to use as a garnish.

WATERZOOI
This soup originated in Belgium where it is traditionally made with freshwater fish, as here, or with chicken. The toasted bread in the bottom of the bowls helps thicken the soup. It is very filling and could be served as a main course if wished.

BOUQUET GARNI
A bouquet garni is the French term for a small bunch of herbs which is used to add flavour to stews, casseroles and soups. Bouquets garnis can be bought ready made, though the flavour of freshly made bouquet is far superior.
    For the basic bouquet garni, tie together 2 parsley sprigs, 1 thyme sprig and 1 bay leaf. If using dried herbs, tie together in a muslin bag, 5 ml (1 tsp) dried parsley, 2.5 ml (½ tsp) dried thyme and ½ bay leaf, crumbled.

Chilled Pea and Mint Soup

CHILLED PEA AND MINT SOUP

SERVES 6

50 g (2 oz) butter or margarine
1 medium onion, skinned and coarsely chopped
450 g (1 lb) frozen peas
568 ml (1 pint) milk
600 ml (1 pint) chicken stock
2 large mint sprigs
pinch of caster sugar
salt and pepper
150 ml (¼ pint) natural yogurt
mint sprigs, to garnish

/ 1 / Put the butter or margarine in a large bowl and microwave on HIGH for 1-2 minutes or until the fat has completely melted.

/ 2 / Add the onion, cover the bowl and microwave on HIGH for 5-7 minutes or until the onion is soft.

/ 3 / Add the peas, milk, stock, 2 mint sprigs and sugar. Re-cover and microwave on HIGH for about 8 minutes or until the liquid is boiling. Reduce the setting to LOW and cook for 15 minutes or until the peas are really tender. Season well with salt and pepper and cool slightly.

/ 4 / Remove about 45 ml (3 tbsp) peas from the soup and put them aside for the garnish. Rub the remaining peas through a sieve, or liquidise them in a blender or food processor until quite smooth.

/ 5 / Pour the purée into a large serving bowl. Adjust the seasoning and leave to cool for 30 minutes. Stir in the yogurt and cover and chill for 2-3 hours before serving. Serve garnished with the reserved peas and mint sprigs.

This recipe for Chilled Pea and Mint Soup uses frozen peas, but in the summer when you can pick fresh peas from the garden or buy them easily at local farms and markets the soup can be made with fresh – you will need 900 g (2 lb). There is nothing like the sweet, fragrant flavour of freshly picked peas in summer, so it is a good idea to make at least a double quantity of this soup and freeze some to remind you of the summer.

TROUT PÂTÉ

C **SERVES 4**

2 pink trout, each weighing about 350 g (12 oz), cleaned
15 ml (1 tbsp) vegetable oil
50 g (2 oz) butter or margarine
15 ml (1 tbsp) lemon juice
45 ml (3 tbsp) single cream
salt and pepper

/ 1 / Brush the trout with oil and arrange in a single layer in a shallow dish. Cover and microwave on HIGH for 8-10 minutes or until tender. Remove and discard the head, skin and bones from the trout and flake the fish.

/ 2 / Cut the butter or margarine into small pieces, put in a small bowl and microwave on HIGH for 1-2 minutes or until melted. Leave to cool slightly.

/ 3 / Meanwhile, put the lemon juice and the trout into a blender or food processor and purée until smooth. Add the melted butter or margarine and cream and season to taste with salt and pepper. Process until well mixed.

/ 4 / Turn the pâté into a serving dish. Leave to cool, then chill for at least 1 hour.

COARSE HERB AND MUSHROOM PÂTÉ

SERVES 6 - 8

25 g (1 oz) butter or margarine
1 garlic clove, skinned and crushed
2 juniper berries, crushed
700 g (1½ lb) mushrooms, roughly chopped
75 g (3 oz) fresh brown breadcrumbs
60 ml (4 tbsp) chopped fresh mixed herbs
lemon juice
salt and pepper
fresh herbs, to garnish

/ 1 / Put the butter or margarine, garlic and juniper berries in a large bowl and microwave on HIGH for 1 minute.

/ 2 / Add the mushrooms and microwave on HIGH for 10-12 minutes or until the mushrooms are really soft, stirring frequently.

/ 3 / Add the breadcrumbs and herbs and season to taste with lemon juice and salt and pepper. Beat thoroughly together, then turn into a serving dish. Cover and chill before serving garnished with fresh herbs.

PORK PÂTÉ

C **SERVES 8**

225 g (8 oz) streaky bacon rashers, rinded
225 g (8 oz) pig's liver
225 g (8 oz) pork belly
225 g (8 oz) lean pork
1 large onion, skinned and roughly chopped
3 garlic cloves, skinned
12 juniper berries
5 ml (1 tsp) salt
2.5 ml (½ tsp) black peppercorns
10 ml (2 tsp) chopped fresh thyme or 5 ml (1 tsp) dried
10 ml (2 tsp) chopped fresh sage or 5 ml (1 tsp) dried
1 egg, beaten
25 g (1 oz) fresh white breadcrumbs
30 ml (2 tbsp) single cream
fresh sage sprigs, to garnish

/ 1 / Using the back of a knife, stretch 100 g (4 oz) of the bacon rashers and use to line a 1.4 litre (2½ pint) soufflé dish.

/ 2 / Put the remaining bacon, the liver, pork belly, pork and onion in a blender or food processor and process until finely chopped. Transfer the mixture to a bowl.

/ 3 / Crush the garlic, juniper berries, salt and peppercorns in a pestle and mortar. Add to the pork mixture with the herbs, egg, breadcrumbs and cream and mix well together. Press into the bacon-lined dish, fold the bacon rasher ends over the mixture and cover the dish with a double layer of greaseproof paper.

/ 4 / Stand the dish on the wire rack and cook on combination at 180°C/MEDIUM LOW for 40-45 minutes or until the juices run clear when the pâté is pierced with a knife. Leave to cool completely in the dish.

/ 5 / When cold, cover the pâté with foil and put a heavy weight on top. Leave in the refrigerator overnight.

/ 6 / Leave to stand at room temperature for 30 minutes before serving garnished with sage.

TROUT PÂTÉ
Fish is cooked when the flesh flakes easily and is opaque. Overcooking fish will toughen the flesh. Unless instructions are given to the contrary, always cover fish when cooking.

PORK PÂTÉ
Home-made pâté tastes a million times better than the over-processed, shrink-wrapped pâtés on sale in the shops. This pork pâté is a delicious well-flavoured pâté with a generous hint of garlic. It's very easy to make and takes half the normal time to cook in the combination oven. Serve with warm toast as a starter or with a mixed salad and chunks of French bread for lunch.

COARSE HERB AND MUSHROOM PÂTÉ
Round, purple-brown juniper berries are about twice the size of peppercorns and have smooth skins. They are always bought whole and are easy to crush or grind as they are soft. Juniper berries are often included in spice mixtures for meat and are particularly good with pork and game. They can be added to casseroles as well as pâtés, and are also good with cabbage. Juniper berries are an important flavouring ingredient in gin.

Picture opposite: Coarse Herb and Mushroom Pâté

Aubergine and Yogurt Purée

AUBERGINE AND YOGURT PURÉE

SERVES 4

1 aubergine, total weight about 450 g (1 lb)
5 ml (1 tsp) vegetable oil
1-2 garlic cloves, skinned and crushed
6 black olives, stoned and roughly chopped
juice of ½ lemon
150 ml (¼ pint) low-fat natural yogurt
wholemeal pitta bread, toast or crudités, to serve

/ 1 / Rub the aubergine with the oil and prick well all over with a fork. Place on absorbent kitchen paper. Microwave on HIGH for 8 minutes or until tender, turning over once.

/ 2 / Leave to stand for 5 minutes, then chop roughly, discarding the stalk. Put in a blender or food processor with the remaining ingredients, except the bread, toast or crudités, and work until smooth.

/ 3 / Turn the purée into a bowl and leave to cool. Serve with wholemeal pitta bread, toast or crudités (see right).

MUSHROOM AND SPINACH PÂTÉ

C ### SERVES 4

about 5 young spinach leaves
25 g (1 oz) butter or margarine
2 garlic cloves, skinned and crushed
450 g (1 lb) flat black mushrooms, finely chopped
75 g (3 oz) fine oatmeal
1 egg yolk
100 g (4 oz) full-fat soft cheese
30 ml (2 tbsp) chopped fresh herbs
15 ml (1 tbsp) lemon juice
wholemeal toast, to serve

/ 1 / Lightly grease a 900 ml (1½ pint) soufflé dish. Remove the stalks from the spinach leaves and use the leaves to line the soufflé dish, reserving 2 leaves for the top.

/ 2 / Put the butter or margarine and garlic in a large bowl and microwave on HIGH for 1 minute or until melted. Add the mushrooms and microwave on HIGH for 5 minutes or until softened. Stir in the oatmeal, egg yolk, soft cheese, herbs and lemon juice and beat well.

/ 3 / Spoon the pâté mixture into the lined soufflé dish and cover with the reserved spinach leaves. Cover the dish, stand on the wire rack and cook on combination at 200°C/ MEDIUM LOW for 20-22 minutes or until firm to the touch. Leave to cool, then chill before serving with wholemeal toast.

PARMESAN MUSHROOMS WITH GARLIC SAUCE

C ### SERVES 2

75 g (3 oz) fine day-old breadcrumbs
30 ml (2 tbsp) freshly grated Parmesan cheese
black pepper
15 ml (1 tbsp) chopped fresh mixed herbs
225 g (8 oz) small button mushrooms
1 egg, beaten
15 ml (1 tbsp) vegetable oil
fresh herb sprigs and lemon wedges, to garnish
SAUCE
60 ml (4 tbsp) natural yogurt
30 ml (2 tbsp) mayonnaise
10 ml (2 tsp) lemon juice
1 garlic clove, skinned and crushed
15 ml (1 tbsp) chopped fresh mixed herbs
salt and pepper

/ 1 / First, make the sauce. Place all the ingredients in a bowl, season to taste with salt and pepper and beat well together. Leave to infuse while cooking the mushrooms.

/ 2 / Spread the breadcrumbs on a large plate, add the Parmesan, pepper and herbs and mix until thoroughly combined.

/ 3 / Dip the mushrooms, 1 at a time, in the beaten egg, then coat in the breadcrumb mixture. Arrange around the edge of a large greased shallow ovenproof dish. Chill for 10 minutes while preheating the oven on convection at 250°C.

/ 4 / Stand the dish of mushrooms on the wire rack and cook on combination at 200°C/ MEDIUM LOW for 3 minutes. Drizzle with the oil and cook for a further 4-6 minutes or until the mushrooms are crisp and lightly browned. Arrange on individual plates, garnish and serve immediately with the garlic sauce.

AUBERGINE AND YOGURT PURÉE
You can warm the pitta bread in the microwave, if wished, but only if you intend to eat it immediately, because when the bread cools it hardens! One large pitta bread takes about 15 seconds on HIGH.

CRUDITÉS
Crudites – French for raw vegetables – can be whatever is available but make sure that they are all as crisp and fresh as possible. A selection for 4 people could be 4 carrots, peeled and cut into thin sticks, 1 small cauliflower, divided into florets, 4 celery sticks, halved, 1 cucumber, seeds removed and cut into sticks, 1 red and 1 green pepper, cored, seeded and sliced, and 1 bunch of radishes, trimmed.

PARMESAN MUSHROOMS WITH GARLIC SAUCE
This quick, easy starter can be made in advance up to the end of step 3. For best results, try to find the really small, compact button mushrooms, and use fresh herbs as the cooking time is very short and the taste of dried herbs is too harsh. Use any favourite herbs you have to hand. These crisp-coated mushrooms look very attractive arranged on individual plates and garnished with fresh green herbs and lemon wedges.

TURKISH AUBERGINES WITH TOMATOES

SERVES 4 - 6

2 aubergines, total weight about 900 g (2 lb), with stalks on
5 ml (1 tsp) olive oil
1 large onion, skinned and thinly sliced
2 garlic cloves, skinned and crushed
4 large ripe tomatoes, chopped
1 green pepper, cored, seeded and chopped
30 ml (2 tbsp) tomato purée
5 ml (1 tsp) ground allspice
5 ml (1 tsp) ground cinnamon
1.25 ml (¼ tsp) cayenne pepper (optional)
45 ml (3 tbsp) chopped fresh parsley
salt and pepper

/ 1 / Rub the aubergines with the olive oil and prick well all over with a fork. Place on a double thickness of absorbent kitchen paper. Microwave on HIGH for 8 minutes. Turn over and microwave on HIGH for a further 6-8 minutes or until the aubergines are very soft.

/ 2 / Put the onion, garlic, tomatoes, green pepper, tomato purée, allspice, cinnamon and cayenne pepper in a large bowl with 100 ml (4 fl oz) water. Cover, and microwave on HIGH for 15-20 minutes or until the onion is soft, stirring once. Stir in half of the parsley and season with salt and pepper to taste.

/ 3 / Transfer the aubergines to a shallow serving dish and make about 5 slashes along the length of each. Fan them out, leaving the stalk intact. Spoon over the filling. Cover, leaving a gap to let steam escape, and microwave on HIGH for 5 minutes.

/ 4 / Leave to cool for 1 hour, then chill for at least 2 hours. Serve garnished with the remaining chopped parsley.

CORN-ON-THE-COB WITH HERB VINAIGRETTE

SERVES 4

4 corn-on-the-cob
15 ml (1 tbsp) vegetable oil
15 ml (1 tbsp) lemon juice
30 ml (2 tbsp) chopped fresh mixed herbs
salt and pepper

/ 1 / Peel back the husks from the corn and remove the silk, then pull back the husks again to cover. If the corn is without husks, wrap separately in greaseproof paper.

/ 2 / Place the corn cobs, side by side, in a shallow dish. Microwave on HIGH for 8-10 minutes until the corn is tender, turning and repositioning 2 or 3 times during cooking.

/ 3 / Meanwhile, whisk the oil, lemon juice and herbs together and season with salt and pepper to taste.

/ 4 / When the corn is cooked, place on 4 warmed serving plates and gently pull back the husks or remove the greaseproof paper. Pour a little dressing over each cob and serve immediately while piping hot.

CROQUE MONSIEUR

C SERVES 2

4 thick slices of white bread
2 thick slices of lean ham
175 g (6 oz) Gruyère cheese, rinded and sliced
butter, for spreading

/ 1 / Preheat the oven on convection at 250°C for 10 minutes.

/ 2 / Meanwhile, make 2 sandwiches with the bread, ham and the cheese. Butter the outside of each sandwich only.

/ 3 / Place the sandwiches on a large ovenproof plate. Stand the plate on the wire rack and cook on convection at 250°C for 10-12 minutes or until brown and crisp, turning over halfway through cooking. Serve immediately.

TURKISH AUBERGINES WITH TOMATOES
This is based on a dish called Imam Bayeldi. The literal translation means 'the imam (priest) fainted', but whether he fainted with delight, or horror at the amount of olive oil used in the dish, is not known.

CORN-ON-THE-COB WITH HERB VINAIGRETTE
Sweetcorn originated in America but it is now grown all over the world. The cob's sweet nutty flavour is at its best just after picking. Once the corn is cut from the plant the natural sugar in the kernels changes to starch and the cob loses the sweetness and flavour quite quickly. When buying, choose cobs with pale green, tightly fitting husk with kernels inside that are not dry.

CROQUE MONSIEUR
The Gruyère cheese gives this recipe its distinctive taste. Gruyère is a hard, large cheese, weighing anything up to 45 kg (100 lb). Originally it came exclusively from Switzerland but is now made in France, Italy and other parts of Europe. It is pale yellow in colour and is honeycombed with 'eyes' or holes, caused by the rapid fermentation of the curd.

HOT BRIE AND PROSCIUTTO SANDWICH

C

SERVES 2

2 long crisp sandwich rolls

100 g (4 oz) Brie

2 thin slices of prosciutto

15 ml (1 tbsp) olive oil

pepper

/ 1 / Preheat the oven on convection at 250°C for 10 minutes.

/ 2 / Meanwhile, cut the rolls in half lengthways and cut the Brie in half. Make 2 sandwiches with the rolls, Brie and prosciutto and place on a large ovenproof plate. Drizzle with the oil and season generously with pepper.

/ 3 / Stand the plate on the wire rack and cook on convection at 250°C for 5 minutes or until the Brie has just melted. Serve immediately.

Prosciutto is the Italian word for ham. Most of the prosciutto on sale in Italian shops is air-dried, which gives it a wonderful smoky flavour. *Prosciutto di Parma* is the most famous of all the hams – and the most expensive! Genuine Parma ham comes from the area around the town of Parma in Emilia-Romagna, and must have its brand burned into the skin.

Croque Monsieur

BAKED POTATOES WITH CHOICE OF FILLINGS

C
SERVES 4
(EACH FILLING IS
ENOUGH FOR 4)

4 medium potatoes, each weighing about 175 g (6 oz)
SMOKED HADDOCK FILLING
225 g (8 oz) smoked haddock fillet
45 ml (3 tbsp) milk
1 hard-boiled egg, chopped
snipped fresh chives
salt and pepper
25 g (1 oz) butter (optional)
CHEESE AND PEANUT FILLING
175 g (6 oz) hard cheese, grated
50 g (2 oz) salted peanuts, chopped
1 large carrot, coarsely grated
25 g (1 oz) butter or margarine
black pepper
paprika
PRAWN FILLING
100 g (4 oz) cooked peeled prawns
25 g (1 oz) butter
chopped mixed fresh herbs of your choice
salt and pepper
60 ml (4 tbsp) mayonnaise
cayenne pepper

/ 1 / Scrub the potatoes and prick all over with a fork. Stand them on the wire rack and cook on combination at 250°C/HIGH for 20-25 minutes. Leave to stand while making the filling of your choice.

/ 2 / Make the smoked haddock filling: put the fish and milk in a large shallow dish, cover and microwave on HIGH for 3-5 minutes or until the fish flakes easily when tested. Remove the fish from the dish, reserving the poaching liquid, and flake.

/ 3 / Cut the cooked potatoes in half, scoop out the flesh and mix with the flaked fish, poaching liquid, egg, chives and salt and pepper. Return to the potato skins. Dot with the butter, if liked. Stand the potato halves on a plate on the wire rack and microwave on HIGH for 2-3 minutes or until hot. Serve.

/ 4 / Make the cheese and peanut filling: cut the cooked potatoes in half, scoop out the flesh and mix with 100 g (4 oz) of the cheese, the peanuts, carrot and butter or margarine. Season to taste with pepper and paprika, spoon back into the potato skins and sprinkle with the remaining cheese.

/ 5 / Stand the potato halves on an ovenproof plate on the wire rack and cook on combination at 200°C/MEDIUM LOW for 3-5 minutes or until the cheese melts and the potatoes are hot. Serve.

/ 6 / Make the prawn filling: put the prawns and butter in a bowl and microwave on HIGH for 3-5 minutes or until hot, stirring occasionally. Cut the cooked potatoes in half. Loosen the flesh with a fork and mash lightly. Place a potato half on each of 4 serving plates.

/ 7 / Add the herbs to the prawn mixture and season to taste with salt and pepper. Spoon on to the potatoes. Top each with a spoonful of mayonnaise and sprinkle with a little cayenne pepper. Serve.

BAKED POTATOES

Now that nutritionists have persuaded us to eat potatoes in their jackets for extra dietary fibre, the baked potato has become a fast snack food with the help of the microwave. Instead of having to wait an hour for baked potatoes to cook conventionally, microwaved potatoes can cook in a fraction of that time, and if they are cooked on combination they have a crisp skin as well! For best results use mature potatoes weighing about 175-225 g (6-8 oz) each. Choose potatoes that are a good, even shape with no blemishes on the skin. As well as the fillings given here, you can improvise and use whatever ingredients you have to hand.

The following are all good potatoes for baking. *Desiree* has pinkish-red skin and pale yellow flesh which is consistently good quality and not as dry as many maincrop varieties. *King Edward* has a patchy red skin and pale yellow floury flesh. *Maris Piper* has a pale skin and creamy white floury flesh which does not discolour after cooking. *Pentland Crown* has pale skin and creamy white flesh but is of only moderate cooking quality as it tends to be wet – its best use is as baked potatoes. *Pentland Dell* has a pale skin and tends to disintegrate. Its best use is as baked potatoes. *Pentland Hawk* has a pale skin and creamy flesh but is of only moderate cooking quality.

Baked potatoes cooked in the combination oven are a delight. They cook quickly, as in the microwave, but instead of having soft skins they are deliciously crisp. They make the perfect hot and filling, high-fibre, snack topped simply with soured cream, grated cheese, baked beans or one of the fillings suggested here.

Picture opposite:
Baked Potatoes with Choice of Fillings

STUFFED MUSHROOMS

SERVES 4 - 6

12 medium cup mushrooms
15 ml (1 tbsp) olive oil
1 garlic clove, skinned and crushed
finely grated rind and juice of 1 lemon
50 g (2 oz) fresh wholemeal breadcrumbs
25 g (1 oz) porridge oats
30 ml (2 tbsp) chopped fresh parsley
30 ml (2 tbsp) grated fresh Parmesan cheese
salt and pepper
fresh herb sprigs, to garnish

/ 1 / Remove the mushroom stalks and finely chop them. Place the chopped stalks in a small bowl with the oil, garlic, lemon rind and half of the lemon juice. Cover and microwave on HIGH for 1-2 minutes until softened.

/ 2 / Stir in the breadcrumbs, oats, parsley and Parmesan cheese. Season with salt and pepper.

/ 3 / Arrange the mushroom caps around the edge of a large shallow dish and spoon a little of the stuffing on to each.

/ 4 / Pour the remaining lemon juice into the dish. Cover and microwave on HIGH for 5-6 minutes. Serve garnished with herbs.

TAGLIATELLE WITH FRESH FIGS

SERVES 1

75 g (3 oz) dried tagliatelle
salt and pepper
3 large ripe fresh figs
15 g (½ oz) butter or margarine
1.25 ml (¼ tsp) medium curry powder
30 ml (2 tbsp) soured cream
30 ml (2 tbsp) grated Parmesan cheese
fresh herbs, to garnish (optional)

/ 1 / Put the tagliatelle and salt to taste in a medium bowl and pour over 600 ml (1 pint) boiling water. Stir, cover and microwave on HIGH for 3-4 minutes or until almost tender, stirring frequently. Leave to stand, covered (do not drain before standing).

/ 2 / Meanwhile, cut 1 of the figs in half lengthways. Reserve 1 of the halves to garnish, then peel and roughly chop the remainder.

/ 3 / Put the butter or margarine, chopped figs and curry powder in a shallow dish and microwave on HIGH for 2 minutes, stirring occasionally during cooking.

/ 3 / Drain the pasta and stir into the fig mixture with the soured cream and Parmesan cheese. Season well with salt and pepper. Carefully mix together with 2 forks and microwave on HIGH for 1-2 minutes or until hot.

/ 5 / Garnish with fresh herbs, if using, and the reserved fig half and serve immediately.

DEVILISH EGGS

[c]   ### SERVES 2

100 g (4 oz) button mushrooms, thinly sliced
1 large green or red pepper, seeded and finely chopped
2 spring onions, trimmed and chopped
15 ml (1 tbsp) tomato purée
2.5 ml (½ tsp) curry paste
5 ml (1 tsp) Worcestershire sauce
5 ml (1 tsp) mustard powder
5 ml (1 tsp) lemon juice
30 ml (2 tbsp) olive oil
4 eggs
60 ml (4 tbsp) double cream

/ 1 / Divide the mushrooms, pepper and onions between 2 small ovenproof dishes.

/ 2 / Whisk the tomato purée, curry paste, Worcestershire sauce, mustard, lemon juice and oil together, then pour over the vegetables. Microwave on HIGH for 3-5 minutes or until the vegetables are softened, stirring once.

/ 3 / Beat 2 of the eggs with the cream and pour half over the vegetables in each dish. Crack 1 of the remaining eggs on top of each. Carefully prick the egg yolks with a fine skewer or cocktail stick to prevent the yolk from bursting during cooking.

/ 4 / Stand the dishes on the wire rack and cook on combination at 180°C/MEDIUM LOW for 7-10 minutes or until the whole egg in the middle is just cooked and the outside mixture is risen and puffy. Serve immediately.

STUFFED MUSHROOMS
These mushrooms make a tasty starter served with Herb, Cheese and Olive Bread (see page 191).

Stuffed Mushrooms can be made in advance up to the end of step 3, then pour over the lemon juice, cover and set aside until ready to serve.

DEVILISH EGGS
'Devilling' was popular in the 18th and 19th century England; it usually involved meat and always involved 'devil' paste, a mixture of spicy ingredients such as Worcestershire sauce, curry powder and mustard. Here a devil paste is added to eggs and vegetables to make a nutritious snack. The beaten egg mixture should puff up rather like a soufflé while the whole egg in the middle is cooked until lightly set. A little chopped ham or salami added to the vegetable mixture tastes good too. Serve with hot buttered toast.

TAGLIATELLE WITH FRESH FIGS
When cooking pasta in the microwave, boil the water for cooking the pasta in a kettle to save time. Always cover the container during cooking. Remove the pasta from the cooker when it is still slightly undercooked, otherwise prolonged cooking will cause it to become soggy. Part of the cooking occurs during the standing time. Large quantities of pasta are better cooked conventionally.

Tagliatelle with Fresh Figs

BRIE AND WATERCRESS TARTS

SERVES 4

100 g (4 oz) plain wholemeal flour
salt and pepper
75 g (3 oz) butter or margarine
2 bunches watercress
275 g (10 oz) ripe Brie
45 ml (3 tbsp) double cream
freshly grated nutmeg

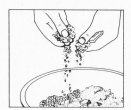

To make the pastry: put the flour and salt to taste in a bowl. Add 50 g (2 oz) of the butter or margarine and rub in until the mixture resembles fine breadcrumbs.

Pastry cooked on inverted dishes keeps its shape better and cools quickly. Roll the pastry very thin for crisp results.

/ 1 / Make the pastry: put the flour and salt to taste in a bowl. Add 50 g (2 oz) of the butter or margarine and rub in until the mixture resembles fine breadcrumbs. Add 30-60 ml (2-4 tbsp) water and mix together using a round-bladed knife. Knead lightly to give a firm, smooth dough.

/ 2 / Roll out the dough thinly. Invert four 10 cm (4 inch) shallow glass flan dishes and cover the bases and sides with the dough. Cover and chill while making the filling.

/ 3 / Put the remaining butter or margarine in a medium bowl and microwave on HIGH for 1 minute or until melted. Trim and discard the tough stalks from the watercress. Reserve a few sprigs to garnish and stir the remainder into the butter. Microwave on HIGH for 1-2 minutes until just wilted.

/ 4 / Remove the rind from the cheese and cut into small pieces. Stir into the watercress with the cream. Microwave on HIGH for 1-2 minutes until melted. Season to taste with nutmeg, salt and pepper.

/ 5 / To cook the tarts, uncover and prick all over with a fork. Arrange pastry side uppermost in a circle in the cooker and microwave on HIGH for 2-3 minutes or until the pastry is firm to the touch.

/ 6 / Leave to stand for 5 minutes, then carefully loosen around the edge and invert on to a large serving plate. Fill with the cheese and watercress mixture and microwave on HIGH for 2-3 minutes or until warmed through. Garnish with watercress.

Brie and Watercress Tarts

TINY CHEESE TRIANGLES

SERVES 4

75 g (3 oz) full-fat soft cheese
15 ml (1 tbsp) lemon or lime juice
1 spring onion, trimmed and finely chopped
25 g (1 oz) chopped dried apricots or dates
salt and pepper
75 g (3 oz) butter or margarine, cut into small pieces
4 sheets of frozen filo pastry, thawed
75 ml (5 tbsp) natural yogurt
15 ml (1 tbsp) lemon juice
¼ cucumber
mint sprigs, to garnish

/ 1 / Make the filling: mix the full-fat soft cheese and lemon or lime juice with the spring onion and chopped fruit and season the mixture to taste with salt and pepper.

/ 2 / Put the butter or margarine in a small bowl and microwave on HIGH for 1-2 minutes or until the fat has melted.

/ 3 / Lay 1 sheet of pastry on top of a second sheet and cut widthways into 6 double layer 7.5 cm (3 inch) strips. Repeat with the remaining 2 sheets of pastry.

/ 4 / Brush the strips of pastry with the melted butter or margarine. Place a generous teaspoonful of filling at 1 end of each strip. Fold the pastry strip diagonally across the filling to form a triangle shape.

/ 5 / Continue folding, keeping the triangle shape, until you reach the end of the strip of pastry. Repeat with the remaining strips of pastry to make a total of 12 triangles.

/ 6 / Heat a browning dish on HIGH for 5-8 minutes or according to the manufacturer's instructions for your particular one.

/ 7 / Meanwhile, brush both sides of each triangle with the melted butter or margarine.

/ 8 / Using tongs, quickly add 6 triangles to the dish and microwave on HIGH for 1-2 minutes until the underside of each triangle is golden brown and the top looks puffy. Turn over and microwave on HIGH for 1-2 minutes until the second side is golden brown.

/ 9 / Reheat the browning dish on HIGH for 2-3 minutes, then repeat with the remaining filo pastry triangles.

/ 10 / While the filo triangles are cooking, make the sauce. Put the yogurt and lemon juice in a bowl and mix together. Grate in the cucumber and season the sauce to taste with salt and pepper.

/ 11 / Serve the filo triangles warm or cold, garnished with mint sprigs, with the yogurt and cucumber sauce handed separately.

PASTA WITH MUSHROOMS AND CHEESE

C   SERVES 4 - 6

450 g (1 lb) dried pasta shapes
50 g (2 oz) butter, cut into pieces
350 g (12 oz) flat black mushrooms, sliced
2 garlic cloves, skinned and crushed
100 g (4 oz) Danish blue cheese, crumbled
225 g (8 oz) curd cheese
salt and pepper
100 g (4 oz) Emmenthal cheese, grated
30 ml (2 tbsp) freshly grated Parmesan cheese

/ 1 / Cook the pasta conventionally in boiling salted water until just tender. Drain and rinse in boiling water.

/ 2 / Meanwhile, put the butter in a large gratin dish and microwave on HIGH for 1 minute or until melted. Add the mushrooms and garlic, cover and microwave on HIGH for 4-6 minutes or until the mushrooms are softened.

/ 3 / Stir the Danish blue cheese into the mushrooms with the curd cheese. Re-cover and microwave on HIGH for 2-3 minutes or until the cheese has melted.

/ 4 / Stir in the pasta and toss together until the pasta is thoroughly coated in the sauce. Season to taste with salt and pepper. Sprinkle with Emmenthal and Parmesan cheese.

/ 5 / Stand the dish on the wire rack and cook on combination at 250°C/MEDIUM LOW for 10-15 minutes or until golden brown. Serve the pasta bake piping hot.

TINY CHEESE TRIANGLES

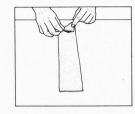

Brush the strips of pastry with the melted butter or margarine. Place a generous teaspoonful of filling at 1 end of each strip. Fold the pastry diagonally across the filling to form a triangle.

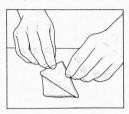

Continue folding, keeping the triangle shape, until you reach the end of the strip of pastry.

Filo pastry, sometimes spelt phyllo, is a paper-thin pastry made of flour and water. It is possible to make it at home but it is a time-consuming task because of the amount of rolling and stretching needed to make it really thin, so buy it ready prepared and keep it in the freezer until required.

PASTA WITH MUSHROOMS AND CHEESE
Use flat mushrooms, if possible, for this recipe as they have more flavour than button mushrooms.

SPINACH TARTS WITH TOMATO AND BASIL SALAD

SERVES 2

Basil is a delicate annual plant that survives only during the summer months. It has small, soft, oval leaves and tiny white flowers. It can be used fresh or dried, in most savoury dishes and is particularly good in those that contain tomatoes.

50 g (2 oz) plain wholemeal flour
salt and pepper
50 g (2 oz) butter or margarine
2 egg yolks
1 small onion, skinned and finely chopped
1 small garlic clove, skinned and crushed
300 g (10.6 oz) packet frozen leaf spinach
75 ml (5 tbsp) freshly grated Parmesan cheese
60 ml (4 tbsp) double cream
freshly grated nutmeg
3 large tomatoes
15 ml (1 tbsp) chopped fresh basil
15 ml (1 tbsp) olive or vegetable oil

/1/ Mix the flour and a pinch of salt in a bowl. Cut half of the butter or margarine into small pieces, add it to the flour and rub in until the mixture resembles fine breadcrumbs.

/2/ Make a well in the centre and stir in 1 of the egg yolks and 15-30 ml (1-2 tbsp) water. Mix together using a round-bladed knife. Knead lightly to give a firm, smooth dough.

/3/ Roll out the dough thinly. Invert two 10 cm (4 inch) shallow glass flan dishes and cover the base and sides with the dough. Cover with cling film and chill in the refrigerator while making the filling.

/4/ Put the remaining butter or margarine in a large bowl and microwave on HIGH for 1 minute or until the fat melts. Stir in the onion and garlic, cover and microwave on HIGH for 4-5 minutes or until the onion is softened.

Spinach Tarts with Tomato and Basil Salad

/ 5 / Add the spinach, re-cover and microwave on HIGH for 8-9 minutes or until it is thawed, stirring frequently. Stir in 60 ml (4 tbsp) Parmesan cheese, the cream and season well with salt, pepper and nutmeg.

/ 6 / Remove the cling film from the pastry cases and prick all over, with a fork. Microwave on HIGH, pastry side uppermost, for 2-2½ minutes or until the pastry is firm to the touch. Leave to stand for 4-5 minutes, then carefully invert the pastry cases on to a wire rack. Remove the flan dishes and leave the pastry cases to crisp on the wire rack.

/ 7 / Meanwhile, thinly slice the tomatoes and arrange on 2 large serving plates. Sprinkle with the basil and drizzle over the olive oil. Season with salt and pepper.

/ 8 / Microwave the spinach filling on HIGH for 2-3 minutes, stirring occasionally. Stir in the remaining egg yolk and microwave on HIGH for 1-1½ minutes or until slightly thickened.

/ 9 / Transfer the pastry cases to the serving plates and carefully spoon the spinach filling into the centres. Sprinkle the tarts with remaining Parmesan cheese and serve immediately with the tomato and basil salad.

CHEESE AND NUT PLAIT

C   S E R V E S   4

FILLING
25 g (1 oz) butter or margarine
1 small onion, skinned and finely chopped
15 ml (1 tbsp) green peppercorns, chopped
175 g (6 oz) chopped mixed nuts
100 g (4 oz) fresh wholemeal breadcrumbs
100 g (4 oz) Cheddar cheese, grated
cayenne pepper
salt
1 egg, beaten
PASTRY
275 g (10 oz) plain flour
salt
150 g (5 oz) butter or margarine
1 egg, beaten
30 ml (2 tbsp) finely chopped mixed nuts

/ 1 / Make the filling: put the butter or margarine in a bowl and microwave on HIGH for 1 minute or until melted. Add the onion, cover and microwave on HIGH for 3 minutes or until the onion has softened.

/ 2 / Stir in the peppercorns, nuts, breadcrumbs and cheese, then season to taste with cayenne and salt. Add enough beaten egg just to bind the ingredients and set aside while making the pastry.

/ 3 / Mix the flour and salt together in a bowl. Rub in the butter or margarine until the mixture resembles fine breadcrumbs, then mix in about 60 ml (4 tbsp) water with a round-bladed knife, adding just enough to form a firm dough. Knead lightly and roll out on a lightly floured surface to a 33 cm (13 inch) square.

/ 4 / Starting with the side of pastry to your right, make 7.5 cm (3 inch) cuts in the pastry at right angles to the edge and at 2.5 cm (1 inch) intervals. Repeat with the opposite side of the pastry square.

/ 5 / Spoon the filling down the centre of the pastry leaving a 4 cm (1¼ inch) border at the top and bottom. Brush the pastry with beaten egg, then fold the top and bottom pieces of pastry down over the filling. Starting from the top, fold the top left hand strip of pastry over the filling, then fold the top right hand strip over. Continue folding over the pastry from alternate sides down the length of the filling to give a plaited effect.

/ 6 / Transfer the plait to a large shallow ovenproof dish and brush with the remaining egg. Sprinkle with the nuts, then chill for 10 minutes in the refrigerator while preheating the oven on convection at 250°C.

/ 7 / Stand the dish on the wire rack and cook on combination at 200°C/MEDIUM LOW for 20-25 minutes or until browned. Serve the plait warm or cold.

CHEESE AND NUT PLAIT
If the instructions given here for rolling out the pastry and wrapping over the filling seem a little complicated at first, don't be put off. You'll find it will all become clear once the pastry and filling are in front of you.

Nuts when mixed with whole grain ingredients, will provide a high protein meal. They contain significant amounts of fibre whilst all but chestnuts have a low carbohydrate content.
    All nuts are rich in minerals, particularly phosphorus, potassium, iron and calcium. In varying quantities, they also contain B vitamins and vitamin E.
    With the exception of chestnuts, nuts have a high fat content. In some the fats are mainly polyunsaturated in others they are monosaturated (which seems to have little effect one way or the other on blood cholesterol) but in some, especially coconut, the fats are mainly saturated which have been linked with higher blood cholesterol levels.

LEEK AND CAMEMBERT TART

[C]   SERVES 4 - 6

PASTRY

175 g (6 oz) plain flour

pinch of salt

75 g (3 oz) butter or margarine

1 egg, beaten

FILLING

50 g (2 oz) butter or margarine

700 g (1½ lb) leeks, trimmed and thinly sliced

2 eggs

150 ml (¼ pint) double cream

175 g (6 oz) Camembert

freshly grated nutmeg

salt and pepper

/ 1 / Make the pastry: mix the flour and salt together in a bowl. Add the butter or margarine and rub in until the mixture resembles fine breadcrumbs. Mix in the egg, using a round-bladed knife and knead lightly to give a firm, smooth dough.

/ 2 / Roll out the pastry thinly on a lightly floured surface and use to line a 20.5 cm (8 inch) cake dish. Chill in the refrigerator while making the filling.

/ 3 / Put the butter or margarine in a large bowl and microwave on HIGH for 1 minute or until melted. Add the leeks, cover and microwave on HIGH for 10 minutes or until softened.

/ 4 / Preheat the oven on convection at 250°C for 10 minutes.

/ 5 / Meanwhile, beat the eggs and cream into the leeks. Remove the rind from the Camembert and cut the cheese into small pieces. Stir most of the cheese pieces into the leek mixture. Season the mixture to taste with nutmeg, salt and pepper.

/ 6 / Fill the pastry case with the filling and sprinkle the reserved cheese on top. Stand the dish on the wire rack and cook on combination at 200°C/MEDIUM LOW for 20-25 minutes or until the filling is set and golden brown. Serve the tart while it is warm.

SPINACH AND RICOTTA FILO PIE

[C]   SERVES 6 - 8

75 g (3 oz) butter or margarine

1 large onion, skinned and finely chopped

2 garlic cloves, skinned and crushed

900 g (2 lb) fresh spinach, washed, trimmed and chopped, or a 450 g (1 lb) packet frozen spinach

450 g (1 lb) ricotta cheese

2.5 ml (½ tsp) dried dill

freshly grated nutmeg

salt and pepper

8 sheets of frozen filo pastry, thawed

sesame seeds

/ 1 / Put 25 g (1 oz) of the butter or margarine in a bowl and microwave on HIGH for 30 seconds or until melted. Stir in the onion and garlic, cover and cook on HIGH for 3-4 minutes or until softened.

/ 2 / Stir the spinach into the onion mixture. If using fresh spinach, cover and microwave on HIGH for 3-4 minutes or until the spinach is just cooked. If using frozen, microwave on HIGH for 8-9 minutes or until thawed. Drain and return to the bowl.

/ 3 / Add the ricotta cheese and dill to the bowl and mix well together. Season generously with nutmeg and salt and pepper.

/ 4 / Put the remaining butter or margarine in a bowl and microwave on HIGH for 1 minute or until melted. Use a little to grease a 23 cm (9 inch) flan dish.

/ 5 / Using 7 sheets of the filo pastry, brush them with melted butter, 1 at a time, and use to line the flan dish letting the pastry fall over the sides. Spoon the filling into the dish. Fold the overlapping pieces of pastry over to cover the filling completely.

/ 6 / Preheat the oven on convection at 250°C for 10 minutes. Meanwhile, cut the remaining filo sheet into 2.5 cm (1 inch) strips. Sprinkle on top of the pie and brush with any remaining butter. Sprinkle with the sesame seeds.

/ 7 / Stand the flan dish on the wire rack and cook on combination at 200°C/MEDIUM LOW for 10 minutes or lightly browned.

Spinach and Ricotta Filo Pie

FILO CHEESE TRIO

C SERVES 4

8 sheets of frozen filo pastry, thawed
50 g (2 oz) butter
100 g (4 oz) Stilton
100 g (4 oz) Brie with herbs
100 g (4 oz) Camembert
salad leaves and cherry tomatoes, to garnish

/ 1 / Using kitchen scissors, cut each sheet of filo pastry into three 15 cm (6 inch) squares.

/ 2 / Put the butter in a small bowl and microwave on HIGH for 1 minute or until melted. Lay 12 of the filo squares on a flat surface and brush with melted butter. Place a second filo square on top and brush the edges with more butter.

/ 3 / Preheat the oven on convection at 250°C for 10 minutes. Meanwhile, cut each cheese into 4 equal-sized pieces and place 1 in the centre of each filo square.

/ 4 / Bring the edges of the pastry up around the cheese and squeeze together at the top to seal. Brush the outside of the parcels with any remaining butter.

/ 5 / Stand the cheese parcels on a large flat ovenproof plate and cook on combination at 200°C/MEDIUM LOW for 3-4 minutes or until golden brown. Serve immediately on individual plates garnished with salad leaves and cherry tomatoes.

These small crisp parcels containing a selection of just melted cheeses, make a tasty dinner party starter. When arranging the parcels for cooking, take care to make a note of which parcels contain which cheese so that each person is served 1 of each rather than 3 the same.

Filo pastry is sold in 450 g (1 lb) packs which usually contain about 24 sheets. You only need 8 for this recipe, so keep the remainder in the refrigerator.

PRAWN AND CHIVE TARTS

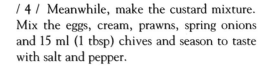

SERVES 6

2 eggs, beaten
150 ml (¼ pint) double cream
100 g (4 oz) cooked peeled prawns
6 spring onions, trimmed and finely chopped
15 ml (1 tbsp) snipped fresh chives
salt and pepper
snipped fresh chives, to garnish
PASTRY
175 g (6 oz) plain flour
pinch of salt
75 g (3 oz) butter or margarine
1 egg, beaten

PRAWN AND CHIVE TARTS

These attractive tarts have pink prawns in a lightly set chive custard all contained in a buttery shortcrust pastry case. The pastry cases can be made and baked blind in advance, but the prawn custard is best cooked just before serving. When garnishing with chives, try not to cut them into tiny pieces, but instead use kitchen scissors to snip them into 5 cm (2 inch) lengths and pile them generously on top of the cooked tarts.

/ 1 / Make the pastry, mix the flour and salt together in a bowl. Rub in the butter or margarine until the mixture resembles fine breadcrumbs. Mix in the egg, using a round-bladed knife, and knead lightly with fingertips to give a firm, smooth dough.

/ 2 / Roll out the pastry thinly on a lightly floured surface and use to line 6 individual 11 cm (4½ inch) fluted flan dishes. Chill for 10 minutes in the refrigerator while preheating the oven on convection at 250°C.

/ 3 / Stand the flan dishes on the wire rack and cook on combination at 200°C/MEDIUM LOW for 8-10 minutes or until lightly set and just beginning to colour.

/ 4 / Meanwhile, make the custard mixture. Mix the eggs, cream, prawns, spring onions and 15 ml (1 tbsp) chives and season to taste with salt and pepper.

/ 5 / Spoon the custard into the pastry cases. Stand the dishes on the wire rack and cook on combination at 200°C/MEDIUM LOW for 8-10 minutes or until lightly set. Garnish with chives and serve warm.

FETA CHEESE AND SPINACH PUFFS

MAKES 8

75 g (3 oz) Feta cheese
15 ml (1 tbsp) Greek yogurt or soured cream
2.5 ml (½ tsp) dried oregano
50 g (2 oz) fresh young spinach
pepper
375 g (13 oz) packet frozen puff pastry, thawed
beaten egg, to glaze

FETA CHEESE AND SPINACH PUFFS

This type of little pie is found all over Greece. The filling is Feta cheese, which is a salty Greek cheese, so don't be tempted to add any extra salt. Fresh spinach leaves are mixed with the Feta and are cooked briefly as the pastry cooks, so retaining a bright green colour. Don't use frozen spinach as it's too watery and would give a rather soggy result.

/ 1 / Put the cheese and yogurt or soured cream in a bowl and mash together with a fork. Stir in the oregano.

/ 2 / Discard any tough stems from the spinach, then wash the leaves in several changes of water. Drain well, chop finely and mix with the cheese. Season to taste with pepper.

/ 3 / Roll out the pastry thinly on a lightly floured surface and cut out 16 rounds, using a 7.5 cm (3 inch) plain round cutter.

/ 4 / Place a heaped teaspoonful of the cheese and spinach mixture in the centre of 8 of the pastry rounds. Brush the edges with beaten egg, then place a second pastry round on top of each. Press down well to seal.

/ 5 / Place on a large flat ovenproof plate and chill for 10 minutes while preheating the oven on convection at 250°C.

/ 6 / Brush the puffs with beaten egg, place the plate on the wire rack and cook on combination at 250°C/MEDIUM LOW for 8-10 minutes or until puffed up and golden brown. Serve these cheese and spinach puffs warm or cold.

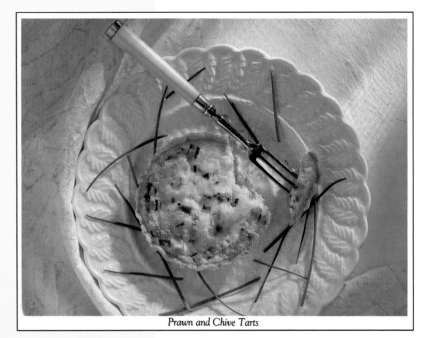

Prawn and Chive Tarts

Feta Cheese and Spinach Puffs

CHEESE AND WATERCRESS MILLE-FEUILLES

C   S E R V E S   6

375 g (13 oz) packet frozen puff pastry, thawed
1 egg yolk, beaten
2 bunches of watercress, trimmed
15 ml (1 tbsp) lemon juice
225 g (8 oz) full-fat soft cheese
salt and pepper
lemon twists, to garnish

/ 1 / Preheat the oven on convection at 250°C for 10 minutes.

/ 2 / Meanwhile, roll out the pastry thinly on a lightly floured surface and cut out 12 rounds, using an 8.5 cm (3½ inch) fluted cutter.

/ 3 / Place 6 pastry rounds on a large ovenproof plate. Prick evenly with a fork and brush with beaten egg yolk, taking care not to brush the edges. Stand the plate on the wire rack and cook on combination at 200°C/MEDIUM LOW for 6-8 minutes or until well risen and golden brown. Transfer to a wire rack and leave to cool. Repeat with the remaining 6 pastry rounds and leave to cool.

/ 4 / Make the filling: place most of the watercress in a bowl, reserving a few sprigs to garnish. Microwave on HIGH for 30 seconds-1 minute or until the watercress is just wilted. Place in a blender or food processor with the lemon juice, cheese and salt and pepper to taste, and purée until smooth.

/ 5 / Just before serving, split each pastry round in half, spread with the watercress filling, then sandwich back together. Serve 2 mille-feuilles per person, garnished with the reserved watercress and lemon twists.

Mille-feuilles are usually made in a large rectangular shape. Here the idea has been adapted to suit a combination oven by making small, round mille-feuilles. When pricking the pastry before cooking, make sure that you prick it evenly all over or the pastry will rise unevenly. take care also when brushing with the egg glaze – if the glaze gets on to the edge of the pastry it will stick it together and prevent it from rising.

Scrambled Egg with Smoked Salmon

SCRAMBLED EGG WITH SMOKED SALMON

SERVES 1

25 g (1 oz) smoked salmon trimmings
2 eggs, size 2
30 ml (2 tbsp) double cream or milk
25 g (1 oz) butter
salt and pepper
buttered toast, to serve
chopped fresh parsley, to garnish

/ 1 / Cut the salmon into small pieces and set aside. Put the eggs, cream or milk and butter into a medium bowl and season with a little salt and lots of pepper. Whisk together well.

/ 2 / Microwave on HIGH for 1 minute or until the mixture just begins to set around the edge of the bowl. Whisk vigorously to incorporate the set egg mixture.

/ 3 / Add the smoked salmon and microwave on HIGH for 1½-2 minutes, whisking every 30 seconds and taking care not to break up the salmon, until the eggs are just set but still soft.

/ 4 / Check the seasoning, then spoon on to the toast. Garnish with chopped parsley and serve immediately.

MUSSELS IN WHITE WINE

SERVES 2

900 g (2 lb) fresh mussels
1 small onion, skinned and finely chopped
1 garlic clove, skinned and crushed
75 ml (5 tbsp) dry white wine
75 ml (5 tbsp) fish stock or water
30 ml (2 tbsp) chopped fresh parsley
salt and pepper
crusty bread, to serve

/ 1 / To clean the mussels, put them in a sink or bowl and scrub thoroughly with a hard brush. Wash them in several changes of water.

/ 2 / Scrape off any 'beards' or tufts protruding from the shells. Discard any damaged mussels or any that do not close when tapped.

/ 3 / Put the onion, garlic, wine, stock or water and mussels in a large bowl. Cover and microwave on HIGH for 3-5 minutes or until all the mussels have opened, removing the mussels on the top as they open and shaking the bowl occasionally. Discard any mussels that have not opened.

/ 4 / Pile the mussels in a warmed serving dish. Stir the parsley into the liquid remaining in the bowl and season to taste with salt and pepper. Pour over the mussels and serve immediately with lots of crusty bread.

POTTED SHRIMPS

SERVES 4

200 g (7 oz) butter
175 g (6 oz) cooked shrimps, peeled
pinch of ground mace
pinch of cayenne pepper
pinch of ground nutmeg
salt and pepper
bay leaves and peppercorns, to garnish
brown bread and lemon wedges, to serve

/ 1 / Cut half of the butter into small pieces, put in a medium bowl and microwave on HIGH for 1-2 minutes until melted.

/ 2 / Add the shrimps, mace, cayenne pepper, nutmeg, salt and plenty of pepper. Stir to coat the shrimps in the butter, then microwave on LOW for 2-3 minutes until the shrimps are hot, stirring occasionally. Do not allow the mixture to boil. Pour into 4 ramekin dishes or small individual pots.

/ 3 / Cut the remaining butter into small pieces, put into a small bowl and microwave on HIGH for 1-2 minutes until melted. Leave to stand for a few minutes to let the salt and sediment settle, then carefully spoon the clarified butter over the shrimps to cover completely.

/ 4 / Garnish with bay leaves and peppercorns, leave until set, then chill in the refrigerator before serving.

/ 5 / Serve straight from the pots with brown bread and lemon wedges, or turn out and arrange on individual plates.

SCRAMBLED EGG WITH SMOKED SALMON

Cut the smoked salmon into small pieces so that it will heat through very quickly.

To serve 2: double the quantities of Scrambled Egg with Smoked Salmon and serve with Bucks Fizz made with 1 part chilled fresh orange juice to 2 parts chilled champagne. Fill a champagne glass about one-third full with orange juice and top up with champagne.

POTTED SHRIMPS
Serve these little pots of shrimps with warm bread rolls instead of brown bread, if preferred. Place the bread rolls in a wicker basket, lined with a paper napkin if liked. Microwave on HIGH for 30-45 seconds until warm. Do not overcook or the rolls will be hard.

MUSSELS IN WHITE WINE
Mussels are usually sold by the quart (1.1 litres) which is approximately the same as 900 g (2 lb). Never buy mussels with cracked or open shells. Mussels are available from September to March.

STUFFED PLAICE TIMBALES WITH LEMON BUTTER

STUFFED PLAICE
TIMBALES WITH LEMON
BUTTER

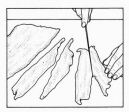

Cut the plaice fillets in half lengthways, to make 2 long fillets from each.

Line the ramekin or soufflé dishes with the fish, then spoon the cooked rice mixture into the centre of each ramekin, pressing down well.

Cover the dishes with absorbent paper and microwave on HIGH for 2-3 minutes until the fish is cooked. Leave to stand for 2-3 minutes, then invert the dishes on to serving plates. With the dishes still in place, pour off any excess liquid, then carefully remove the dishes.

BAKED CRAB RAMEKINS
This recipe uses cooked crab meat; use half a frozen 450 g (1 lb) block for convenience.

SERVES 4

25 g (1 oz) butter
5 ml (1 tsp) lemon juice
30 ml (2 tbsp) chopped fresh parsley
salt and pepper
175 g (6 oz) mushrooms
15 ml (1 tbsp) vegetable oil
75 g (3 oz) long-grain white rice
300 ml (½ pint) hot chicken stock
2 large double plaice fillets, skinned or 1 plaice, filleted
parsley sprigs, to garnish

/ 1 / Make the lemon herb butter: put the butter in a small bowl and beat until soft. Add the lemon juice, half of the parsley and season well with salt and pepper. Beat together well. Push to the side of the bowl to form a small pat and then leave to chill in the refrigerator while making the timbales.

/ 2 / Finely chop the mushrooms and put in a medium bowl with the oil. Cover and microwave on HIGH for 2-3 minutes or until the mushrooms are softened.

/ 3 / Stir in the rice and the stock, re-cover and microwave on HIGH for 10-12 minutes or until the rice is tender and the stock absorbed, stirring occasionally.

/ 4 / Meanwhile, cut the plaice fillets in half lengthways, to make 2 long fillets from each. Place 1 fillet, skinned side in, around the inside of each of 4 buttered 150 ml (¼ pint) ramekin or individual soufflé dishes. The fish should line the dish leaving a hole in the centre for the mushroom and rice filling.

/ 5 / When the rice is cooked, stir in the remaining parsley and salt and pepper to taste. Spoon this mixture into the centre of each ramekin, pressing down well. Cover loosely with absorbent kitchen paper and microwave on HIGH for 2-3 minutes or until the fish is cooked (looks opaque).

/ 6 / Leave to stand for 2-3 minutes, then invert the ramekin dishes on to serving plates. With the dishes still in place pour off any excess liquid, then carefully remove the dishes.

/ 7 / Garnish the timbales with parsley sprigs, then serve hot, with a knob of the lemon herb butter on top of each.

BAKED CRAB RAMEKINS WITH PAPRIKA

C · SERVES 6

25 g (1 oz) butter or margarine
1 small onion, skinned and finely chopped
225 g (8 oz) white (or white and brown) crab meat
50 g (2 oz) fresh wholemeal breadcrumbs
150 ml (¼ pint) soured cream
1 egg, beaten
finely grated rind and juice of 2 limes
salt
paprika
40 g (1½ oz) Cheddar cheese, grated
lime slices and parsley sprigs, to garnish

/ 1 / Put the butter or margarine in a medium bowl and microwave on HIGH for 45 seconds or until melted. Add the onion, cover and microwave on HIGH for 4 minutes or until the onion has softened.

/ 2 / Flake the crab meat, taking care to remove any membrane or shell particles. Add the crab meat to the onion with the breadcrumbs and mix well together. Stir in the soured cream, beaten egg and lime rind and juice. Season to taste with salt and paprika.

/ 3 / Spoon the mixture into 6 ramekin dishes and sprinkle with paprika and the grated cheese. Stand the dishes on the wire rack and cook on combination at 200°C/MEDIUM LOW for 8-12 minutes or until lightly set. Serve the ramekins while they are still warm, garnished with a few lime slices and parsley sprigs.

Baked Crab Ramekins with Paprika

CHILLED COURGETTE
MOUSSE WITH SAFFRON
SAUCE
Use a swivel-type potato peeler to get the best courgette slices. Make sure the slices are neat because they show when the mousse is turned out (see page 12).

If you don't have any saffron, you can use turmeric to colour the sauce a pretty yellow, but the flavour will not be the same.

GRATIN OF MUSSELS
AND SPINACH
For convenience and speed, precooked mussels have been used in this recipe. They are sold frozen in 450 g (1 lb) bags. If you prefer, you can cook fresh mussels for this recipe. You will need about 900 g (2 lb) mussels in the shell.

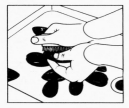

To clean the mussels put them in a sink or bowl and scrub thoroughly with a hard brush. Wash them in several changes of water.

Scrape off any 'beards' or tufts protruding from the shells. Discard any damaged mussels or any that do not close when tapped with a knife. Put the mussels in a large bowl with 150 ml (¼ pint) dry white wine, cover and microwave on HIGH for 3-5 minutes or until the mussels open. Dis~~~ ~~~ any that do not op~~~ ~~~ve from the shell a~~~ ~~~eed with the recipe, u~~~ the wine to make the ~~~ uce.

CHILLED COURGETTE MOUSSE WITH SAFFRON SAUCE

SERVES 2

275 g (10 oz) small courgettes, trimmed
15 g (½ oz) butter or margarine
7.5 ml (1½ tsp) lemon juice
100 g (4 oz) low-fat soft cheese
salt and pepper
5 ml (1 tsp) gelatine
45 ml (3 tbsp) natural yogurt
pinch of saffron strands
1 egg yolk
fresh herb sprigs, to garnish

/ 1 / Cut 1 of the courgettes into very thin slices lengthways, using a potato peeler or sharp knife. Put the slices in a medium bowl with 30 ml (2 tbsp) water.

/ 2 / Cover and microwave on HIGH for 2-3 minutes or until the slices are just tender, stirring once during cooking. Drain and dry thoroughly with absorbent kitchen paper.

/ 3 / Use the courgettes slices to line 2 oiled 150 ml (¼ pint) ramekin dishes. Set aside while making the courgette and cheese filling.

/ 4 / Finely chop the remaining courgettes and put into a medium bowl with half of the butter or margarine and the lemon juice.

/ 5 / Cover and microwave on HIGH for 5-6 minutes or until tender, stirring occasionally.

/ 6 / Allow to cool slightly, then liquidise in a blender or food processor with the remaining butter and the cheese until smooth. Season well with salt and pepper.

/ 7 / Put the gelatine and 15 ml (1 tbsp) water into a small bowl or cup and cook on LOW for 1-1½ minutes or until the gelatine has dissolved, stirring occasionally. Add to the courgette purée and mix together thoroughly.

/ 8 / Pour into the lined dishes and leave to cool. Chill for at least 1 hour or until set.

/ 9 / Meanwhile, make the sauce. Put the yogurt, saffron, egg yolk, salt and pepper into a small bowl and cook on LOW for 1-1½ minutes, or until slightly thickened, stirring frequently. Strain, then leave to cool.

/ 10 / To serve, loosen the courgette moulds with a palette knife, then turn out on to 2 individual serving plates. Pour over the sauce, garnish each plate with a herb sprig and serve immediately.

GRATIN OF MUSSELS AND SPINACH

C   SERVES 4

1 small onion, skinned and finely chopped
50 g (2 oz) butter
225 g (8 oz) fresh spinach or 100 g (4 oz) frozen spinach, thawed
150 ml (¼ pint) dry white wine
15 ml (1 tbsp) potato flour
450 g (1 lb) cooked shelled mussels, thawed if frozen
60 ml (4 tbsp) Greek yogurt
salt and pepper
75 g (3 oz) fresh breadcrumbs

/ 1 / Put the onion and half of the butter in a bowl, cover and microwave on HIGH for 5-7 minutes or until softened.

/ 2 / Meanwhile, thoroughly wash the fresh spinach in several changes of clean water. Trim off any coarse stems and roughly chop.

/ 3 / Add the wine and fresh or frozen spinach to the onion, re-cover and microwave on HIGH for 3-4 minutes or until the fresh spinach has just wilted or the frozen spinach is hot.

/ 4 / Transfer the mixture to a blender or food processor and purée until smooth. Return to the bowl and sprinkle with the potato flour. Microwave on HIGH for 2 minutes or until thickened, stirring occasionally.

/ 5 / Stir in the mussels and yogurt and season to taste with salt and pepper. Divide the mixture between 4 individual ovenproof serving dishes, or 1 large dish, sprinkle with the breadcrumbs and dot with the remaining butter.

/ 6 / Stand the dishes on the wire rack and cook on combination at 250°C/MEDIUM LOW for 10-15 minutes or until the breadcrumbs are brown and crisp. Serve hot.

SMOKED SALMON IN GOLDEN BOXES

C   SERVES 4

half a large, stale, unsliced white sandwich loaf
50 g (2 oz) butter
2 eggs
22.5 ml (1½ tbsp) plain flour
150 ml (¼ pint) milk
salt and pepper
15 ml (1 tbsp) lemon juice
150 ml (¼ pint) single cream
15 ml (1 tbsp) chopped fresh chervil
50 g (2 oz) smoked salmon, cut into thin strips
lemon wedges or chervil sprigs, to garnish

/ 1 / Cut 2 slices, about 5 cm (2 inches) thick, from the loaf and remove the crusts. Trim the slices into rectangular blocks, measuring 7.5 cm (3 inches) by 10 cm (4 inches). Cut each slice in half across the width to make a total of four pieces, each measuring 7.5 cm (3 inches) by 5 cm (2 inches) by 5 cm (2 inches).

/ 2 / Remove the centre of 1 bread piece by making a cut about 1 cm (½ inch) in from each edge. Scoop out this middle section to make a neat bread box. Repeat with the remaining bread slices to make 4 boxes.

/ 3 / Put the butter in a medium bowl and microwave on HIGH for 1 minute or until melted. Preheat the oven on convection at 250°C for 10 minutes. Meanwhile, cook the eggs conventionally in boiling water for about 10 minutes or until hard-boiled. Drain, shell and roughly chop.

/ 4 / Brush the outsides and tops of the bread cases with some of the melted butter and stand them on an ovenproof plate. Place the plate on the wire rack and cook on combination at 200°C/MEDIUM LOW for 5-7 minutes or until crisp and golden. Remove from the oven and place on 4 individual serving plates.

/ 5 / Stir the flour, milk and salt and pepper to taste into the remaining melted butter in the bowl. Microwave on HIGH for 3-4 minutes or until boiling and thickened, whisking frequently. Stir in the lemon juice, cream, chopped chervil and chopped egg. Spoon into the golden boxes allowing the mixture to spill out on to the plates.

/ 6 / Sprinkle with the smoked salmon, garnish with lemon or chervil and serve immediately.

SMOKED SALMON IN GOLDEN BOXES
Don't be put off by the length of this recipe. If you follow the steps carefully, it's very simple to make and the result is well worth the extra effort. Make sure you use stale bread (fresh is impossible to cut accurately). The golden boxes can be made in advance and reheated before filling.

Smoked Salmon in Golden Boxes

DEVILLED HERRINGS IN OATMEAL

SERVES 2

10 ml (2 tsp) tomato purée
2.5 ml (½ tsp) mild mustard
2.5 ml (½ tsp) brown sugar
dash of Worcestershire sauce
pinch of cayenne pepper
salt and pepper
4 small herring fillets
60 ml (4 tbsp) medium oatmeal
15 ml (1 tbsp) vegetable oil
15 g (½ oz) butter or margarine
lemon wedges and mustard and cress, to garnish

/ 1 / Heat a browning dish on HIGH for 5-8 minutes or according to the manufacturer's instructions for your particular one.

/ 2 / Meanwhile, mix the tomato purée, mustard, sugar, Worcestershire sauce and cayenne pepper together. Season with salt and pepper. Spread the paste thinly on to both sides of each herring fillet, then coat in the oatmeal.

/ 3 / Put the oil and butter or margarine in the browning dish and swirl to coat the base.

/ 4 / Quickly add the fillets, skin side down, and microwave on HIGH for 1½ minutes. Turn over and microwave on HIGH for 1-2 minutes or until the fish is cooked. Serve garnished with lemon wedges and mustard and cress.

BAKED SAUSAGES WITH ONIONS

C

SERVES 3 - 4

2 medium onions, skinned and thinly sliced
450 g (1 lb) sausages
10 ml (2 tsp) Dijon mustard
30 ml (2 tbsp) redcurrant jelly
150 ml (¼ pint) hot beef stock
pepper
French bread, to serve

/ 1 / Put the onions in an ovenproof dish large enough to hold the sausages in a single layer.

/ 2 / Whisk the mustard and jelly into the hot stock and season to taste with pepper. Pour over the onions, cover and microwave on HIGH for 5-7 minutes or until the onions are softened, stirring occasionally.

/ 3 / Arrange the sausages on top of the onions. Stand the dish on the wire rack and cook on combination at 250°C/MEDIUM LOW for 20-25 minutes or until the sausages are cooked and browned. Serve with French bread.

PRAWNS COOKED IN BRANDY AND CREAM

SERVES 1

175 g (6 oz) medium raw prawns, in the shell
15 g (½ oz) butter or margarine
salt and pepper
25 ml (1½ tbsp) brandy
45 ml (3 tbsp) double cream
4 green Cos lettuce leaves, shredded
lime twists, to garnish

/ 1 / Prepare the prawns. Remove the shells, leaving the tail shells intact. With kitchen scissors or a sharp knife, split the prawns along the curved underside towards the tail, stopping at the tail shell, and cutting deep enough to expose the dark vein.

/ 2 / Spread each prawn wide open, remove the dark vein, then rinse under cold running water. Dry thoroughly on kitchen paper.

/ 3 / Put the butter or margarine into a medium bowl and microwave on HIGH for 45 seconds or until the butter melts. Stir in the prawns and microwave on HIGH for 1½-2½ minutes or until the prawns just turn pink, stirring frequently. Remove with a slotted spoon and set aside.

/ 4 / Season with salt and pepper and quickly stir in the brandy and the cream. Microwave on HIGH for 4-4½ minutes or until the mixture is thickened and reduced.

/ 5 / Stir in the prawns and lettuce and mix together carefully. Microwave on HIGH for 30-45 seconds or until the prawns are just heated through. Garnish with lime twists and serve.

DEVILLED HERRINGS IN OATMEAL
Herrings are a neglected fish, yet they are a good source of protein, the minerals calcium and phosphorus and, because they are oily fish, vitamins A and D.

BAKED SAUSAGES WITH ONIONS
Sausages baked in the oven are much nicer than when grilled or fried. The trouble is they take so long to cook in a conventional oven. With the benefits of combined microwave and convection cooking, however, they take only 20-25 minutes. Use good quality beef or pork sausages for this recipe.

PRAWNS COOKED IN BRANDY AND CREAM

To prepare the prawns: remove the shells, leaving the shells intact. With kitchen scissors or a sharp knife, split the prawns along the curved underside towards the tail, stopping at the tail shell, and cutting deep enough to expose the dark vein.

If you find it difficult to buy raw prawns, buy the best quality cooked prawns in the shell and omit step 1.

Prawns Cooked in Brandy and Cream

FISHCAKES

Cut the potatoes in half, scoop out the flesh and put in a bowl.

Don't discard the potato skins, use them to make crispy potato skins, by baking or frying, to serve with dips as a starter.

Fishcakes can also be made with smoked fish or canned fish such as tuna or salmon.

SPICED CHICKEN WITH CHILLI MAYONNAISE
These delicious strips of chicken in a crunchy oatmeal coating are served warm with a tangy mayonnaise for dunking. This is an ideal starter to prepare in advance. Make the mayonnaise and store in the refrigerator, covered, and prepare the chicken goujons up to the end of step 2. When your guests are seated, simply pop the chicken in the preheated oven and in just 5-10 minutes they are ready to serve.

Whole oat grains are ground to make a meal of varying textures. Pinhead oatmeal is the coarsest; soaked overnight and cooked gently in the morning, it makes superb porridge. Medium oatmeal and fine oatmeal are used for baking. Rolled oats are used mainly for muesli; they are produced by steaming and rolling either whole or pinhead oats. Porridge oats have been rolled and partially cooked. Instant oats are made from a mixture of oatflakes and refined oat flour. Use fine oatmeal for this recipe.

Picture opposite: Fishcakes

FISHCAKES

MAKES 4

2 potatoes, each weighing 100 g (4 oz)
225 g (8 oz) fish fillets, such as smoked haddock, cod, salmon or coley
30 ml (2 tbsp) milk
25 g (1 oz) butter or margarine
finely grated rind of ½ lemon
30 ml (2 tbsp) chopped fresh parsley
a few drops anchovy essence (optional)
salt and pepper
beaten egg
30 ml (2 tbsp) seasoned plain flour
30 ml (2 tbsp) vegetable oil
lime twists, to garnish

/ 1 / Scrub the potatoes and prick all over with a fork. Microwave on HIGH for 7 minutes, turning over once during cooking.

/ 2 / Put the fish and the milk in a small shallow dish. Cover and put in the cooker with the potatoes. Microwave on HIGH for 4-5 minutes until the fish flakes easily and the potatoes are soft when pierced with a fork.

/ 3 / Cut the potatoes in half, scoop out the flesh and put in a bowl. Flake the fish, discarding the skin, and add to the potato with the cooking liquid.

/ 4 / Heat a browning dish on HIGH for 5-8 minutes or according to the manufacturer's instructions for your particular one.

/ 5 / Meanwhile, mix the fish and potato with the butter or margarine, lemon rind, half the parsley, the anchovy essence, if using, and salt and pepper to taste. Mash thoroughly together, then mix with enough beaten egg to bind the mixture together.

/ 6 / Shape into 4 fishcakes about 2.5 cm (1 inch) thick. Mix the remaining chopped parsley with the seasoned flour and use to coat the fishcakes.

/ 7 / Add the oil to the browning dish, then quickly add the fishcakes and microwave on HIGH for 2½ minutes. Turn over and microwave on HIGH for a further 2 minutes. Serve immediately, garnished with lime twists.

SPICED CHICKEN WITH CHILLI MAYONNAISE

C   SERVES 4

450 g (1 lb) chicken breast fillets, skinned
100 g (4 oz) fine oatmeal
7.5 ml (1½ tsp) garam masala
2.5 ml (½ tsp) paprika
salt and pepper
60 ml (4 tbsp) plain flour
1 egg, beaten
vegetable oil
parsley sprigs, to garnish
CHILLI MAYONNAISE
90 ml (6 tbsp) mayonnaise
60 ml (4 tbsp) Greek yogurt
1 garlic clove, skinned and crushed
15 ml (1 tbsp) lemon juice
2.5 ml (½ tsp) chilli powder

/ 1 / Cut the chicken fillets into strips 1 cm (½ inch) wide and 7.5 cm (3 inches) long.

/ 2 / Mix together the oatmeal, garam masala, paprika, salt and pepper on a large plate. Coat the strips of chicken in flour, dip in the beaten egg, then coat in the spiced oatmeal. Place in a shallow ovenproof dish. Chill for 10 minutes in the refrigerator while preheating the oven on convection at 250°C.

/ 3 / Make the chilli mayonnaise: place all the ingredients in a bowl and mix well. Set aside while cooking the chicken strips.

/ 4 / Lightly drizzle the chicken with oil. Stand the dish on the wire rack and cook on combination at 250°C/MEDIUM LOW for 5-10 minutes or until the chicken is tender and the coating crisp. Arrange on 4 individual serving plates, garnish with parsley sprigs and serve immediately with the chilli mayonnaise.

Kidneys are the perfect basis for a healthy snack as they are quick to prepare and cook and rich in protein, iron and B vitamins. The simplest way to prepare them is with kitchen scissors. After removing the outer membrane and splitting them in half, use the scissors to snip out the white core and any tubes. Take care not to overcook the kidneys or they will be tough. If your local baker does not sell small buttery brioches, use crisp white rolls instead (cut them in half and hollow out the insides as for brioches) or serve the kidneys with chunks of warmed French bread.

MUSTARD KIDNEYS EN BRIOCHE

SERVES 6

50 g (2 oz) butter or margarine
450 g (1 lb) lamb's kidneys, skinned, cored and roughly chopped
4 rashers streaky bacon, rinded and chopped
45 ml (3 tbsp) plain flour
300 ml (½ pint) chicken stock
30 ml (2 tbsp) wholegrain mustard
6 small brioches
60 ml (4 tbsp) single cream
salt and pepper

/ 1 / Put the butter or margarine in a medium bowl and microwave on HIGH for 1 minute or until melted. Add the kidneys and bacon and microwave on HIGH for 3-5 minutes or until the kidneys just change colour.

/ 2 / Add the flour and microwave on HIGH for 1 minute. Gradually stir in the stock and the mustard, then microwave on HIGH for 3-4 minutes or until the mixture is boiling and thickened and the kidneys are cooked, stirring frequently to ensure even cooking.

/ 3 / While the kidneys are cooking, remove the small knob from the top of each brioche and scoop out the soft insides. (Use the insides to make breadcrumbs to use in another recipe.)

/ 4 / When the kidneys are ready, place the brioches on the wire rack and cook on convection at 250°C for 4-5 minutes or until the brioches are crisp and hot.

/ 5 / Stir the cream into the kidney mixture and season to taste with salt and pepper. Place the warm brioches on serving plates and fill with the mustard kidneys. Replace the lids and serve the filled brioches immediately.

Mustard Kidneys en Brioche

BARBECUED SPARERIBS

C   S E R V E S   4

1.8 kg (4 lb) Chinese style pork spareribs
salt and pepper
120 ml (8 tbsp) clear honey
60 ml (4 tbsp) dark soft brown sugar
60 ml (4 tbsp) tomato ketchup
30 ml (2 tbsp) Worcestershire sauce
30 ml (2 tbsp) French mustard
30 ml (2 tbsp) wine vinegar
2 garlic cloves, skinned and crushed
chopped spring onions, to garnish

/ 1 / Put the spareribs in a large shallow oven-proof dish and season to taste with salt and pepper.

/ 2 / Stand the dish on the wire rack and cook on combination at 200°C/MEDIUM LOW for 10-15 minutes or until the fat just starts to run. Drain off the fat.

/ 3 / Mix together all the remaining ingredients, except the spring onions, pour over the ribs and stir to make sure they are all coated.

/ 4 / Continue to cook for 35-45 minutes or until the ribs are crisp and the sauce is thick and sticky, stirring occasionally. Sprinkle with spring onions and serve immediately.

HOT BAGUETTE SANDWICH WITH SALAMI

S E R V E S   2

15 ml (1 tbsp) olive or vegetable oil
1 small onion, skinned and chopped
5 ml (1 tsp) paprika
2.5 ml (½ tsp) sugar
pinch of cayenne pepper
1 small red pepper, cored, seeded and chopped
15 ml (1 tbsp) plain flour
150 ml (¼ pint) chicken stock
1 small baguette, about 30.5 cm (12 inches) long
225 g (8 oz) Mozzarella cheese
4 thin slices of Danish salami
pepper
a few black olives, stoned (optional)

Hot Baguette Sandwich with Salami

/ 1 / Put the oil, onion, paprika, sugar, cayenne pepper and chopped red pepper in a medium bowl. Cover and microwave on HIGH for 5-7 minutes or until softened, stirring occasionally. Stir in the flour and microwave on HIGH for 30 seconds.

/ 2 / Gradually stir in the chicken stock and microwave on HIGH for 5-6 minutes, stirring frequently, until the pepper is soft and the sauce has thickened.

/ 3 / Meanwhile, cut the baguette in half widthways, then cut each half in half lengthways. Cut the Mozzarella into thin slices and remove the rind from the salami. Arrange a layer of Mozzarella on 2 halves. Top with a layer of salami. Season with pepper.

/ 4 / When the sauce is cooked, let it cool a little, then purée in a blender or food processor until smooth. Spoon on top of the salami. Top with a few olives, if using. Put the other half of the baguette on top of each half to make 2 sandwiches.

/ 5 / Wrap each sandwich in greaseproof paper and microwave on HIGH for 1-1½ minutes or until the sandwiches are just warmed through. Serve immediately.

BARBECUED SPARERIBS
Spareribs are one of the most economical cuts of meat you can buy. Not all butchers display them because they are so bulky, but they are well worth asking for. The quantity of ribs given here will serve 4 as a starter for a Chinese-style meal. As they are eaten with the fingers, be sure to provide finger bowls and plenty of napkins.

HOT BAGUETTE SANDWICH WITH SALAMI

Cut the baguette in half widthways, then cut each half in half lengthways.

47

Meat

This chapter has a wide range of meat recipes illustrating how to cook by microwave alone, as well as showing you how to use the combination oven to full effect with succulent roasts, pies and melt-in-the-mouth casseroles and stews.

Remember, too, that meat dishes can be reheated very successfully by microwave. Indeed, the flavour is often improved if cooking is done in advance and the flavours given time to develop before the dish is reheated and served.

Poultry and game definitely benefit from the combination method of cooking. The flesh remains moist while the skin cooks until deliciously crisp and brown. Quick-cooking small game birds, such as pheasant, pigeon or grouse, are best cooked on convection, remembering to reduce your usual oven setting by 10°C to allow for the fast-cooking fan-assisted system. Small chicken portions, such as in Chicken Cordon Bleu or Sesame Drumsticks, are most successful if put into a hot oven, so preheat the oven while preparing the ingredients.

Sage and Bacon-stuffed Pork

THAWING MEAT IN THE MICROWAVE

Frozen meat exudes a lot of liquid during thawing and because microwaves are attracted to water, the liquid should be poured off or mopped up with absorbent kitchen paper when it collects, otherwise thawing will take longer. Start thawing a joint in its wrapper and remove it as soon as possible – usually after one-quarter of the thawing time. Place the joint on a microwave roasting rack so that it does not stand in liquid during thawing.

Remember to turn over a large piece of meat. If the joint shows signs of cooking give the meat a 'rest' period of 20 minutes. A joint is thawed when a skewer can easily pass through the thickest part of the meat. Chops and steaks should be re-positioned during thawing; test them by pressing the surface with your fingers – the meat should feel cold to the touch and give in the thickest part. Allow to stand for the times given in the chart below before cooking.

Type	Time on Low or Defrost Setting	Notes
Beef		
Boned roasting joints (sirloin, topside)	8-10 minutes per 450 g (1 lb)	Turn over regularly during thawing and rest if the meat shows signs of cooking. Stand for 1 hour.
Joints on bone (rib of beef)	10-12 minutes per 450 g (1 lb)	Turn over joint during thawing. The meat will still be icy in the centre but will complete thawing if you leave it to stand for 1 hour.
Minced beef	8-10 minutes per 450 g (1 lb)	Stand for 10 minutes.
Cubed steak	6-8 minutes per 450 g (1 lb)	Stand for 10 minutes.
Steak (sirloin, rump)	8-10 minutes per 450 g (1 lb)	Stand for 10 minutes.
Lamb/Veal		
Boned rolled joint (loin, leg, shoulder)	5-6 minutes per 450 g (1 lb)	As for boned roasting joints of beef above. Stand for 30-45 minutes.
On the bone (leg and shoulder)	5-6 minutes per 450 g (1 lb)	As for beef joints on bone above. Stand for 30-45 minutes.
Minced lamb or veal	8-10 minutes per 450 g (1 lb)	Stand for 10 minutes.
Chops	8-10 minutes per 450 g (1 lb)	Separate during thawing. Stand for 10 minutes.
Pork		
Boned rolled joint (loin, leg)	7-8 minutes per 450 g (1 lb)	As for boned roasting joints of beef above. Stand for 1 hour.
On the bone (leg, hand)	7-8 minutes per 450 g (1 lb)	As for beef joints on bone above. Stand for 1 hour.
Tenderloin	8-10 minutes per 450 g (1 lb)	Stand for 10 minutes.
Chops	8-10 minutes per 450 g (1 lb)	Separate during thawing and arrange 'spoke' fashion. Stand for 10 minutes.
Offal		
Liver	8-10 minutes per 450 g (1 lb)	Separate during thawing. Stand for 5 minutes.
Kidney	6-9 minutes per 450 g (1 lb)	Separate during thawing. Stand for 5 minutes.

COOKING MEAT IN THE MICROWAVE

Type	Time/Setting	Microwave Cooking Technique(s)
Beef		
Boned roasting joint (sirloin, topside)	per 450 g (1 lb) Rare: 5-6 minutes on HIGH Medium: 7-8 minutes on HIGH Well done: 8-10 minutes on HIGH	Turn over joint halfway through cooking time. Stand for 15-20 minutes, tented in foil.
On the bone roasting joint (fore rib, back rib)	per 450 g (1 lb) Rare: 5 minutes on HIGH Medium: 6 minutes on HIGH Well done: 8 minutes on HIGH	Turn over joint halfway through cooking time. Stand as for boned joint.
Lamb/Veal		
Boned rolled joint (loin, leg, shoulder)	per 450 g (1 lb) Medium: 7-8 minutes on HIGH Well done: 8-10 minutes on HIGH	Turn over joint halfway through cooking time. Stand as for beef.
On the bone (leg and shoulder)	per 450 g (1 lb) Medium: 6-7 minutes on HIGH Well done: 8-9 minutes on HIGH	Position fatty side down and turn over halfway through cooking time. Stand as for beef.
Chops	1 chop: 2½-3½ minutes on HIGH 2 chops: 3½-4½ minutes on HIGH 3 chops: 4½-5½ minutes on HIGH 4 chops: 5½-6½ minutes on HIGH	Cook in preheated browning dish. Position with bone ends towards centre. Turn over once during cooking.
Bacon		
Joints	12-14 minutes on HIGH per 450 g (1 lb)	Cook in a pierced roasting bag. Turn over joint partway through cooking time. Stand for 10 minutes, tented in foil.
Rashers	2 rashers: 2-2½ minutes on HIGH 4 rashers: 4-4½ minutes on HIGH 6 rashers: 5-6 minutes on HIGH	Arrange in a single layer. Cover with greaseproof paper to prevent splattering. Cook in preheated browning dish if liked. Remove paper immediately after cooking to prevent sticking.
Pork		
Boned rolled joint (loin, leg)	8-10 minutes on HIGH per 450 g (1 lb)	As for boned rolled lamb above.
On the bone (leg, hand)	8-9 minutes on HIGH per 450 g (1 lb)	As for lamb on the bone above.
Chops	1 chop: 4-4½ minutes on HIGH 2 chops: 5-5½ minutes on HIGH 3 chops: 6-7 minutes on HIGH 4 chops: 6½-8 minutes on HIGH	Cook in preheated browning dish. Prick kidney, if attached. Position with bone ends towards centre. Turn over once during cooking.
Offal		
Liver (lamb and calves)	6-8 minutes on HIGH per 450 g (1 lb)	Cover with greaseproof paper to prevent splattering.
Kidneys	8 minutes on HIGH per 450 g (1 lb)	Arrange in a circle. Cover to prevent splattering. Re-position during cooking.

ROAST LOIN OF PORK

C
SERVES 6

1.8 kg (4 lb) loin of pork, boned, with rind on

salt

/ 1 / Calculate the cooking time using the chart on the right. Score the rind of the joint and rub all over with salt.

/ 2 / Place the joint, fat side uppermost, in a large shallow dish and stand on the wire rack, or stand directly on the wire rack with the splash trivet in position below.

/ 3 / Cook for the calculated time, basting frequently. If cooking in a dish, drain off the excess fat halfway through cooking. (If using a splash trivet, this is not necessary because the trivet shields the fat from the microwave energy during cooking.)

/ 4 / Leave the joint in a warm place to rest for 10-15 minutes before carving. Meanwhile, use the cooking juices in the dish to make gravy in the conventional way.

/ 5 / Cook accompanying vegetables by microwave on HIGH for the times given in the chart on pages 124 and 125. To roast potatoes at the same time as meat, see the instructions in the menu on page 212.

POT ROAST OF PORK WITH RED CABBAGE

C
SERVES 4

450 g (1 lb) red cabbage, finely shredded

60 ml (4 tbsp) orange juice

225 g (8 oz) cooking apples, peeled, cored and sliced

30 ml (2 tbsp) demerara sugar

30 ml (2 tbsp) red wine vinegar

15 ml (1 tbsp) plain flour

salt and pepper

900 g (2 lb) boneless pork shoulder, rinded and rolled

/ 1 / Place the red cabbage in a large bowl with the orange juice. Cover and microwave on HIGH for 3-4 minutes or until just softened.

ROASTING MEAT IN A COMBINATION OVEN

If your oven comes with a splash trivet and wire rack, then you can roast meat standing on the rack, with the splash trivet in position below, on the turntable. Roast potatoes can then be cooked on the splash trivet. Alternatively, place the joint in a large shallow dish and stand the dish on the wire rack. This second method is preferable since it reduces splashing and it is simpler and safer to handle the meat in a dish rather than placing it directly on the rack.

Small joints weighing less than 1.1 kg (2½ lb), other than rack of lamb, are best cooked on convection only. It is not necessary to preheat the oven when cooking large joints, but when cooking chops, or other small items with a short cooking time, the results are better if the oven is preheated on convection at 250°C for 10 minutes. Turning the joint halfway through cooking is sometimes recommended, but is not really necessary.

Meat roasting times per 450 g (1 lb) on combination at 200°C/MEDIUM LOW	Minutes
Lamb	
Leg:	
medium	10-12
well done	12-14
Rack of lamb:	
medium	10-12
Chops	10-12
Beef	
Rib or Topside:	
rare	8-10
medium	10-12
well done	12-14
Pork	
Leg, Loin or Shoulder	15-18
Chops	11-12

/ 2 / Place the cabbage in a casserole with the apples. Add the sugar, vinegar and flour and season to taste with salt and pepper. Mix well to combine the ingredients.

/ 3 / Slash the fat side of the pork joint several times and sprinkle with plenty of salt and pepper. Place on top of the cabbage and apple mixture in the casserole and cover.

/ 4 / Stand the casserole on the wire rack and cook on combination at 200°C/MEDIUM LOW for 1¼ hours or until the pork is tender. Serve the pork on a warm serving platter, surrounded by the cabbage.

POT ROAST OF PORK WITH RED CABBAGE

Ask your butcher to bone, rind and roll the pork shoulder for you so that it cooks evenly in the combination oven and is a neat shape for carving.

ROAST LOIN OF PORK

To bone a loin of pork yourself; place the loin on a board with the skin side down and trim away any loose fat. Cut along both sides of 1 rib at a time. Gently pull the rib upwards away from the meat and insert the knife under the bone. Work down the bone to free the meat.

Twist the bone sharply to break it away from the spine. Repeat with each rib. Remove the fillet from the spine through the strip of connective tissue. Keep the knife close to the spine as you go. Work down the spine with the point of the knife to free it from the meat. Roll up the meat and tie into a neat shape with trussing string.

Picture opposite:
Roast Loin of Pork

PORK WITH FRESH PLUM SAUCE

SERVES 2

350 g (12 oz) pork fillet
50 ml (2 fl oz) chicken stock
50 ml (2 fl oz) fruity white wine
225 g (8 oz) fresh ripe red or purple plums, halved and stoned
15 ml (1 tbsp) dark soft brown sugar
5 ml (1 tsp) lemon juice
salt and pepper
15 ml (1 tbsp) vegetable oil
fresh parsley sprigs, to garnish

/ 1 / Cut the pork into 1 cm (½ inch) slices. Place between sheets of greaseproof paper and flatten, using a meat mallet or a rolling pin, to a thickness of 0.5 cm (¼ inch). Set aside.

/ 2 / Make the sauce: put the stock and wine into a medium bowl and microwave on HIGH for 5 minutes or until the sauce is boiling and slightly reduced.

/ 3 / Reserve 2 plum halves for the garnish, finely chop the remainder and stir into the hot liquid with the sugar and lemon juice. Cover and microwave on HIGH for 3-4 minutes or until the plums are tender. Season to taste with salt and pepper.

/ 4 / Allow to cool a little, then purée the sauce in a blender or food processor until smooth. Pour back into the bowl and microwave on HIGH for 5-7 minutes or until thickened and is further reduced.

/ 5 / Put the oil in a shallow dish and microwave on HIGH for 1-2 minutes or until hot. Stir in the pork and microwave on HIGH for 4-5 minutes or until tender, turning once during cooking. Season to taste with salt and pepper.

/ 6 / Reheat the sauce on HIGH for 1-2 minutes or until hot, then spoon on to 2 warmed plates. Arrange the pork on the sauce, garnish with the reserved plum halves and the parsley sprigs and serve immediately.

CHEESE AND HAM PIE

C   SERVES 6

450 g (1 lb) curd or ricotta cheese
50 g (2 oz) freshly grated Parmesan cheese
100 g (4 oz) Gruyère cheese, grated
225 g (8 oz) piece of cooked ham, diced
2 eggs
salt and pepper
beaten egg, to glaze
PASTRY
275 g (10 oz) plain flour
pinch of salt
150 g (5 oz) butter or margarine

/ 1 / Make the pastry: mix the flour and salt together in a bowl. Add the butter or margarine and rub it in until the mixture resembles fine breadcrumbs. Add 45-60 ml (3-4 tbsp) cold water and mix together with a round-bladed knife, adding just enough of the water to give a firm dough.

/ 2 / Roll out two thirds of the pastry on a lightly floured surface and use to line a 20.5 cm (8 inch) cake dish. Trim the pastry so that it stands slightly above the rim of the cake dish.

/ 3 / Put the cheeses in a bowl with the ham, eggs and salt and pepper to taste and mix well together. Spoon the mixture into the pastry case and fold the pastry edges over the filling. Brush the pastry edges with beaten egg.

/ 4 / Roll out the remaining pastry to a 20.5 cm (8 inch) circle and place over the filling. Seal the edges by pressing lightly together. Roll out any pastry trimmings and cut out leaves to decorate. Glaze the top of the pie with beaten egg, then chill in the refrigerator for 10 minutes to allow the pastry to rest. Meanwhile, preheat the oven on convection at 250°C.

/ 5 / Stand the pie on the wire rack and cook on combination at 200°C/MEDIUM LOW for 10-15 minutes or until golden brown. Serve the pie hot or cold.

PORK WITH FRESH PLUM SAUCE
Pork fillet is a tender, lean cut from underneath the back bone of the loin. It is also called tenderloin. It can be stuffed and rolled for roasting, cubed for kebabs or grilled, as well as being cut into cubes for conventional frying.

Pork is highly perishable, and should be eaten as soon as possible after buying. To store in the refrigerator, wrap in foil or cling film, to prevent the meat drying out. Never leave fresh meat in the polythene bag in which it was bought. Cook within 2 days of purchase.

CHEESE AND HAM PIE
For this pie, it's best to use a large piece of cooked ham cut from a roast gammon joint so that you can cut it into chunky cubes. Sliced cooked ham does not give such a good result as it tends to disintegrate during cooking.

Cold Cheese and Ham Pie makes an excellent summer lunch dish. The flavour of the different cheeses is quite strong, so salad accompaniments should have definite flavours. Fennel, chicory and spring onions will all hold their own against the sharpness of the cheese. Serve with a robust red wine such as a Chianti or Valpolicella.

Cheese and Ham Pie

HONEY ROAST GAMMON

SERVES 6 - 8

1.4 kg (3 lb) gammon or collar
30 ml (2 tbsp) clear honey
30 ml (2 tbsp) orange marmalade
a few drops of Tabasco sauce

/ 1 / Weigh the gammon and calculate the cooking time, allow 7-8 minutes per 450 g (1 lb). Put the gammon in a roasting bag. Seal the end and prick the bag in several places. Stand on a roasting rack and place in a large shallow dish. Microwave on HIGH for the calculated cooking time.

/ 2 / Five minutes before the end of the cooking time, remove the rind from the gammon and discard. Mix the honey, marmalade and Tabasco together and brush all over the joint. Continue cooking, uncovered, for the remaining calculated time, brushing frequently with the honey marinade.

/ 3 / Cover tightly with foil and leave to stand for 10 minutes before serving hot or cold.

PORK AND VEGETABLES

SERVES 4

30 ml (2 tbsp) vegetable oil
60 ml (4 tbsp) soy sauce
15 ml (1 tbsp) dry sherry
12.5 ml (2½ tsp) cornflour
6.25 ml (1¼ tsp) sugar
2.5 ml (½ tsp) finely chopped fresh ginger or 1.25 ml (¼ tsp) ground ginger
1 garlic clove, skinned and crushed
450 g (1 lb) pork fillet, cut into thin strips
2 large carrots, peeled and cut into thin strips
1 green pepper, cored, seeded and cut into thin strips
3 spring onions, cut into 2.5 cm (1 inch) lengths
225 g (8 oz) mushrooms, sliced
cooked rice, to serve

/ 1 / Stir the oil, soy sauce, sherry, cornflour, sugar, chopped fresh or ground ginger and garlic together in a large bowl.

/ 2 / Add the pork, mix well and leave to marinate for at least 30 minutes.

/ 3 / Stir in the vegetables and microwave on HIGH for 7-8 minutes until the pork is tender and the juices run clear and the vegetables are tender but still firm, stirring occasionally. Serve with cooked rice.

SAGE AND BACON-STUFFED PORK

SERVES 6 - 8

about 1.8 kg (4 lb) boned loin of pork
8 streaky bacon rashers, rinded
12 fresh sage leaves
2 garlic cloves, skinned and cut into slivers
salt and pepper
fresh sage, to garnish

/ 1 / Cut the rind off the pork, together with all but a very thin layer of fat next to the meat. Score the remaining fat with a sharp knife.

/ 2 / Turn over the meat and lay half of the bacon, the sage leaves and the garlic over the flesh. Season well with salt and pepper. Roll up and lay the remaining bacon on top.

/ 3 / Secure the joint with fine string. Weigh the joint and cook for the calculated time (see the chart on page 53). If cooking in a dish, drain off the excess fat halfway through cooking. (If using a splash trivet, this is not necessary because the trivet shields the fat from the microwave energy.)

/ 4 / Leave the joint in a warm place to rest for 10-15 minutes before carving. Serve cut into slices, garnished with fresh sage leaves.

Gammon is the name given to the entire hind leg of a bacon pig after curing. When cooked and served cold, it is usually called ham. Speciality hams, such as York Ham, are produced from whole legs separated from the carcass before being cured and cooked by traditional methods. Cooked ham is sold freshly sliced or as vacuum-packed slices. Uncooked gammon is usually sold as joints or steaks.

SAGE AND BACON-STUFFED PORK
To cook this joint by microwave; weigh the joint and calculate the cooking time allowing 8 minutes per 450 g (I lb). Place on a roasting rack, bacon side down, and cover with a split roasting bag. Stand the rack in a shallow dish to catch the juices. Microwave on HIGH for half of the calculated cooking time, then turn over and cook for the remaining time.

PORK AND VEGETABLES
Cook rice to serve with this dish in the microwave if wished. Cook while the pork is marinating. Put the rice and salt to taste in a large bowl, then pour over enough boiling water to cover the rice by 2.5 cm (I inch). Stir and cover the bowl, then microwave on HIGH for 10-12 minutes for 225 g (8 oz) white rice, 30-35 minutes for brown rice. Drain, rinse in cold water, then turn into a serving dish. Reheat once the pork is cooked: dot with butter, cover and microwave on HIGH for 2-4 minutes, stirring once.

Picture opposite:
Honey Roast Gammon

ROAST BEEF WITH YORKSHIRE PUDDINGS

Ⓒ   S E R V E S   6

1.6 kg (3½ lb) topside of beef
mustard, for spreading
salt and pepper
YORKSHIRE PUDDINGS
100 g (4 oz) plain flour
1 egg
300 ml (½ pint) milk

/ 1 / Spread the joint with a little mustard and season to taste with salt and pepper. Place the joint in a large shallow dish and stand on the wire rack, or stand directly on the wire rack with the splash trivet in position below.

/ 2 / Cook for the calculated time (see the chart on page 53). If cooking in a dish, drain off the excess fat halfway through cooking. (If using a splash trivet, this is not necessary because the trivet shields the fat from the microwave energy during cooking.)

/ 3 / Meanwhile, make the Yorkshire puddings. Mix the flour and a pinch of salt together in a bowl. Make a well in the centre, add the egg and half the milk and gradually work in the flour, beating until smooth. Gradually beat in the remaining milk and beat until smooth.

/ 4 / Leave the joint in a warm place to rest for 10-15 minutes before carving.

/ 5 / Meanwhile, grease 6 ramekin dishes or a 6-hole muffin dish with oil or lard. Pour in the batter mixture, stand on the wire rack and cook on combination at 250°C/MEDIUM LOW for 10-15 minutes or until the puddings are well risen and golden brown.

MILD BEEF CURRY

Ⓒ   S E R V E S   4 - 6

1 medium onion, skinned and roughly chopped
2 garlic cloves, skinned
2.5 cm (1 inch) piece of fresh root ginger, peeled
1 cinnamon stick
5 ml (1 tsp) ground turmeric
5 ml (1 tsp) ground fenugreek
7.5 ml (1½ tsp) ground coriander
7.5 ml (1½ tsp) ground cumin
7.5 ml (1½ tsp) garam masala
4 cloves
4 green cardamom pods, crushed
15 ml (1 tbsp) vegetable oil
900 g (2 lb) braising steak
60 ml (4 tbsp) plain flour
450 ml (¾ pint) beef stock
60 ml (4 tbsp) desiccated coconut
salt and pepper

/ 1 / Put the onion, garlic and ginger in a blender or food processor and process until very finely chopped. Turn into a large bowl and add all the spices and the oil. Cover and microwave on HIGH for 5-7 minutes or until the onion has softened and the spices are sizzling.

/ 2 / Meanwhile, trim the meat and cut into 2.5 cm (1 inch) cubes. Toss in the flour.

/ 3 / Add the meat and any loose flour to the bowl and stir together to coat the meat. Microwave, uncovered, on HIGH for 4-5 minutes or until the meat just starts to change colour.

/ 4 / Stir in the stock and mix thoroughly. Cover, stand on the wire rack and cook on combination at 180°C/MEDIUM LOW for 50-60 minutes or until the meat is tender.

/ 5 / Stir in the coconut and season to taste with salt and pepper. Re-cover and continue to cook for 5 minutes. Serve hot with boiled rice.

ROAST BEEF WITH YORKSHIRE PUDDINGS
Meat will always splash during cooking and, because the capacity of the oven is much smaller than a conventional oven, it is concentrated on a smaller area and seems worse. Draining off excess fat halfway through cooking, placing the meat in a shallow dish rather than directly on the wire rack, and reducing the microwave setting all help to reduce splashing.

In Yorkshire, 'batter pudding' was traditionally served as a first course with gravy, then beef and vegetables followed on as a separate course. The idea behind this was to fill hungry stomachs before the beef was served.

MILD BEEF CURRY
Don't be tempted to substitute ready-prepared curry powder for the spices. The flavour just will not be as good. This mixture of spices makes a curry with a good strong spicy flavour, but it's still mild.

SHEPHERD'S PIE
Shepherd's Pie is best made with leftover minced roast beef, in which case you will only need to cook it for 5 minutes in step 4. However, as leftover roast beef is not always available, this recipe uses raw lean minced beef, and provided you add Worcestershire sauce, tomato purée and plenty of salt and pepper the result will be just as good.

SHEPHERD'S PIE

SERVES 4

900 g (2 lb) potatoes, peeled
1 small onion, skinned and chopped
1 small carrot, finely chopped
1 celery stick, finely chopped
65 g (2½ oz) butter or margarine
45 ml (3 tbsp) milk
salt and pepper
450 g (1 lb) lean minced beef
30 ml (2 tbsp) plain flour
30 ml (2 tbsp) Worcestershire sauce
30 ml (2 tbsp) tomato purée
300 ml (½ pint) beef stock

/ 1 / Cook the potatoes in boiling salted water, in the usual way, for about 20 minutes or until the potatoes are tender.

/ 2 / Meanwhile, put the onion, carrot, celery and 15 g (½ oz) butter or margarine in a large bowl and microwave on HIGH for 5 minutes or until softened.

/ 3 / Drain the potatoes and mash with the remaining butter or margarine and the milk. Season to taste with salt and pepper. Set aside.

/ 4 / Add the beef and the remaining ingredients to the softened vegetables in the bowl, season to taste with salt and pepper, cover and microwave on HIGH for 12-15 minutes or until tender, stirring occasionally.

/ 5 / Spoon the meat mixture into an ovenproof dish and cover the top with the mashed potato. Decorate the top by marking with a fork. Stand the dish on the wire rack and cook on combination at 200°C/MEDIUM LOW for 15-20 minutes or until the potato is golden brown. Serve hot.

───────── V A R I A T I O N ─────────

Add a few sliced mushrooms and a crushed garlic clove to the chopped onion, carrot and celery in step 2 for extra flavour, if wished.

Shepherd's Pie

STEAK AND KIDNEY PUDDING

C   S E R V E S   6

900 g (2 lb) braising steak, trimmed
8 lamb's kidneys, skinned, cored and chopped
1 large onion, skinned and finely chopped
60 ml (4 tbsp) seasoned plain flour
60 ml (4 tbsp) vegetable oil
225 g (8 oz) button mushrooms, halved
600 ml (1 pint) beef stock
P A S T R Y
275 g (10 oz) self-raising flour
150 g (5 oz) shredded suet
pinch of salt

/ 1 / Cut the steak into 1 cm (½ inch) cubes. Toss the cubed steak, chopped kidneys and onion in the seasoned flour.

/ 2 / Heat the oil in a frying pan, add the meat and onion and fry until lightly browned. Transfer the mixture to a large casserole and add the mushrooms.

/ 3 / Gradually pour the stock into the frying pan and bring to the boil, stirring to loosen any sediment on the bottom of the pan. Pour over the meat. Cover the casserole, stand on the wire rack and cook on combination at 180°C/ MEDIUM LOW for 1-1¼ hours or until the meat is tender. Leave to cool completely in the casserole before making the pudding.

/ 4 / When the steak and kidney is cold, make the pastry. In a large bowl, mix together the flour, suet and salt. Stir in enough cold water to mix to a soft dough, about 200 ml (7 fl oz), and knead lightly. Turn out on to a lightly floured surface and roll out to a circle 35 cm (14 inches) in diameter. Cut out a quarter of the circle of dough.

/ 5 / Lightly grease a 1.7 litre (3 pint) pudding basin. Lightly dust the large piece of dough with flour and fold in half, then in half again. Lift the dough carefully into the basin, then unfold and press into the base and up the sides, taking care not to stretch the pastry. The pastry should overlap the basin top by about 2.5 cm (1 inch).

/ 6 / Spoon the meat mixture into the lined pudding basin. Roll out the remaining piece of dough to a circle 2.5 cm (1 inch) larger than the top of the basin. Dampen the edges and place on top of the filling in the basin. Pinch the pastry edges together, then trim.

/ 7 / Cover the pudding with a plate and microwave on HIGH for 10-12 minutes or until the pastry is cooked. Leave to stand for 5 minutes, then loosen around the edges and carefully turn the pudding out on to a serving plate.

BEEF WITH GINGER AND GARLIC

S E R V E S   2

350 g (12 oz) fillet steak
2.5 cm (1 inch) piece of fresh root ginger, peeled and finely grated
1 garlic clove, skinned and crushed
150 ml (¼ pint) dry sherry
30 ml (2 tbsp) soy sauce
2 medium carrots
15 ml (1 tbsp) vegetable oil
30 ml (2 tbsp) cornflour
2.5 ml (½ tsp) light soft brown sugar
cooked rice, to serve

/ 1 / Cut the steak across the grain into 1 cm (½ inch) strips, and put into a bowl. Mix the ginger with the garlic, sherry and soy sauce, then pour over the steak, making sure that all the meat is coated. Cover and leave to marinate for at least 1 hour. Using a potato peeler, cut the carrots into thin slices lengthways.

/ 2 / Put the oil in a large bowl and microwave on HIGH for 1 minute or until hot. Using a slotted spoon, remove the steak from the marinade and stir into the hot oil. Microwave on HIGH for 1-2 minutes until just cooked, stirring once.

/ 3 / Meanwhile, blend the cornflour and the sugar with a little of the marinade to make a smooth paste, then blend in all the marinade.

/ 4 / Stir the carrots into the steak and microwave on HIGH for 1-2 minutes, then gradually stir in the marinade mixture. Microwave on HIGH for 2-3 minutes until boiling and thickened, stirring frequently. Serve with rice.

STEAK AND KIDNEY PUDDING
Using the combination oven, steak and kidney pudding can be made in half the usual time. It should be served immediately after cooking and standing because the pastry tends to toughen.

BEEF WITH GINGER AND GARLIC
Fresh root ginger has a warm citrus-like flavour. It is usually peeled and grated or finely chopped and used to flavour fish, poultry, soups and casseroles as well as curries and oriental and South-east Asian dishes.

Good sharp knives are the cook's most important tools, especially in recipes like Beef with Garlic and Ginger when you need to cut meat into thin strips. Knives vary enormously in quality, the best ones have taper ground blades – the blade, bolster and tang is forged from a single piece of steel, and the handle is fixed securely in place with rivets.

BEEF IN STOUT

C

SERVES 4

900 g (2 lb) braising steak

4 celery sticks

50 g (2 oz) plain flour

salt and pepper

45 ml (3 tbsp) vegetable oil

600 ml (1 pint) stout

225 g (8 oz) button mushrooms

finely grated rind of 1 orange

50 g (2 oz) chopped walnuts

/ 1 / Trim the steak and cut into 2.5 cm (1 inch) cubes. Cut the celery into 2.5 cm (1 inch) lengths. Season the flour with salt and pepper and use to coat the meat.

/ 2 / Heat the oil in a frying pan and quickly fry the meat until browned on all sides. Using a slotted spoon, transfer the browned steak cubes to a casserole.

/ 3 / Stir the stout into the frying pan and bring to the boil, stirring to loosen any sediment on the botton of the pan. Pour over the steak. Add the button mushrooms, celery pieces and orange rind to the casserole and season to taste with salt and pepper.

/ 4 / Cover the casserole, stand it on the wire rack and cook on combination at 180°C/ MEDIUM LOW for 1 hour 20 minutes-1½ hours or until the steak is tender, stirring occasionally. Sprinkle with the chopped walnuts and serve the casserole immediately.

Braising meat in stout is a good trick since the meat becomes mouthwateringly tender and the stout makes a good rich gravy. A few chopped walnuts add texture and crunch.

Beef with Ginger and Garlic

Meatballs with Tomato Sauce

MEATBALLS WITH TOMATO SAUCE

SERVES 2

1 small onion, skinned and quartered
1 garlic clove, skinned and crushed
2.5 cm (1 inch) piece of fresh root ginger, peeled and crushed
350 g (12 oz) lean minced beef
15 ml (1 tbsp) mango chutney
2.5 ml (½ tsp) ground cumin
2.5 ml (½ tsp) ground coriander
30 ml (2 tbsp) chopped fresh coriander
salt and pepper
1 egg, size 6, beaten
200 g (7 oz) can tomatoes
15 ml (1 tbsp) chicken stock
10 ml (2 tsp) tomato purée
5 ml (1 tsp) sugar
fresh coriander, to garnish

/ 1 / Put the onion, garlic and ginger in a blender or food processor and liquidise until very finely chopped.

/ 2 / Add the beef, chutney, cumin, ground coriander and half the fresh chopped coriander and season with salt and pepper. Pour in the egg and blend until well mixed.

/ 3 / Shape the mixture into 16 small balls. Arrange in a single layer in a shallow dish. Microwave on HIGH for 5-6 minutes or until the meat is cooked, rearranging once during cooking. Leave to stand, covered, while making the sauce.

/ 4 / Put the tomatoes and their juice into a large bowl. Stir in the chicken stock, tomato purée, sugar, salt and pepper.

/ 5 / Microwave on HIGH for 5 minutes, stirring occasionally, then stir in the remaining fresh coriander and microwave on HIGH for 2-3 minutes or until the tomato sauce is reduced and has thickened.

/ 6 / Microwave the meatballs on HIGH for 1-2 minutes or until reheated. Serve the meatballs with the sauce, garnished with coriander.

MEAT LOAF

SERVES 4 - 6

1 medium onion, skinned and chopped
15 ml (1 tbsp) vegetable oil
900 g (2 lb) lean minced beef
30 ml (2 tbsp) tomato purée
30 ml (2 tbsp) Worcestershire sauce
50 g (2 oz) coarse oatmeal
Tabasco sauce
salt and pepper
2 small onions, skinned and thinly sliced
15 ml (1 tbsp) plain flour
lemon juice
paprika

/ 1 / Put the chopped onion and oil in a large bowl and microwave on HIGH for 5 minutes or until the onion has softened. Stir in the minced beef, tomato purée, Worcestershire sauce and oatmeal. Season generously with Tabasco and pepper and a little salt.

/ 2 / Spoon into a 1.7 litre (3 pint) loaf dish and level the surface. Arrange the small onion slices on top.

/ 3 / Stand the dish on the wire rack and cook on combination at 200°C/MEDIUM LOW for 20-25 minutes or until the juices run clear when the loaf is pierced with a knife. Baste the onion slices on the top with the juices halfway through cooking.

/ 4 / When the meat loaf is cooked, pour the juices into a heatproof jug and add the flour and 300 ml (½ pint) cold water. Microwave on HIGH for 3-4 minutes or until boiling and thickened, whisking frequently. Season to taste with lemon juice, Tabasco sauce and salt and pepper.

/ 5 / Turn the meat loaf out on to a plate, then invert on to a serving plate so that the onions are on top. Sprinkle with a little paprika and serve with the gravy.

MEAT LOAF
This is a quick and easy family supper dish that is more tasty than its image suggests, provided you season generously with Worcestershire sauce, Tabasco sauce and salt and pepper. You could also add a little garlic or chopped fresh herbs. Instead of using breadcrumbs to bind the mixture, this recipe uses coarse oatmeal to add some texture and absorb some of the liquid produced during cooking.

The top of the meat loaf is covered with a layer of onions which cook until deliciously soft and sweet. Turning the loaf out, so that the onions are on top isn't as tricky as you might think. Carefully invert the loaf on to a plate and then turn back over on to a serving plate, so that the onions are on top (replacing any onions left on the plate). Serve with a gravy made from the cooking juices as in the recipe, or with a tomato or onion sauce.

MEATBALLS WITH TOMATO SAUCE

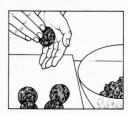

Shape the beef and onion mixture into 16 small balls. Arrange in a single layer in a shallow dish.

Small foods such as these meatballs benefit from being rearranged halfway through cooking, as it ensures they cook evenly.

LAMB CUTLETS EN CROÛTE

C	SERVES 4
8 lamb cutlets, trimmed	
egg yolk, to glaze	
PASTRY	
275 g (10 oz) plain flour	
pinch of salt	
150 g (5 oz) butter or margarine	
1 egg	

/ 1 / Grill the cutlets under a very hot grill for 2-3 minutes only on each side. They should be just lightly browned on the outside but not cooked. Leave to cool.

/ 2 / Make the pastry: mix the flour and salt together in a bowl. Rub in the butter or margarine until the mixture resembles fine breadcrumbs. Mix in the egg and about 30-45 ml (2-3 tbsp) water, using a round-bladed knife, adding only enough water to form a soft dough.

/ 3 / Knead lightly, then cut the pastry in half. Roll out each piece of pastry on a lightly floured surface to a 25.5 cm (10 inch) square. Divide each into 4 squares. Place each of the lamb cutlets on a square of pastry so that the bone extends over the edge of the pastry. Dampen the pastry edges, wrap the pastry over the cutlets and seal well.

/ 4 / Place the pastry parcels in a shallow ovenproof dish, folded sides underneath. Use any pastry trimmings to decorate the cutlets. Brush with egg yolk, then chill for 20 minutes.

/ 5 / Stand the cutlets on the wire rack and cook on combination at 200°C/MEDIUM LOW for 12-15 minutes or until pastry is golden.

HERBY ROAST RACK OF LAMB

C	SERVES 2
1 best end neck of lamb with 6-8 cutlets, chined	
25 g (1 oz) butter or margarine	
5 ml (1 tsp) chive mustard	
45 ml (3 tbsp) chopped fresh herbs	
25 g (1 oz) fresh white breadcrumbs	
salt and pepper	

/ 1 / If necessary, trim back the fat and meat on each cutlet bone to a depth of 2.5 cm (1 inch).

/ 2 / In a small bowl, beat together the butter or margarine, mustard, herbs and breadcrumbs. Season to taste with salt and pepper. Spread the mixture evenly over the fat side of the lamb. Weigh the lamb, then place it in a shallow ovenproof dish.

/ 3 / Stand the dish on the wire rack and cook on combination at 200°C/MEDIUM LOW for 10-12 minutes per 450 g (1 lb).

/ 4 / Leave in a warm place to rest for 10-15 minutes before carving.

LAMB PARCELS

	SERVES 4
8 medium cabbage leaves	
450 g (1 lb) lean minced lamb	
1 small onion, skinned and finely chopped	
1 garlic clove, skinned and crushed	
30 ml (2 tbsp) chopped fresh mint	
1.25 ml (¼ tsp) ground cinnamon	
100 g (4 oz) fresh breadcrumbs	
salt and pepper	
about 15 ml (1 tbsp) lemon juice	
10 ml (2 tsp) cornflour	
397 g (14 oz) can chopped tomatoes, sieved	
15 ml (1 tbsp) soft light brown sugar	
30 ml (2 tbsp) chopped fresh parsley	
mint sprigs, to garnish	

/ 1 / Cut out the centre stem of each cabbage leaf and place the leaves in a large shallow casserole. Cover and microwave on HIGH for 2-3 minutes or until the leaves are soft.

/ 2 / Mix the lamb, onion, garlic, mint, cinnamon, breadcrumbs and seasoning together with enough lemon juice to bind. Shape into 8 even-sized cigar-shaped rolls.

/ 3 / Wrap each roll in a cabbage leaf and place in the casserole, seam side down.

/ 4 / Mix the cornflour to a smooth paste with a little of the tomato liquid, add the remaining tomatoes, the sugar and parsley. Spoon the tomato mixture over the cabbage rolls, cover and microwave on HIGH for 20 minutes. Serve garnished with mint.

LAMB CUTLETS EN CROÛTE

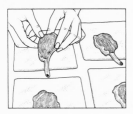

Place each of the lamb cutlets on a square of pastry so that the bone extends over the edge of the pastry.

Dampen the pastry edges, wrap the pastry over the cutlets and seal well. Place the pastry parcels in a shallow ovenproof dish, folded sides underneath. Use any pastry trimmings to decorate the cutlets.

HERBY ROAST RACK OF LAMB
Rack of lamb is sometimes known as best end of neck. It's a small roasting joint consisting of 6 or 8 cutlets joined together. Two racks of lamb, roasted facing each other, usually with a stuffing in the middle, make the classic Guard of Honour. If your butcher has not already chined the joint for you, it should be sliced down between the bones and the fat trimmed away. The fat and meat should be removed from the ends of each cutlet bone down to a depth of about 2.5 cm (1 inch). Rack of lamb should always be served still slightly pink on the inside.

Picture opposite: Lamb Parcels

Lamb with Aubergine

LAMB WITH AUBERGINE

SERVES 4

1 large aubergine, weighing about 400 g (14 oz)
salt and pepper
450 g (1 lb) lean boneless lamb, such as fillet or leg
30 ml (2 tbsp) olive oil
397 g (14 oz) can tomatoes, drained
a few allspice berries, crushed
a small bunch of fresh mint

/ 1 / Cut the aubergine into 2.5 cm (1 inch) cubes. Put in a colander, sprinkling each layer generously with salt. Stand the colander on a large plate, cover with a small plate and place a weight on top. Leave for about 20 minutes to extract the bitter juices.

/ 2 / Meanwhile, trim the meat of all excess fat and cut into 2.5 cm (1 inch) cubes. Rinse the aubergine and pat dry.

/ 3 / Heat a large browning dish on HIGH for 5-8 minutes or according to manufacturer's instructions for your particular type.

/ 4 / Put the oil in the browning dish, then quickly add the cubes of meat. Microwave on HIGH for 2 minutes.

/ 5 / Turn the pieces of meat over and microwave on HIGH for a further 2 minutes. Add the aubergine to the browning dish and microwave on HIGH for 5 minutes, stirring once.

Cut the aubergine into 2.5 cm (1 inch) cubes. Put in a colander, sprinkling each layer generously with salt. Stand the colander on a large plate, cover with a small plate and place a weight on top. Leave for about 20 minutes to extract the bitter juices.

66

/ 6 / Add the tomatoes, breaking them up with a fork, the allspice and pepper to taste. Cover and microwave on HIGH for about 15 minutes or until the lamb and aubergine are very tender, stirring occasionally.

/ 7 / Coarsely chop the mint and stir into the lamb with salt to taste. Re-cover and microwave on HIGH for 1 minute.

ITALIAN LAMB WITH ANCHOVIES

C   S E R V E S   4 - 6

50 g (2 oz) can anchovy fillets
2 garlic cloves, skinned and crushed
10 ml (2 tsp) chopped fresh rosemary or 5 ml (1 tsp) dried
15 ml (1 tbsp) white wine vinegar
pepper
1.8-2.3 kg (4-5 lb) leg of lamb
15 ml (1 tbsp) plain flour
150 ml (¼ pint) dry white wine

/ 1 / Crush the anchovies with their oil in a pestle and mortar. Add the garlic, rosemary, vinegar and pepper and mix to a smooth paste.

/ 2 / Using a sharp knife, make random incisions all over the leg of lamb. Spread the anchovy paste over the lamb, working it into the incisions.

/ 3 / Place the joint in a casserole, stand on the wire rack and cook on combination at 200°C/ MEDIUM LOW for 15-18 minutes per 450 g (1 lb).

/ 4 / Transfer the lamb to a serving plate, cover with foil and keep warm.

/ 5 / Pour off most of the fat remaining in the casserole, leaving about 15 ml (1 tbsp), then sprinkle in the flour. Microwave on HIGH for 1 minute. Gradually stir in the wine and season with a little pepper. Microwave on HIGH for 3-4 minutes or until boiling and thickened, stirring frequently. Serve with lamb.

LAMB IN RED WINE

C   S E R V E S   4 - 6

1.6 kg (3½ lb) shoulder of lamb, boned
450 ml (¾ pint) red wine
thinly pared rind of 1 lemon
15 ml (1 tbsp) coriander seeds, crushed
1 bay leaf
30 ml (2 tbsp) plain flour
45 ml (3 tbsp) vegetable oil
425 g (14 oz) can chick-peas, drained and rinsed
salt and pepper
chopped fresh coriander or parsley, to garnish

/ 1 / Cut the lamb into bite-sized pieces, discarding any excess fat. Put the meat in a large bowl with the wine, 150 ml (¼ pint) water, pared lemon rind, coriander seeds and bay leaf. Cover and leave to marinate in the refrigerator for at least 2-3 hours, or overnight.

/ 2 / Just before cooking, use a slotted spoon to remove the meat from the marinade. Reserve the marinade. Toss the meat in the flour.

/ 3 / Heat the oil in a frying pan and quickly brown the meat on all sides. Transfer to a casserole. Pour the marinade into the pan and bring to the boil, stirring to loosen any sediment on the bottom of the pan. Pour over the meat, cover, stand on the wire rack and cook on combination at 180°C/MEDIUM LOW for 40-45 minutes or until the meat is tender.

/ 4 / Ten minutes before the end of cooking, stir in the chick-peas. Season to taste with salt and pepper and serve garnished with chopped coriander or parsley.

LAMB IN RED WINE
This is another recipe with Greek influence. Reminiscent of the Greek Afelia, this casserole is flavoured with lemon, bay and coriander. For a really authentic flavour, use a robust Greek wine such as retsina. Serve with rice or sauté potatoes and salad.

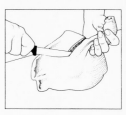

To bone a shoulder of lamb yourself: free the meat from the flat blade bone. Scrape the meat away from the bone, rolling it back until you reach the joint. Turn the joint around and free the meat from around the shank bone. If necessary split the flesh up to the bone a little to make it easier. Scrape the flesh away from the shank end until the joint is reached. Pull the bone out from the cavity.

ITALIAN LAMB WITH ANCHOVIES
This is so called because the lamb is coated in a delicious mixture of garlic, rosemary and anchovies – ingredients all widely used in Italian cookery. If time permits, the flavour is improved by leaving the joint to stand for 1-2 hours once coated in the paste mixture. Serve in thin slices with Cream Baked Celery (see page 128).

Spread the anchovy paste all over the lamb, working it into the incisions as much as possible.

ROSEMARY LAMB CHOPS WITH BAKED APPLES

ROSEMARY LAMB CHOPS WITH BAKED APPLES
Marinating these lamb chops before cooking not only ensures that they are tender but that the flavour goes right through. Served with lightly baked apple halves filled with cranberries (or blackberries or raspberries), they make a delicious and attractive meal.

C   S E R V E S   4

4 lean lamb chump chops
150 ml (¼ pint) apple juice
15 ml (1 tbsp) chopped fresh rosemary
1 garlic clove, skinned and crushed
2 large eating apples
juice of 1 small lemon
60 ml (4 tbsp) cranberries
10 ml (2 tsp) clear honey
rosemary sprigs, to garnish

/ 1 / Put the lamb chops in a large shallow ovenproof dish with the apple juice, rosemary and garlic. Cover and leave to marinate in the refrigerator for at least 2-3 hours, or overnight.

/ 2 / When ready to cook, preheat the oven on convection at 250°C for 10 minutes. Stand the dish on the wire rack and cook on combination at 200°C/MEDIUM LOW for 7 minutes. Drain off the marinade into a jug and turn the chops over, then re-cover and continue to cook for 8-13 minutes or until tender. Skim the fat from the marinade.

/ 3 / Meanwhile, halve the apples crossways, then core and brush with the lemon juice. Fill each apple half with 15 ml (1 tbsp) cranberries and top with a little honey.

/ 4 / Stand the stuffed apples on an ovenproof plate and place the plate on top of the chops so that they are covered. Microwave on HIGH for 5-6 minutes or until the apples and cranberries are just soft. Leave the chops and apples to stand while reheating the marinade.

/ 5 / Microwave the marinade on HIGH for 2 minutes or until boiling. Spoon a little of the marinade over the chops and serve the remainder separately. Arrange the stuffed apple halves on the dish with the chops and garnish with rosemary sprigs.

Rosemary Lamb Chops with Baked Apples

LAMB NOISETTES WITH ONION PURÉE

S E R V E S   2

15 g (½ oz) butter or margarine
1 medium onion, skinned and finely chopped
75 ml (3 fl oz) chicken stock
2.5 ml (½ tsp) chopped fresh sage
5 ml (1 tsp) lemon juice
salt and pepper
45 ml (3 tbsp) soured cream
4 lamb noisettes, each about 4 cm (1½ inches) thick
15 ml (1 tbsp) plain flour
15 ml (1 tbsp) vegetable oil
fresh sage leaves, to garnish

/ 1 / To make the purée, put the butter or margarine in a medium bowl and microwave on HIGH for 30 seconds or until melted.

/ 2 / Stir in the onion, cover and microwave on HIGH for 4-6 minutes or until the onion is really soft, stirring occasionally.

/ 3 / Stir in the stock, sage and lemon juice, re-cover and microwave on HIGH for 3 minutes, stirring occasionally. Season to taste with salt and pepper. Leave to cool slightly, then add the soured cream.

/ 4 / Heat a browning dish on HIGH for 5-8 minutes or according to the manufacturer's instructions for your particular type.

/ 5 / Meanwhile, purée the onion mixture in a blender or food processor, then turn into a clean ovenproof serving bowl. Set aside.

/ 6 / Lightly coat the noisettes with the flour and season with salt and pepper. Add the oil to the browning dish, then quickly add the noisettes, arranging them in a circle in the dish. Microwave on HIGH for 2 minutes. Turn over and microwave on HIGH for 1-2 minutes or until cooked as desired. They should still be slightly pink in the centre. Arrange the noisettes on a warmed serving plate and garnish with fresh sage leaves.

/ 7 / Microwave the onion purée on HIGH for 1-2 minutes or until hot and adjust the seasoning if necessary. Serve immediately with the hot lamb noisettes.

LAMB BURGERS

SERVES 4

450 g (1 lb) lean minced lamb or beef
1 large onion, skinned and finely grated
5 ml (1 tsp) salt
1.25 ml (¼ tsp) cayenne pepper
30 ml (2 tbsp) vegetable oil
plain or toasted hamburger buns, to serve
tomato ketchup, to serve

/ 1 / Mix the lamb or beef and onion together in a bowl and season to taste with the salt and cayenne pepper.

/ 2 / Divide the lamb mixture into 4 and with your hands shape each portion into a neat burger about 2.5 cm (1 inch) thick.

Lamb Noisettes with Onion Purée

/ 3 / Heat a large browning dish on HIGH for 5-8 minutes or according to manufacturer's instructions for your particular type.

/ 4 / Add the oil, then quickly press 2 lamb burgers flat on to the hot surface and microwave on HIGH for 2-3 minutes. Turn the burgers over, re-position them and microwave on HIGH for a further 2-3 minutes or until cooked. Repeat with the remaining burgers.

/ 5 / Serve the lamb burgers in plain or toasted hamburger buns, with tomato ketchup.

Divide the lamb mixture into 4 and shape each portion into a neat burger about 2.5 cm (1 inch) thick.

Lamb's Heart Casserole

LAMB'S HEART CASSEROLE

C SERVES 8

50 g (2 oz) butter or margarine
1 medium onion, skinned and chopped
100 g (4 oz) mushrooms, finely chopped
100 g (4 oz) lean ham, finely chopped
15 ml (1 tbsp) chopped fresh sage or 2.5 ml (½ tsp) dried
225 g (8 oz) fresh white breadcrumbs
finely grated rind of 1 lemon
salt and pepper
1 egg
8 lambs' hearts, washed and trimmed
60 ml (4 tbsp) plain flour
30 ml (2 tbsp) vegetable oil
300 ml (½ pint) chicken stock
45 ml (3 tbsp) dry sherry
finely pared lemon rind or fresh sage leaves, to garnish

/ 1 / Make the stuffing: put half the butter or margarine in a medium bowl and microwave on HIGH for 1 minute or until melted. Add the onion and mushrooms, cover and cook on HIGH for 5 minutes or until the onion has softened. Stir in the ham, sage, breadcrumbs, lemon rind and salt and pepper to taste. Finally, stir in the egg to bind the mixture together.

/ 2 / Fill the hearts with the stuffing and sew up neatly. Toss in the flour.

/ 3 / Heat the remaining butter or margarine with the oil in a frying pan and brown the hearts on all sides. Transfer the hearts to a casserole. Pour the stock and sherry into the frying pan and bring to the boil, stirring to loosen any sediment on the bottom of the pan. Pour over the hearts.

/ 4 / Cover the dish, stand on the wire rack and cook on combination at 200°C/MEDIUM LOW for 50-60 minutes or until tender.

/ 5 / Serve the hearts, sliced, with a little of the cooking juice poured over, and garnished with lemon rind or fresh sage leaves.

RABBIT CIDER HOTPOT

C SERVES 4 - 6

1 rabbit, weighing about 1.1 kg (2½ lb), jointed
60 ml (4 tbsp) plain flour
60 ml (4 tbsp) vegetable oil
600 ml (1 pint) dry cider
30 ml (2 tbsp) chive mustard
3 bay leaves
450 g (1 lb) parsnips, peeled and cut into chunks
2 medium onions, skinned and cut into chunks
salt and pepper
425 g (14 oz) can red kidney beans, drained and rinsed

/ 1 / Coat the rabbit pieces in the flour. Heat the oil in a frying pan and cook the rabbit quickly until brown on all sides. Transfer to a casserole, using a slotted spoon.

/ 2 / Add the cider, mustard and bay leaves to the frying pan and bring to the boil, stirring to loosen any sediment on the bottom of the pan. Pour over the rabbit.

/ 3 / Add the parsnips and onions to the casserole and season to taste with salt and pepper. Mix thoroughly, then cover and cook on combination at 200°C/MEDIUM LOW for 40-45 minutes or until the rabbit is tender.

/ 4 / Add the kidney beans and continue to cook, uncovered, for 10 minutes. Serve the hotpot immediately.

— RABBIT CIDER HOTPOT —

Rabbits are available both fresh or frozen. Unlike hares, they are paunched (entrails removed) within a few hours of killing and are not hung. Tame rabbits, which have a delicate flavour, are always tender. Wild rabbits have darker stronger flavoured flesh and they should be eaten young. Frozen rabbit is best used for pies and casseroles. Fresh rabbit can be roasted.

RABBIT CIDER HOTPOT
Rabbit can take forever to cook in the conventional oven, so the combination of microwave and convection heat suits it perfectly, reducing the cooking time to just 40-45 minutes. Serve this satisfying winter casserole with a purée of potatoes and carrots, or with ribbon noodles tossed in butter and chopped fresh parsley.

LAMB'S HEART CASSEROLE
Whole lambs' hearts make a tasty meal when stuffed with a well flavoured filling, then cooked gently until melt-in-the-mouth tender. Don't be put off by the thought of the preparation, it's quite simple to do (see below).

To prepare lambs' hearts: wash each heart in water to remove any blood. Snip out the arteries and tendons. Soak in salted water for 1 hour, then drain and pat dry before stuffing.

THAWING POULTRY AND GAME IN THE MICROWAVE

Poultry or game should be thawed in its freezer wrapping, which should be pierced first and the metal tag removed. During thawing, pour off liquid that collects in the bag. Finish thawing in a bowl of cold water with the bird still in its bag. Shop-bought chicken portions can be thawed in their polystyrene trays, if wished.

Type	Time on Low or Defrost Setting	Notes
Whole chicken or duckling	6-8 minutes per 450 g (1 lb)	Remove giblets. Stand in cold water for 30 minutes.
Whole turkey	10-12 minutes per 450 g (1 lb)	Remove giblets. Stand in cold water for 2-3 hours.
Chicken portions	5-7 minutes per 450 g (1 lb)	Separate during thawing. Stand for 10 minutes.
Poussin, grouse, pheasant, pigeon, quail	5-7 minutes per 450 g (1 lb)	

ROAST CHICKEN

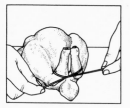

Truss the chicken into a neat compact shape using fine string.

Roast Chicken

COOKING POULTRY IN THE MICROWAVE

Type	Time/Setting	Microwave Cooking Technique(s)
Chicken		
Whole chicken	8-10 minutes on HIGH per 450 g (1 lb)	Cook in a roasting bag, breast side down, and turn halfway through cooking. Stand for 10-15 minutes.
Portions	6-8 minutes on HIGH per 450 g (1 lb)	Position skin side up with thinner parts towards the centre. Re-position halfway through cooking time. Stand for 5-10 minutes.
Boneless breast	2-3 minutes on HIGH	
Duck		
Whole	7-9 minutes on HIGH per 450 g (1 lb)	Turn over as for whole chicken. Stand for 10-15 minutes.
Portions	4×300 g (11 oz) pieces: 10 minutes on HIGH, then 30-35 minutes on MEDIUM	Position and re-position as for portions above.
Turkey		
Whole	9-11 minutes on HIGH per 450 g (1 lb)	Turn over 3 or 4 times, depending on size, during cooking: start cooking breast side down. Stand for 10-15 minutes.

ROAST CHICKEN

C   SERVES 4

1.8 kg (4 lb) oven-ready roasting chicken
salt and pepper
a few fresh herbs (optional)
stuffing (optional)

/ 1 / Season the inside of the chicken with salt and pepper. Place herbs inside the chicken and stuff the neck end, if wished.

/ 2 / Truss the chicken into a neat compact shape using fine string. Weight the bird and calculate the cooking time allowing 8-10 minutes per 450 g (1 lb).

/ 3 / Stand the bird in a large shallow dish and stand on the wire rack, or stand the bird directly on the wire rack with the splash trivet in position below. Cook on combination at 200°C/MEDIUM LOW for the calculated cooking time, basting frequently. If cooking in a shallow dish, drain off excess fat halfway through cooking. (If using a splash trivet, this is not necessary.) Leave to stand for 5-10 minutes before serving.

ROASTING POULTRY AND GAME IN A COMBINATION OVEN

Poultry and game can be roasted either in a large shallow dish or by standing directly on the wire rack with the splash trivet in position (see page 53). If cooking a whole chicken, duck or turkey, it should be trussed into a neat shape before roasting (don't use metal skewers). Stuff with your favourite stuffing or simply place a skinned onion and some herbs or a halved lemon in the body cavity. Game birds are best cooked on convection only as they tend to become dry and tough if cooked on combination.

Poultry and Game roasting times per 450 g (1 lb) on combination at 200°C/MEDIUM LOW. Weigh the bird when it has been stuffed.

	Minutes
Chicken	
whole	8-10
quarters	8-10
drumsticks	10-12
Turkey whole	6-8
Duck	
whole	8-10
finish cooking on convection at 250°C for 5 minutes if skin is not crisp enough.	
quarters	8-10
Goose whole	9-11
Game birds whole cook on convection only.	

CHICKEN WITH PEPPERS AND MARJORAM

SERVES 2

2 chicken breast fillets, skinned
1 garlic clove, skinned and crushed
10 ml (2 tsp) lemon juice
pinch of sugar
45 ml (3 tbsp) olive or vegetable oil
15 ml (1 tbsp) chopped fresh marjoram or 5 ml (1 tsp) dried
1 small onion, skinned and thinly sliced into rings
salt and pepper
1 small red pepper, cored, seeded and coarsely chopped
1 small yellow pepper, cored, seeded and coarsely chopped
50 g (2 oz) black olives, halved and stoned
15 ml (1 tbsp) capers
fresh marjoram, to garnish

CHICKEN WITH PEPPERS AND MARJORAM
The difference between the different colours of peppers is in their botanical variety and degree of ripeness: green peppers become red when they are fully ripe, yellow and purple peppers were white before they became ripe! If you like peppers to taste sweet, then choose red or purple ones.

*Picture opposite:
Chicken and Prune Kebabs*

/ 1 / Cut the chicken breasts in half widthways, and put into a shallow dish just large enough to hold them in a single layer.

/ 2 / Put the garlic, lemon juice and sugar in a small bowl and whisk together. Gradually whisk in the oil. Stir in the marjoram, onion rings, salt and pepper.

/ 3 / Pour over the chicken, cover and leave to marinate for at least 30 minutes.

/ 4 / Meanwhile, put the peppers into a shallow dish with 30 ml (2 tbsp) water, cover and microwave on HIGH for 5-6 minutes or until the peppers are just soft, stirring occasionally. Drain and set aside.

/ 5 / To cook the chicken, cover and microwave on HIGH for 5-6 minutes or until the chicken is tender, turning once.

/ 6 / Add the peppers, olives and capers and microwave on HIGH for 1-2 minutes or until heated through, stirring once. Serve immediately, garnished with fresh marjoram.

CHICKEN AND PRUNE KEBABS

SERVES 4

16 prunes, stoned
75 ml (5 tbsp) chicken stock
1 small garlic clove, skinned and crushed
15 ml (1 tbsp) dry sherry
4 chicken breast fillets, skinned and cut into 2.5 cm (1 inch) cubes
15 ml (1 tbsp) vegetable oil
450 g (1 lb) leeks, trimmed and thinly sliced
30 ml (2 tbsp) smetana
salt and pepper
chopped fresh parsley, to garnish

/ 1 / Put the prunes, chicken stock, garlic and sherry in a medium bowl. Cover and microwave on HIGH for 2 minutes to plump.

/ 2 / Stir in the chicken and mix thoroughly together. Set aside while cooking the leeks.

/ 3 / Put the oil and leeks in a large shallow dish and stir to coat the leeks in the oil. Cover and microwave on HIGH for 10-12 minutes until the leeks are really tender, stirring occasionally.

/ 4 / Thread the chicken and prunes on to 8 wooden skewers. Place the kebabs on top of the leeks. Cover and microwave on HIGH for 5-7 minutes until the chicken is tender, repositioning once during cooking.

/ 5 / Stir the smetana into the leeks and season with salt and pepper to taste. Spoon on to 4 warmed serving plates, then arrange 2 kebabs on each plate. Garnish with chopped parsley and serve immediately.

Chicken with Peppers and Marjoram

The sight and smell of bright reddish-orange pieces of chicken as they come sizzling to your table is enough to make anybody want to create this Indian-restaurant experience at home. Unfortunately, the authentic red colour usually comes from a mixture of orange and yellow food colouring, which you may prefer to omit. You can settle for a pale tandoori, or colour the spice and yogurt mixture pink with a little tomato purée – don't use too much or the flavour will be spoilt. Serve tandoori chicken with basmati rice, poppadoms, chutney and raita and enjoy a truly Indian style evening.

BAKED TANDOORI CHICKEN

C   S E R V E S   4

| 3 garlic cloves, skinned and crushed |
| 2.5 cm (1 inch) piece of fresh root ginger, peeled and grated |
| 10 ml (2 tsp) ground coriander |
| 5 ml (1 tsp) ground cumin |
| 2.5 ml (½ tsp) ground turmeric |
| 1.25 ml (¼ tsp) chilli powder |
| 5 ml (1 tsp) sweet paprika |
| 300 ml (½ pint) thick natural yogurt |
| 30 ml (2 tbsp) lemon juice |
| salt |
| tomato purée (optional) |
| 4 chicken quarters, skinned |
| lemon wedges and onion rings, to garnish |

/ 1 / Put the garlic, ginger, coriander, cumin, turmeric, chilli powder, paprika, yogurt, lemon juice and salt in a large bowl. Add a little tomato purée, if wished, to colour the mixture red.

/ 2 / Make several deep cuts all over the chicken pieces, then spoon over the yogurt mixture to coat them completely. Leave to marinate for at least 3-4 hours or overnight.

/ 3 / Just before cooking, preheat the oven on convection at 250°C for 10 minutes.

/ 4 / Arrange the chicken pieces in a large ovenproof dish with the thinner pieces towards the centre. Cook on combination at 250°C/ MEDIUM LOW for 25-30 minutes or until the juices run clear when the chicken is pierced with a knife. Serve hot, garnished with lemon wedges and onion rings.

Baked Tandoori Chicken

Chicken Cordon Bleu

CHICKEN CORDON BLEU

c SERVES 4

| 4 chicken breast fillets, skinned |
| 100 g (4 oz) full-fat soft cheese with herbs and garlic |
| 100 g (4 oz) Gouda or Edam cheese, grated |
| 4 thin slices of ham |
| 30 ml (2 tbsp) plain flour |
| salt and pepper |
| 1 egg, beaten |
| 100 g (4 oz) fresh breadcrumbs |
| 15 g (½ oz) butter |

/ 1 / Using a sharp knife, carefully cut a horizontal slice three-quarters of the way through each chicken fillet. Open out each fillet like a book and place between 2 sheets of greaseproof paper or cling film. Beat out each fillet evenly, using a rolling pin, until very thin, being careful not to tear the flesh.

/ 2 / Place the full-fat soft cheese and the grated cheese in a bowl and beat well together. Lay the ham slices on a flat surface and spread a quarter of the cheese mixture over each. Roll up each slice of ham and place on one half of a flattened fillet. Carefully fold each of the chicken fillets over to completely enclose the filled rolls of ham.

/ 3 / Season the flour with salt and pepper and spread on a plate. Place the beaten egg and breadcrumbs on 2 more plates. Coat the fillets with flour, 1 at a time, and brush with beaten egg, then place on the crumbs and pat crumbs all over them. Place in a shallow ovenproof dish and chill for 10 minutes. Preheat the oven on convection at 250°C.

/ 4 / Dot the chicken fillets with the butter, stand the dish on the wire rack and cook on combination at 200°C/MEDIUM LOW for 15-20 minutes or until golden brown. Serve hot.

This method of preparing chicken has gained enormous popularity. It is now being manufactured en masse and sold in every supermarket, either chilled or frozen, and can be seen on the menu in many local cafés. It's very easy to make at home and is much tastier than the shop-bought version. Make sure that you coat the chicken fillets thoroughly with breadcrumbs or the delicious cheese filling will ooze out during cooking.

Sesame Drumsticks

SESAME DRUMSTICKS
Serve these crisp and crunchy chicken drumsticks with a mixed salad for a light lunch, or with a salad, such as coleslaw, and French fries for a more substantial evening meal. The drumsticks can be prepared in advance up to the end of step 3.

Picture opposite:
Spanish Chicken in Red
Wine

S E S A M E
D R U M S T I C K S

C   S E R V E S   4

50 g (2 oz) plain flour
salt and pepper
8 chicken drumsticks, skinned
1 egg, beaten
about 100 g (4 oz) sesame seeds
finely grated rind of 1 lemon
25 g (1 oz) butter

/ 1 / Preheat the oven for 10 minutes on convection at 250°C.

/ 2 / Season the flour with salt and pepper and use to coat the drumsticks, then dip in the beaten egg. Finally, mix together the sesame seeds and lemon rind and pat all over the flour- and egg-coated drumsticks.

/ 3 / Arrange the drumsticks in a circle around the edge of a large ovenproof plate, with the thick ends towards the outside. Dot all over with the butter.

/ 4 / Stand the plate on the wire rack and cook on combination at 200°C/MEDIUM LOW for 15-18 minutes or until the chicken is golden brown and the juices run clear when the chicken is pierced with a knife. Serve hot.

S P A N I S H
C H I C K E N I N R E D
W I N E

S E R V E S   4

15 ml (1 tbsp) vegetable oil
4 chicken pieces
100 g (4 oz) bacon rashers, rinded and chopped
225 g (8 oz) button mushrooms
45 ml (3 tbsp) plain flour
150 ml (¼ pint) red wine
salt and pepper
50 g (2 oz) black or green olives, stoned

/ 1 / Preheat a browning dish to maximum according to the manufacturer's instructions, adding the oil for the last 30 seconds. Add the chicken and quickly brown.

/ 2 / Add the bacon and mushrooms and microwave on HIGH for 2 minutes. Stir in the flour and microwave on HIGH for 30 seconds.

/ 3 / Gradually stir in the red wine and microwave on HIGH for 5 minutes or until boiling, stirring occasionally during cooking. Season to taste with salt and pepper.

/ 4 / Pour the sauce over the chicken and add the olives. Cover and microwave on HIGH for 10 minutes. Turn chicken over and microwave, uncovered, on HIGH for 8 minutes or until the chicken is tender.

MARINATED CHICKEN WITH PEANUT SAUCE

MARINATED CHICKEN WITH PEANUT SAUCE

A marinade is a convenient, trouble-free way of flavouring and tenderising poultry. It is ideal to use in conjunction with quick cooking methods such as microwaving. Soak the poultry in the flavoursome liquid for a few hours, then use any remaining marinade in a sauce.

A marinade is generally based on a fat or oil to give dry meat extra moisture. Olive oil is a good choice, but other more or less highly flavoured oils are also suitable. As well as the oil, you need an acid ingredient to break down the fibres in the meat – wine, vinegar or lemon juice are the usual choices for this. Add spices or herbs for flavour.

SERVES 4

60 ml (4 tbsp) olive oil
30 ml (2 tbsp) herb vinegar
10 ml (2 tsp) Dijon mustard
grated rind and juice of ½ lemon
15 ml (1 tbsp) soy sauce
1 garlic clove, skinned and crushed
salt and pepper
4 chicken breast fillets, skinned and the flesh cut into 2.5 cm (1 inch) cubes
lemon and lime slices, to garnish

SAUCE

1 small onion, skinned and chopped
2 large tomatoes, skinned, seeded and chopped
1 garlic clove, skinned and chopped
15 ml (1 tbsp) tomato purée
1.25-2.5 ml (¼-½ tsp) cayenne pepper
75 ml (3 fl oz) chicken stock
15 ml (1 tbsp) soy sauce
60 ml (4 tbsp) peanut butter

/ 1 / Make the marinade: whisk together the oil, vinegar, mustard, lemon rind and juice, soy sauce, garlic and salt and pepper until well blended.

/ 2 / Thread the chicken cubes on to 8 wooden kebab sticks. Place these in a shallow oven-proof dish and pour the marinade over. Cover and leave to stand for 2 hours or overnight in the refrigerator.

/ 3 / In a blender or food processor liquidise all the ingredients for the sauce until smooth. Pour the sauce into an ovenproof glass bowl, cover and set aside until it is needed.

/ 4 / Place the covered chicken in the cooker and microwave on HIGH for 10-12 minutes or until the chicken is cooked, turning and re-positioning the kebabs at least twice during the cooking time.

/ 5 / Arrange the chicken in a serving dish, re-serve the cooking liquid. Keep the chicken hot while heating the sauce.

/ 6 / Add the reserved cooking liquid to the sauce mixture in the glass bowl, cover and microwave on HIGH for 5-6 minutes until the sauce boils, stirring frequently. Garnish the chicken and serve with the sauce.

CHICKEN FRICASSÉE

SERVES 4

1 oven-ready roasting chicken, weighing about 1.4 kg (3 lb)
25 g (1 oz) butter or margarine
salt and pepper
225 g (8 oz) carrots, peeled and thinly sliced
45 ml (3 tbsp) vegetable oil
45 ml (3 tbsp) plain flour
300 ml (½ pint) chicken stock
45 ml (3 tbsp) chopped fresh coriander
425 g (15 oz) can chick-peas
chopped fresh coriander, to garnish

/ 1 / Place the chicken, breast side down, in a 2.3 litre (4 pint) microwave dish and spread it with the butter or margarine, then sprinkle it with a little pepper.

Marinated Chicken with Peanut Sauce

/ 2 / Cover the chicken loosely with grease-proof paper and microwave on HIGH for 6 minutes per 450 g (1 lb), turning halfway through cooking. Leave it to stand for 15 minutes.

/ 3 / Cut all the flesh off the bone and divide it into pieces. Reserve the skin and bones for stock, if wished.

/ 4 / Place the carrots in a casserole dish with the oil. Cover, then microwave on HIGH for 4 minutes until just tender.

/ 5 / Stir in the flour, followed by the stock, salt and pepper and the chopped coriander. Add the chicken and the drained chick-peas, stirring well to mix.

/ 6 / Cover and microwave on HIGH for 4 minutes, then stir well. Re-cover and microwave on HIGH for a further 4 minutes.

/ 7 / Leave the chicken to stand for 5 minutes. Adjust the seasoning, then garnish with fresh coriander and serve.

SHREDDED TURKEY WITH COURGETTES

SERVES 4

450 g (1 lb) turkey or chicken breast fillet
450 g (1 lb) courgettes, trimmed
1 red pepper, cored, seeded and thinly sliced
45 ml (3 tbsp) vegetable oil
45 ml (3 tbsp) dry sherry
15 ml (1 tbsp) soy sauce
salt and pepper
60 ml (4 tbsp) natural yogurt or soured cream

/ 1 / Cut the turkey or chicken, courgettes and pepper into fine strips.

/ 2 / Place all the ingredients except the yogurt or soured cream in a 2.3 litre (4 pint) microwave dish, season and stir well to mix.

/ 3 / Cover and microwave the chicken and vegetables on HIGH for 4 minutes.

/ 4 / Leave to stand for 5 minutes, then add the yogurt or soured cream, adjust the seasoning and serve immediately.

STUFFED QUAIL WITH MUSHROOMS AND JUNIPER

SERVES 2

4 quail, cleaned
15 ml (1 tbsp) olive or vegetable oil
150 ml (¼ pint) chicken stock
4 juniper berries
5 ml (1 tsp) chopped fresh thyme or 2.5 ml (½ tsp) dried
15 ml (1 tbsp) gin
100 g (4 oz) button mushrooms, sliced
salt and pepper
watercress, to garnish

/ 1 / Preheat a browning dish to maximum according to the manufacturer's instructions for your particular type of dish.

/ 2 / Meanwhile, using a rolling pin, beat each quail 3 or 4 times to flatten slightly, to ensure they cook evenly in the microwave.

/ 3 / Add the oil to the dish. Quickly add the quail, breast side down, and microwave on HIGH for 2 minutes. Turn over and microwave on HIGH for 1 minute.

/ 4 / Stir in the stock, juniper berries, thyme, gin, mushrooms, salt and pepper. Microwave on HIGH for 6 minutes or until tender, turning the quail once during cooking.

/ 5 / Transfer the quail to a warmed serving dish, then microwave the cooking liquid in the browning dish on HIGH for 3 minutes or until it is slightly reduced.

/ 6 / Season, if necessary, with salt and pepper, then pour over the quail. Garnish with watercress and serve immediately.

STUFFED QUAIL WITH MUSHROOMS AND JUNIPER
Serve the quail with matchstick potatoes which can be made conventionally while the quail are cooking. To make matchstick potatoes: cut potatoes into very small matchstick-size chips. Soak them in cold water, dry and fry conventionally in deep fat at 190°C (375°F) for about 3 minutes. Remove and drain on absorbent paper.

SHREDDED TURKEY WITH COURGETTES
Using yogurt in this recipe gives it a lovely tangy flavour. Yogurt is made by introducing 2 harmless bacteria, Lactobacillus bulgaricus and Streptococcus thermophilus, into either whole or skimmed milk. These bacteria feed on the milk sugars and produce an acid which coagulates the protein, resulting in the thick consistency of yogurt. Vitamins and minerals remain similar in proportion to those in whole or semi-skimmed milk.

Peking-style Duck

PEKING-STYLE DUCK

SERVES 4

The English Aylesbury duck is the most famous breed. It is believed to be a strain of the original Peking duck, and takes its name from the Vale of Aylesbury in Buckinghamshire where it was originally bred. If you see Aylesbury duckling for sale, then you can be sure of buying a good quality, meaty bird with tender flesh and superb flavour.

1 bunch of spring onions, trimmed
½ cucumber
2 kg (4-4½ lb) oven-ready duckling
soy sauce to taste
100 ml (4 fl oz) hoisin sauce
PANCAKES
450 g (1 lb) plain flour
pinch of salt
15 ml (1 tbsp) vegetable oil, plus extra for brushing

/ 1 / Trim off the root end of the spring onions, and trim the green leaves down to about 5 cm (2 inches). Skin, then cut twice lengthways to within 2.5 cm (1 inch) of the end. Place in a bowl of iced water and refrigerate for 1-2 hours or until the onion curls. Cut the cucumber into 5 cm (2 inch) fingers.

/ 2 / Make the pancakes: put the flour and salt in a large bowl. Gradually mix in 15 ml (1 tbsp) oil and 375 ml (13 fl oz) boiling water, stirring vigorously with a wooden spoon. When the dough is slightly cool, shape into a ball and turn on to a lightly floured surface. Knead for about 5 minutes to make a soft smooth dough. Leave to stand in a bowl for 30 minutes covered with a damp cloth or cling film.

82

/ 3 / Cut the dough in half and shape each half into a roll 40 cm (16 inches) long. Cut each roll into 16 even slices. On a lightly floured surface, roll out 2 slices of dough into circles about 7.5 cm (3 inches) across. Brush the tops with oil. Put the oiled surfaces together and roll out to a thin 15 cm (6 inch) circle. Repeat with the remaining roll of dough cut into 16 slices to make a total of 16 pairs of pancakes.

/ 4 / Heat an ungreased frying pan or griddle and cook each pair of pancakes for about 1-2 minutes on each side, turning when air bubbles start to form. Remove from the frying pan and while they are still hot separate the pancakes. Stack in a clean damp tea-towel.

/ 5 / Pat the duck dry with absorbent kitchen paper. Calculate the cooking time at 10 minutes per 450 g (1 lb). Place the duck, breast side down, on a microwave roasting rack and brush with soy sauce.

/ 6 / Cover and microwave on HIGH for half the calculated cooking time. Turn the duck over, brush with soy sauce and continue to microwave on HIGH, uncovered, for the remaining cooking time, until the duck is tender. Leave the duck to stand for 10-15 minutes loosely covered with foil.

/ 7 / Grill the duck under a hot grill for about 2 minutes or until the duck is golden brown and the skin is crisp on all sides.

/ 8 / Microwave the hoisin sauce on HIGH for about 2 minutes or until the sauce is hot and just beginning to bubble.

/ 9 / Cut the duck into small pieces. Meanwhile, microwave the pancakes wrapped in the damp tea-towel on HIGH for 2 minutes or until they are just warm.

/ 10 / Serve each person with 8 pancakes and some of the duck, including the skin. Hand the vegetables and sauce separately. To eat, spread a little sauce on a pancake and top with vegetables and pieces of duck and skin. Roll up and eat with your fingers.

SWEET AND SOUR DUCK BREASTS WITH PEPPERS

C   S E R V E S   2

2 duck breast fillets, each weighing about 150 g (5 oz)
25 ml (1½ tbsp) soy sauce
25 ml (1½ tbsp) port
15 ml (1 tbsp) garlic or white wine vinegar
15 ml (1 tbsp) clear honey
10 ml (2 tsp) dark brown sugar
2.5 cm (1 inch) piece of fresh root ginger, peeled and finely grated
salt
½ red pepper, cored and seeded
½ green pepper, cored and seeded
½ yellow pepper, cored and seeded

/ 1 / Put the duck breasts, skin side up, in a shallow dish. Mix the soy sauce, port, vinegar, honey, sugar and ginger together and pour over the duck. Leave to marinate for at least 2-3 hours or overnight.

/ 2 / Just before cooking, preheat the oven on convection at 250°C for 10 minutes.

/ 3 / Remove the duck from the marinade and place, breast side up, on a large ovenproof plate. Sprinkle the skin with salt. Cook on combination at 200°C/MEDIUM LOW for 8-12 minutes or until the duck is cooked but still pink in the middle.

/ 4 / While the duck is cooking, cut the peppers into very thin strips and put in a bowl with 15 ml (1 tbsp) water.

/ 5 / Remove the duck from the oven. Cover the bowl containing the peppers and microwave on HIGH for 2-3 minutes or until the peppers are just tender.

/ 6 / While the peppers are cooking, slice the duck and arrange on 2 plates. Drain the peppers and arrange on the plates with the duck.

/ 7 / Microwave the marinade on HIGH for 1-2 minutes or until boiling. Spoon a little over the duck and serve immediately.

SWEET AND SOUR DUCK BREASTS WITH PEPPERS
This is really quick and simple to make but looks rather impressive. Perfectly cooked duck breasts, still slightly pink on the inside, in a rich sauce are served with a julienne of colourful peppers. Serve for a special meal with a selection of baby vegetables, such as corn or carrots, for maximum impact.

The Chinese were the first to eat ducklings – as long ago as 168 BC! The nobles of the Han dynasty used to breed domestic white ducks for the table – especially for banquets and royal feasts, and they also enjoyed wild duck in stews for more humble occasions. In those days duck meat was served completely unseasoned, and was recommended as a sacrificial offering to appease the gods. Duck soup was also recommended as a remedy for estranged husbands and wives – a drop of duck soup was supposed to bring the couple back together again!

Henry the Eighth had a passion for duck, and was said to retire to bed at night on a supper of roast duckling – not the ideal food for a good night's sleep, but certainly rich enough to satisfy his notoriously large appetite!

Fish

Current thinking on healthy eating recommends a reduction in the amount of red meat we eat, so fish is making a comeback. Fish has both a low saturated fat content and a low calorie content; it's a cheaper source of protein than red meat and it can be prepared in a huge variety of ways.

Fish cooks quickly and easily in the microwave, retaining a deliciously moist and firm texture. The result is similar to that obtained when fish is steamed conventionally or poached. It is ideal for cooking fish ready for flaking to include in pies, pâtés, fish cakes and kedgeree, or for plainly cooking fish fillets for serving with white, parsley or onion sauce or herb butters. The combination setting will help to crisp the outside of small items such as fish cakes or to give gratins a lovely golden finish.

Red Snapper and Root Vegetables

COMBINATION AND MICROWAVE COOKING

THAWING FISH AND SHELLFISH IN THE MICROWAVE

Separate cutlets, fillets or steaks as soon as possible during thawing, and remove pieces from the cooker as soon as they are thawed. The exact timing for thawing will depend on the thickness of the whole fish or the fish pieces.

Type	Time/Setting	Notes
Whole round fish (mullet, trout, carp, bream, whiting)	4-6 minutes per 450 g (1 lb) on LOW or DEFROST	Stand for 5 minutes after each 2-3 minutes. Very large fish are thawed more successfully if left to stand for 10-15 minutes after every 2-3 minutes.
White fish fillets or cutlets (cod, coley, haddock, halibut, monkfish) whole plaice or sole	3-4 minutes per 450 g (1 lb) on LOW or DEFROST	Stand for 5 minutes after each 2-3 minutes.
Lobster, crab, crab claws	6-8 minutes per 450 g (1 lb) on LOW or DEFROST	Stand for 5 minutes after each 2-3 minutes.
Crab meat	4-6 minutes per 450 g (1 lb) block on LOW or DEFROST	Stand for 5 minutes after each 2-3 minutes.
Prawns, shrimps, scampi, scallops	2-3 minutes per 100 g (4 oz) 3-4 minutes per 225 g (8 oz) on LOW or DEFROST	Arrange in a circle on a double sheet of absorbent kitchen paper to absorb liquid. Separate during thawing with a fork and remove pieces from cooker as they thaw.

COOKING FISH AND SHELLFISH IN THE MICROWAVE

The cooking time depends on the thickness of the fish as well as the amount being cooked and whether it is cooked whole, in fillets or cut up into smaller pieces. This chart is a guide only. Always check before the end of the calculated cooking time to prevent overcooking. Simply put the fish in a single layer in a shallow dish with 30 ml (2 tbsp) stock, wine, milk or water per 450 g (1 lb) of fish (unless otherwise stated in the recipes), then cover and cook as instructed below and right.

Type	Time/Setting	Microwave Cooking Technique(s)
Whole round fish (whiting, mullet, trout, carp, bream, small haddock)	4 minutes on HIGH per 450 g (1 lb)	Slash skin to prevent bursting. Turn fish over halfway through cooking time if fish weighs more than 1.4 kg (3 lb). Re-position fish if cooking more than 2.
Whole flat fish (plaice, sole)	3 minutes on HIGH per 450 g (1 lb)	Slash skin. Check fish after 2 minutes.
Cutlets, steaks, thick fish fillets (cod, coley, haddock, halibut, monkfish fillet)	4 minutes on HIGH per 450 g (1 lb)	Position thicker parts towards the outside of the dish. Turn halfway through cooking if steaks are very thick.
Flat fish fillets (plaice, sole)	2-3 minutes on HIGH per 450 g (1 lb)	Check fish after 2 minutes.

Type	Time/Setting	Microwave Cooking Technique(s)
Dense fish fillets, cutlets, steaks (tuna, swordfish, conger eel), whole monkfish tail	5-6 minutes on HIGH per 450 g (1 lb)	Position thicker parts towards the outside of the dish. Turn halfway through cooking if thick.
Skate wings	6-7 minutes on HIGH per 450 g (1 lb)	Add 150 ml (¼ pint) stock or milk. Cook more than 900 g (2 lb) in batches.
Smoked fish	Cook as appropriate for type of fish, e.g. whole, fillet or cutlet. See above	
Squid	Put prepared squid, cut into rings, in a large bowl with 150 ml (¼ pint) wine, stock or water per 450 g (1 lb) of squid. Cook, covered, on HIGH for 5-8 minutes per 450 g (1 lb)	Time depends on size of squid – larger, older, squid are tougher and may take longer to cook.
Octopus	Put prepared octopus, cut into 2.5 cm (1 inch) pieces, in a large bowl with 150 ml (¼ pint) wine, stock or water per 450 g (1 lb) of octopus. Cook, covered, on HIGH until liquid is boiling, then on MEDIUM for 15-20 minutes per 450 g (1 lb)	Tenderise octopus before cooking by beating vigorously with a meat mallet or rolling pin. Marinate before cooking to help tenderise. Time depends on age and size of octopus.
Scallops (shelled)	2-4 minutes on HIGH per 450 g (1 lb)	Do not overcook or scallops will be tough. Add corals for 1-2 minutes at end of cooking time.
Scallops in their shells	Do not cook in the microwave	Cook conventionally.
Mussels	Put up to 900 g (2 lb) mussels in a large bowl with 150 ml (¼ pint) wine, stock or water. Cook, covered, on HIGH for 3-5 minutes	Remove mussels on the top as they cook. Shake the bowl occasionally during cooking. Discard any mussels which do not open.
Cockles	Put cockles in a large bowl with a little water. Cook, covered, on HIGH for 3-4 minutes until the shells open. Take cockles out of their shells and cook for a further 2-3 minutes or until hot	Shake the bowl occasionally during cooking.
Oysters	Do not cook in the microwave	
Raw prawns	2-5 minutes on HIGH per 450 g (1 lb), stirring frequently	Time depends on the size of the prawns. Cook until their colour changes to bright pink.
Live lobster	Do not cook in the microwave	Cook conventionally.
Live crab	Do not cook in the microwave	Cook conventionally.
Small clams	Cook as mussels	As mussels.
Large clams	Do not cook in the microwave	Cook conventionally.

COOKING FISH IN A COMBINATION OVEN

In a combination oven, fish may be cooked by any one of the three methods available – by microwave, combination or in the usual way, by convection.

Fish cooks quickly and easily on the microwave setting, retaining a deliciously moist and firm texture. The result is similar to that obtained when fish is conventionally steamed or poached. It is ideal for cooking fish ready for flaking to include in pies, pâtés, fish cakes and kedgeree, or for plainly cooking fish fillets for serving with white, parsley or onion sauce or herb butters.

The combination setting cooks fish just as quickly but gives whole fish a crisper skin. The cooking time for each method depends on the thickness of the fish as well as the amount being cooked and whether it is cooked whole, in fillets or cut into smaller pieces. A whole fish should have the skin slashed before cooking to prevent it from bursting.

To cook on microwave only, place the fish in a large shallow dish with 30 ml (2 tbsp) stock, wine, milk or water per 450 g (1 lb) fish (unless otherwise stated), then cover and cook as shown in the chart. Alternatively, cook whole fish on a combination setting. Place the fish in a large shallow dish, slash the skin and brush with butter. Cook as directed in the chart.

FISH AND SHELLFISH COOKING CHART

Microwave times are given where this is preferable to combination cooking. Always check before the end of the calculated cooking time to prevent over-cooking.

Type	Time/Setting	Notes
Whole round fish (whiting, mullet, trout, carp, bream, small haddock)	6-8 minutes per 450 g (1 lb) on combination at 200°C/MEDIUM LOW	Slash skin to prevent bursting. Turn fish over halfway through cooking time if fish weighs more than 1.4 kg (3 lb). Re-position fish if cooking more than 2.
Whole flat fish (plaice, sole)	4-5 minutes per 450 g (1 lb) on combination at 200°C/MEDIUM LOW	Slash skin. Check fish after 2 minutes.
Cutlets, steaks, thick fish fillets (cod, coley, haddock, halibut, monkfish fillet)	5-6 minutes per 450 g (1 lb) on combination at 200°C/MEDIUM LOW	Position thicker parts towards the outside of the dish. Turn halfway through the cooking time if the steaks are very thick.
Flat fish fillets (plaice, sole)	2-3 minutes on microwave HIGH per 450 g (1 lb)	Check fish after 2 minutes.
Dense fish fillets, cutlets, steaks (tuna, swordfish, conger eel), whole monkfish tail	7-8 minutes per 450 g (1 lb) on combination at 200°C/MEDIUM LOW	Position thicker parts towards the outside of the dish. Turn halfway through the cooking time if the steaks are thick.
Skate wings	6-7 minutes on microwave HIGH per 450 g (1 lb)	Add 150 ml (¼ pint) stock or milk. If cooking more than 900 g (2 lb) cook in batches.
Smoked fish	Cook as appropriate for type of fish, e.g. whole, fillet or cutlet. See above	

Type	Time/Setting	Notes
Squid	Put prepared squid, cut into rings, in a large bowl with 150 ml (¼ pint) wine, stock or water per 450 g (1 lb). Cook, covered, on microwave HIGH for 5-8 minutes per 450 g (1 lb)	Time depends on size of squid – larger, older, squid are tougher and may take longer to cook.
Octopus	Put prepared octopus, cut into 2.5 cm (1 inch) pieces, in a large bowl with 150 ml (¼ pint) wine, stock or water per 450 g (1 lb). Cook, covered, on microwave HIGH until liquid is boiling, then on MEDIUM for 15-20 minutes per 450 g (1 lb)	Tenderise octopus before cooking by beating vigorously with a meat mallet or rolling pin. Marinate before cooking to help tenderise. Time depends on age and size of octopus.
Scallops (shelled)	2-4 minutes on microwave HIGH per 450 g (1 lb)	Do not overcook or scallops will be tough. Add corals for 1-2 minutes at end of cooking time.
Scallops in their shells	Do not cook in the combination oven	Cook conventionally.
Mussels	Put up to 900 g (2 lb) mussels in a large bowl with 150 ml (¼ pint) wine, stock or water. Cook, covered, on microwave HIGH for 3-5 minutes	Remove mussels on the top as they cook. Shake the bowl occasionally during cooking. Discard any mussels which do not open.
Cockles	Put cockles in a large bowl with a little water. Cook, covered, on microwave HIGH for 3-4 minutes until the shells open. Take cockles out of their shells and cook for a further 2-3 minutes or until hot	Shake the bowl occasionally during cooking.
Raw pawns	2-5 minutes on microwave HIGH per 450 g (1 lb), stirring frequently	Time depends on the size of the prawns. Cook until their colour changes to bright pink.
Live crab or lobster	Do not cook in the combination oven	Cook conventionally.
Small clams	Cook as mussels	As mussels.
Large clams	Do not cook in the combination oven	Cook conventionally.

Creamy Cod Bake

This is the perfect dish to serve for the children's lunch or supper – they will love the combination of soft spinach, fish and cheese sauce and the crunchy, crisp topping. Even if you normally find it difficult to persuade them to eat fish and spinach – with this dish they won't realise what they are eating.

Spinach is a nutritious vegetable. It is a valuable source of vitamins A and C, and has a high iron and calcium content. The frozen spinach used in this recipe is just as good as fresh and much quicker to prepare, but if you prefer to use the fresh vegetable, you will need double the quantity. Wash it thoroughly in several changes of water, discarding any yellow or damaged leaves and thick stalks. Cook as on the chart on page 125.

CREAMY COD BAKE

C   SERVES 4

450 g (1 lb) packet frozen leaf spinach
50 g (2 oz) butter
2.5 ml (½ tsp) freshly grated nutmeg
4 frozen cod steaks
salt and pepper
100 g (4 oz) Cheddar cheese, grated
two 25 g (0.88 oz) packets cheese and onion crisps, finely crushed
SAUCE
25 g (1 oz) butter
25 g (1 oz) plain flour
450 ml (¾ pint) milk
50 g (2 oz) Cheddar cheese, finely grated

/ 1 / Put the frozen spinach in a medium bowl and microwave on HIGH for 6-8 minutes, stirring halfway through the cooking time. Drain off any cooking juices and stir in 25 g (1 oz) of the butter and half the nutmeg. Arrange in an ovenproof dish and set aside.

/ 2 / Put the remaining butter in a shallow dish and microwave on HIGH for 45 seconds or until melted. Add the cod, cover and microwave on HIGH for 10-12 minutes, turning halfway through cooking. Flake the fish and place on top of the spinach with any cooking juices.

/ 3 / Make the sauce: put the butter, flour and milk in a medium bowl and whisk together. Microwave on HIGH for 4-5 minutes or until the sauce has boiled and thickened, whisking frequently. Stir in the cheese, remaining nutmeg and salt and pepper to taste, then pour over the fish to cover it completely.

/ 4 / Mix the 100 g (4 oz) grated cheese with the crushed crisps and sprinkle over the top. Stand the dish on the wire rack and cook on combination at 200°C/MEDIUM for 10-15 minutes or until golden brown and bubbling. Serve hot, straight from the dish.

FISH WITH CORIANDER MASALA

SERVES 2 - 3

1 medium onion, skinned and chopped
2 garlic cloves, skinned
1 green chilli, seeded (optional)
2.5 cm (1 inch) piece fresh root ginger, peeled
15 ml (1 tbsp) coriander seeds
5 ml (1 tsp) ground turmeric
5 ml (1 tsp) fenugreek seeds
45 ml (3 tbsp) chopped fresh coriander
juice of 2 limes
30 ml (2 tbsp) vegetable oil
4 large tomatoes, finely chopped
15 ml (1 tbsp) garam masala
salt
1 whole fish, such as whiting, codling or pollack, weighing about 700-900 g (1½-2 lb), scaled and cleaned
fresh coriander, to garnish

/ 1 / Put the onion, garlic, chilli, ginger, coriander seeds, turmeric, fenugreek seeds, fresh coriander and lime juice in a blender or food processor and process until smooth.

/ 2 / Put the oil in a large shallow dish (large enough to hold the fish) and microwave on HIGH for 1 minute until hot. Add the spice paste and microwave on HIGH for 5 minutes, or until the onion has softened, stirring occasionally during cooking.

/ 3 / Add the tomatoes, garam masala and salt to taste and microwave on HIGH for 3-4 minutes until the sauce is reduced and slightly thickened, stirring occasionally.

/ 4 / Meanwhile, using a sharp knife, make deep cuts in a criss-cross pattern on each side of the fish. If the fish is too large for the microwave, push a long bamboo skewer through the tail and then into the body of the fish so that the tail is curved upwards.

/ 3 / Lay the fish in the dish containing the sauce and spoon the sauce over the fish to coat it. Cover and microwave on HIGH for 10-15 minutes depending on the thickness of the fish, or until the fish is tender. Serve garnished with coriander.

BRILL WITH GREEN SAUCE

SERVES 4 - 6

8 brill, plaice or sole fillets, each weighing about 75 g (3 oz), skinned
30 ml (2 tbsp) fish or vegetable stock or milk
225 g (8 oz) broccoli
100 g (4 oz) French beans
2 medium courgettes
45 ml (3 tbsp) mayonnaise
45 ml (3 tbsp) natural yogurt
15 ml (1 tbsp) lemon juice
45 ml (3 tbsp) chopped fresh herbs
salt and pepper
fresh herbs, to garnish

/ 1 / Cut each fillet into 2 pieces and arrange around the edge of a shallow dish. Pour over the stock or milk, cover and microwave on HIGH for 3-4 minutes until tender. Leave to cool, covered.

/ 2 / Trim the broccoli and cut into tiny florets. Top and tail the beans and cut into 5 cm (2 inch) pieces. Slice the courgettes into 0.5 cm (¼ inch) slices.

/ 3 / Put the vegetables into a bowl with 15 ml (1 tbsp) water. Cover and microwave on HIGH for 2-3 minutes until softened but still crisp. Drain, rinse with cold water and leave to cool.

/ 4 / Make the sauce: put the mayonnaise, yogurt, lemon juice and herbs into a bowl and beat together. Season to taste with salt and pepper. Chill until ready to serve.

/ 5 / To serve: arrange the fish and vegetables on a plate, spoon over a little of the green sauce and serve immediately, garnished with fresh herbs and with the remaining sauce handed separately.

BRILL WITH GREEN SAUCE
Brill is a flat fish with a good flavour and texture which resembles turbot. The flesh is firm and slightly yellowish: avoid any with a bluish tinge. It is sold whole or as fillets.

FISH WITH CORIANDER MASALA
The seeds of the coriander are used as a spice and the leaves as a herb. The round, light brown seeds have a fresh spicy flavour and can be used whole or ground in many Indian dishes. Coriander leaves are a favourite Indian herb and are often chopped and stirred into dishes at the end of the cooking time to retain the flavour.

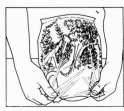

To store fresh coriander leaves: place the roots of the bunch in a container of water, such as a jam jar or jug. The leaves should not be in the water. Place a large polythene bag over the coriander and its container to completely enclose it. Place in the refrigerator or in a cool place. The coriander will last for 2-3 weeks. Remove any yellowing leaves before use.

Trout with Sesame Cream

TROUT WITH SESAME CREAM

SERVES 2

When buying the fish for this recipe, choose between salmon trout and rainbow trout – both are available in different sizes. Both are members of the salmon family, although the salmon trout, also called the sea trout because it spends the major part of its life at sea, is the closest to the salmon or 'king of the river'.

2 trout, total weight about 275 g (10 oz)
15 ml (1 tbsp) vegetable oil
60 ml (4 tbsp) tahini (sesame seed paste)
30 ml (2 tbsp) lemon juice
150 ml (¼ pint) soured cream
1 garlic clove, skinned and crushed (optional)
30 ml (2 tbsp) finely chopped fresh parsley
salt and pepper
tarragon or flat leaf parsley and black olives, to garnish
salad or rice pilaff, to serve

/ 1 / Brush the trout with the oil and arrange in a single layer in a shallow dish. Cover and microwave on HIGH for 5-7 minutes or until tender. Carefully peel off the skin, leaving the head and tail intact. Leave to cool.

/ 2 / Make the sauce: put the tahini, lemon juice, soured cream, garlic, if using, and parsley into a bowl and mix together. Season to taste with salt and pepper.

/ 3 / Carefully transfer the fish to 2 plates. Coat in some of the sauce, leaving the head and tail exposed. Garnish with tarragon or parsley leaves and olives. Serve with the remaining sauce and a salad or rice pilaff.

STUFFED TROUT WITH CUCUMBER SAUCE

C SERVES 4

25 g (1 oz) butter or margarine
1 medium onion, skinned and finely chopped
75 g (3 oz) fresh breadcrumbs
30 ml (2 tbsp) chopped fresh parsley
finely grated rind and juice of 1 lemon
salt and pepper
4 whole trout, about 225 g (8 oz) each, cleaned
lemon wedges and chopped fresh parsley or tarragon, to garnish
CUCUMBER SAUCE
50 g (2 oz) butter or margarine
1 large cucumber, peeled, seeded and finely chopped
5 ml (1 tsp) plain flour
15 ml (1 tbsp) white wine vinegar
150 ml (¼ pint) fish stock or water
10 ml (2 tsp) finely chopped fresh tarragon
salt and pepper

/ 1 / Make the sauce: put the butter or margarine in a large ovenproof glass bowl and microwave on HIGH for 1-2 minutes or until it has completely melted.

/ 2 / Stir the cucumber into the butter or margarine, cover and microwave on HIGH for 6 minutes or until the cucumber is very soft, stirring 2 or 3 times.

/ 3 / Blend the flour with the vinegar and stir in the fish stock or water, then stir this into the cucumber and add the tarragon. Microwave on HIGH for 3-4 minutes or until the sauce is boiling, stirring frequently. Season well with salt and pepper and set aside.

/ 4 / Make the stuffing: put the butter or margarine in a medium ovenproof glass bowl and microwave on HIGH for 1 minute or until melted. Stir in the onion. Cover and microwave on HIGH for 5-7 minutes until the onion has softened. Stir in the breadcrumbs, parsley, lemon rind and juice and the salt and pepper and mix together well until all the ingredients are combined.

/ 5 / Fill each trout with the stuffing, dividing it equally between them. Place the trout side by side in a large ovenproof dish.

Stuffed Trout with Cucumber Sauce

/ 6 / Cover and cook on combination at 200°C/ MEDIUM LOW for 14-15 minutes, or until the fish flakes easily when tested with a fork, turning the trout over and repositioning them halfway through cooking.

/ 7 / Reheat the sauce on HIGH for 1 minute. Garnish the fish with lemon wedges and parsley and serve with the cucumber sauce.

PIQUANT PURPLE SALAD

SERVES 4

450 g (1 lb) baby new potatoes, scrubbed
60 ml (4 tbsp) olive oil
30 ml (2 tbsp) white wine vinegar
salt and pepper
450 g (1 lb) whiting fillets, skinned
30 ml (2 tbsp) milk
2 large pickled dill cucumbers or 4 pickled gherkins
½ cucumber
175 g (6 oz) cooked beetroot
selection of red salad leaves, such as radicchio, red lalola, oak leaf lettuce
30 ml (2 tbsp) capers
6 anchovy fillets
30 ml (2 tbsp) chopped fresh dill
crusty bread, to serve

To cook the beetroot for Piquant Purple Salad in the microwave: put in a bowl, prick the skin with a fork and microwave on HIGH for 7-9 minutes (for 2 medium beetroot), rearranging halfway through cooking.

Use ready-prepared mixed salad leaves sold in bags in supermarkets for this recipe.

Capers are used whole or crushed in many Italian dishes, particularly in fish recipes, sauces and stuffings. They are always sold pickled in brine, and should be used sparingly as their flavour is very pungent.

/1/ Put the potatoes into a medium bowl with 30 ml (2 tbsp) water. Cover and microwave on HIGH for 8-10 minutes until tender, stirring occasionally during cooking.

/2/ While the potatoes are cooking, make the dressing. Whisk the oil and vinegar together and season to taste with salt and pepper. When the potatoes are cooked, drain well and pour the dressing over them. Leave to cool while preparing the rest of the salad.

/3/ Cut the fish into small strips about 1 cm (½ inch) wide and 7.5 cm (3 inches) long and put into a shallow dish with the milk. Cover and microwave on HIGH for 3-4 minutes until just cooked. Do not overcook or the fish will break up and spoil the appearance of the salad. Leave to cool in the dish.

/4/ When the potatoes and fish are cold, slice the pickled dill cucumbers or gherkins and the cucumber and mix with the potatoes. Peel the beetroot and cut into chunks.

/5/ Arrange the salad leaves on a serving platter. Spoon over the potato mixture, then the fish and then the beetroot. Mix lightly together. Sprinkle with the capers, anchovies and dill. Serve with crusty bread.

Piquant Purple Salad

KEDGEREE IN A CRUST

C   SERVES 6

450 g (1 lb) white fish fillet, such as cod, haddock, whiting or coley
45 ml (3 tbsp) milk
100 g (4 oz) long-grain white or basmati rice, cooked
2 hard-boiled eggs, chopped
50 g (2 oz) butter
15 ml (1 tbsp) capers, drained and chopped
45 ml (3 tbsp) chopped fresh parsley
50 g (2 oz) can anchovy fillets
salt and pepper
PASTRY
225 g (8 oz) self-raising flour
2.5 ml (½ tsp) salt
5 ml (1 tsp) baking powder
100 g (4 oz) shredded suet
1 egg
beaten egg or milk, to glaze

/ 1 / Put the fish in a large shallow dish with the milk. Cover and microwave on HIGH for 4-5 minutes or until the fish flakes easily when tested with a fork.

/ 2 / Flake the fish with a fork, discarding the skin, and mix with the rice, chopped boiled eggs, butter, capers and parsley. Chop the anchovy fillets and add to the fish mixture with the oil from the can. Season to taste.

/ 3 / Make the pastry: mix together the flour, salt and baking powder in a bowl. Stir in the suet and the egg, then add enough cold water to mix to a firm dough. Knead lightly, then cut in half. Roll out 1 half on a lightly floured surface to an oval 26.5 cm (10½ inches) wide. Place in a large shallow ovenproof dish.

/ 4 / Spoon the fish filling on to the pastry in the dish, leaving a 2.5 cm (1 inch) border around the edge. Roll out the remaining pastry to an oval large enough to cover the filling. Dampen the border of pastry with water and place the second piece on top. Press together to seal, then crimp the edges. Brush the top with beaten egg or milk, then chill for 10 minutes while preheating the oven on convection at 250°C.

/ 5 / Stand the pie on the wire rack and cook on combination at 200°C/MEDIUM LOW for 10-20 minutes or until golden. Serve hot or cold.

RED SNAPPER AND ROOT VEGETABLES

SERVES 4

1 green chilli
5 ml (1 tsp) ground aniseed
2 allspice berries
60 ml (4 tbsp) vegetable oil
225 g (8 oz) celeriac
225 g (8 oz) parsnips
225 g (8 oz) carrots
4 red snapper or red mullet, each weighing about 275 g (10 oz), cleaned and scaled
salt and pepper
chopped fresh parsley, to garnish

/ 1 / Remove the seeds from the chilli and discard. Finely chop the chilli and put into a small bowl with the aniseed. Crush the allspice berries and add with the oil. Microwave on HIGH for 1-2 minutes or until hot, then leave to infuse while cooking the vegetables.

/ 2 / Peel the celeriac, parsnips and carrots. Cut the celeriac and parsnips into neat strips about 7.5 cm (3 inches) long and 1 cm (½ inch) wide. Cut the carrots into diagonal slices about 1 cm (½ inch) thick. Put all of the vegetables in a medium bowl with 45 ml (3 tbsp) water. Cover and microwave on HIGH for 5-6 minutes or until slightly softened, stirring once during cooking.

/ 3 / Using a sharp knife, slash the fish twice on each side and arrange in a single layer in a large dish. Brush with a little of the spicy oil, cover and put in the cooker on top of the bowl containing the vegetables. Microwave on HIGH for 7-8 minutes or until the fish is tender, rearranging the fish once during cooking.

/ 4 / Microwave the remaining oil on HIGH for 1 minute or until hot, then drain the vegetables and toss in half the hot oil. Season to taste with salt and pepper.

/ 5 / Arrange the vegetables on a serving platter with the fish. Spoon the remaining hot oil over the fish, garnish with chopped parsley and serve immediately.

RED SNAPPER AND ROOT VEGETABLES
When buying root vegetables, choose them carefully and make sure they are firm and unwrinkled. Store them in a cool, airy place, such as a vegetable rack, so that air can circulate round them.

KEDGEREE IN A CRUST
As its name suggests, this is a variation on the classic breakfast dish. A kedgeree-like mixture of fish, egg and rice is enclosed in a crisp suet pastry crust. If you have not tried making suetcrust pastry before, do try it – it's very easy to make and produces a pastry with lots of texture and flavour. In this recipe the pie is an oval, but you could make a round, square or even a fish shape. As the pastry is easy to handle any shape is possible, but remember to keep the diameter to about 26.5 cm (10½ inches).

Fillets of fish may be cooked flat or rolled up. Reposition during cooking. When cooking fish fillets flat, overlap thin parts to prevent overcooking of the thinner ends.

If you boil potatoes conventionally for mashing, then when you've drained them you find they are still too hard for mashing, simply leave the potatoes in a bowl, add milk and butter as usual, then mash as much as possible. Cover the bowl with a plate, then microwave on HIGH for 3-4 minutes. You will find the potatoes are then soft enough to mash.

PARSLEY POTATO FISH PIE

C   SERVES 4

4 large potatoes, each weighing about 225 g (8 oz)
900 g (2 lb) smoked haddock fillet
about 568 ml (1 pint) milk
100 g (4 oz) butter or margarine
45 ml (3 tbsp) chopped fresh parsley
salt and pepper
100 g (4 oz) cooked peeled prawns
50 g (2 oz) plain flour

/ 1 / Scrub the potatoes and prick all over with a fork. Arrange in the oven in a circle. Microwave on HIGH for 18-20 minutes or until the potatoes feel soft when gently squeezed, turning them over once during cooking. Leave to cool slightly.

/ 2 / While the potatoes are cooling, put the fish in a large shallow dish with 60 ml (4 tbsp) of the milk. Cover and microwave on HIGH for 8-10 minutes or until the fish flakes easily when tested with a fork.

/ 3 / Peel the potatoes and mash the flesh with half of the butter or margarine. Add about 75 ml (5 tbsp) of the milk to make a soft mashed potato. Stir in half of the parsley and season to taste with salt and pepper.

/ 4 / Strain the cooking liquid from the fish into a measuring jug and make up to 450 ml (¾ pint) with milk. Set aside. Flake the fish with a fork and place in an ovenproof dish with the cooked peeled prawns.

/ 5 / Make the sauce: put the milk mixture in a medium bowl with the remaining butter or margarine and the flour. Microwave on HIGH for 5-6 minutes or until boiling and thickened, whisking frequently. Season to taste with salt and pepper. Pour the sauce evenly over the fish and prawns.

/ 6 / Spoon or pipe the mashed potato over the top of the fish mixture. Sprinkle with the remaining parsley. Stand the dish on the wire rack and cook on combination at 200°C/ MEDIUM for 10-15 minutes or until hot and lightly browned. Serve at once.

VARIATIONS

Use unsmoked fish instead of smoked haddock, and add other cooked shellfish, such as cockles or mussels, instead of the prawns. Alternatively, add other vegetable ingredients, such as finely chopped peppers or thinly sliced mushrooms. Vary the potato topping by mixing it with cheese, sprinkling it with cheese before cooking, or flavouring it with other fresh herbs of your choice.

Parsley Potato Fish Pie

STUFFED HERRINGS

SERVES 4

4 herrings or mackerel, each weighing about 225 g (8 oz), cleaned and scaled
15 ml (1 tbsp) chopped fresh rosemary
15 ml (1 tbsp) chopped fresh dill
15 ml (1 tbsp) chopped fresh chives
15 ml (1 tbsp) chopped fresh sage
2 garlic cloves, skinned and chopped
50 g (2 oz) walnut halves, finely chopped
25 g (1 oz) fresh white breadcrumbs
salt and pepper
30 ml (2 tbsp) olive oil
30 ml (2 tbsp) lemon juice
walnut halves and fresh herbs, to garnish

/ 1 / Remove the head and the fins from the herrings or mackerel, then cut completely along the underside. Open the fish out and lay cut side down on a board. Press lightly along the middle of the back to loosen the bone.

/ 2 / Turn the fish over and ease out the backbone and as many small bones as possible. Wash and dry the fish.

/ 3 / Arrange the fish, skin side down, in a large shallow dish, placing the wider end towards the outside. Sprinkle the fish with the herbs, garlic, walnuts and half the breadcrumbs. Season generously with pepper and a little salt. Carefully fold each fish in half.

/ 4 / Mix the oil and lemon juice together and pour over the fish. Sprinkle with the remaining breadcrumbs. Cover and microwave on HIGH for 8-10 minutes or until the fish is tender.

/ 5 / Serve with a little of the cooking liquid spooned over, garnished with a few walnut halves and herb sprigs.

Stuffed Herrings

RAIE AU BEURRE NOIR

SERVES 2

75 g (3 oz) unsalted butter
30 ml (2 tbsp) white wine vinegar
30 ml (2 tbsp) capers (optional)
1 skate wing, weighing about 700 g (1½ lb)
1 small onion, skinned and sliced
30 ml (2 tbsp) chopped fresh parsley
salt and pepper

/ 1 / Cut the butter into small pieces and put into a medium bowl. Cover and microwave on HIGH for 4-5 minutes until light brown (do not overcook or the butter will burn). Carefully add half the vinegar and the capers, if using, and cook for a further 1 minute until hot. Set aside while cooking the fish.

/ 2 / Cut the skate in half and put into a large shallow dish with the onion and remaining vinegar. Pour over about 150 ml (¼ pint) water, then cover and microwave on HIGH for 9-10 minutes or until the fish is tender.

/ 3 / Remove the fish from the stock and arrange on 2 plates. Sprinkle with the parsley and salt and pepper to taste. Microwave the sauce on HIGH for 1 minute to reheat. Pour over the fish and serve immediately.

RAIE AU BEURRE NOIR
Skate is a flat-bodied, kite-shaped fish. Its upper side is bluish-grey and its belly is greyish-white. Only the wings (side parts) and nuggets of flesh known as 'nobs' are eaten and they are usually sold already cut from the body.

STUFFED HERRINGS
The fishmonger will nearly always prepare fish for you, but you can do it yourself. Using the back of a knife, remove any scales, scraping from tail to head (the opposite way to the direction the scales lie). Do this in the sink, then rinse under cold running water.
  To remove the entrails, make a slit along the belly from the gills to the tail vent. Draw out the insides and clean away any blood. Rub with a little salt to remove any black skin. Rinse under cold water.

MIXED SEAFOOD WITH SAFFRON SAUCE

SERVES 4

large pinch of saffron
50 ml (2 fl oz) dry white wine
strip of orange rind
1 bay leaf
4 plaice quarter-cut fillets, each weighing about 50 g (2 oz)
450 g (1 lb) cod fillet
4 cooked unpeeled jumbo prawns (optional)
15 ml (1 tbsp) Greek strained yogurt
salt and pepper
fresh herbs, to garnish

/ 1 / Put the saffron, wine, orange rind and bay leaf in a small bowl. Microwave on HIGH for 2-3 minutes or until boiling. Set aside to infuse while cooking the fish.

/ 2 / Skin the plaice fillets: lay them flat, skin side down, on a board or work surface. Dip your fingers in salt and grip the tail end, then separate the flesh from the skin at this point with a sharp knife. Work the knife slowly between the skin and flesh using a sawing action until the opposite end of the fillet is reached. Cut each fillet in half widthways. Skin and cut the cod fillets into large chunks.

/ 3 / Arrange the fish and prawns, if using, in a single layer in a large shallow dish, placing the thinner pieces and the prawns towards the centre of the dish.

/ 4 / Pour over 30 ml (2 tbsp) of the infused sauce. Cover and microwave on HIGH for 5-6 minutes or until the fish is tender. Transfer the fish to 4 warmed serving plates.

/ 5 / Strain the remaining wine mixture into the cooking juices remaining in the dish and stir in the yogurt. Season to taste with salt and pepper. Microwave on HIGH for 1-2 minutes or until hot. Pour over the fish, garnish with herbs and serve immediately.

CITRUS BAKED MACKEREL WITH MUSTARD

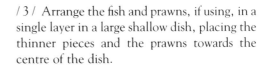

C SERVES 4

4 mackerel, each weighing about 350 g (12 oz), cleaned
thinly pared rind and juice of 1 lime
2 tangerines
5 ml (1 tsp) clear honey
15 ml (1 tbsp) wholegrain mustard
½ small lemon, thinly sliced

/ 1 / Remove and discard the heads from the fish. Slash the fish twice on each side and arrange in a large shallow ovenproof dish.

/ 2 / Remove and discard any white pith from the lime rind and cut the rind into very fine shreds. Sprinkle over the fish.

/ 3 / Peel and segment 1 tangerine and add to the fish and rind shreds. Squeeze the juice from the remaining tangerine.

/ 4 / Mix the lime and tangerine juice with the honey and mustard and pour evenly over the fish. Arrange the lemon slices on top.

/ 5 / Stand the dish on the wire rack and cook on combination at 200°C/MEDIUM LOW for 20 minutes or until the fish flakes easily when tested with a fork, basting with the citrus juices during cooking. Spoon a little of the cooking juice over the fish when serving.

MIXED SEAFOOD WITH SAFFRON SAUCE

To skin the plaice fillets: lay them flat, skin side down, on a board or work surface. Dip your fingers in salt and grip the tail end, then separate the flesh from the skin at this point with a sharp knife. Work the knife slowly between the skin and flesh using a sawing action until the opposite end of the fillet is reached.

Mixed Seafood with Saffron Sauce

Avocado, Prawn and Potato Salad

A V O C A D O ,
P R A W N   A N D
P O T A T O   S A L A D

S E R V E S   4

350 g (12 oz) small new potatoes,
scrubbed and quartered

1 small ripe avocado

150 ml (¼ pint) natural yogurt

15 ml (1 tbsp) lemon juice

5 ml (1 tsp) wholegrain mustard

salt and pepper

225 g (8 oz) cooked peeled prawns

4 large radishes, trimmed and thinly sliced

2 spring onions, trimmed and thinly sliced

few lettuce leaves, to garnish

/ 1 / Put the potatoes into a medium bowl with 30 ml (2 tbsp) water. Cover and microwave on HIGH for 7-8 minutes or until tender, stirring occasionally.

/ 2 / Meanwhile, cut the avocado in half and mash half of the flesh with the yogurt, lemon juice and wholegrain mustard. Season to taste.

/ 3 / Pour the dressing over the potatoes and toss together with the prawns. Cut the remaining avocado into cubes and mix into the salad with the radishes and spring onions.

/ 4 / Serve while still slightly warm, garnished with a few lettuce leaves.

Avocados may have a shiny green or bumpy brown skin, according to variety, but a ripe avocado always 'gives' slightly when pressed at the pointed end.

99

STUFFED TROUT WITH GINGER AND PEAR

C SERVES 4

30 ml (2 tbsp) vegetable oil
1 medium onion, skinned and finely chopped
2 pears, peeled, cored and roughly chopped
1 cm (½ inch) piece of fresh root ginger, peeled and finely grated
75 g (3 oz) coarse oatmeal
salt and pepper
4 trout, each weighing about 275 g (10 oz), cleaned
15 g (½ oz) butter or margarine
chopped fresh parsley, to garnish

/ 1 / Put the oil and onion in a medium bowl. Cover and microwave on HIGH for 4-5 minutes or until softened. Add the pears, ginger and oatmeal. Re-cover and microwave on HIGH for 1 minute. Season to taste with salt and pepper.

/ 2 / Remove and discard the head, tails and fins from the fish, then cut completely along the underside. Open each fish out and lay it, inside down, on a board. Press firmly down the length of the back to loosen the backbone. Turn the fish over and ease out the backbone with as many small bones as possible.

/ 3 / Spoon half the pear mixture on to each fish, then fold the fish over to enclose the stuffing. Arrange side by side in a large, shallow ovenproof dish. Dot the fish evenly with the butter or margarine.

/ 4 / Stand the dish on the wire rack and cook on combination at 200°C/MEDIUM LOW for 15 minutes or until the fish flakes easily when tested with a fork. Serve hot garnished with chopped parsley.

SWEDISH HERRINGS

C SERVES 2

4 fresh herrings, filleted
salt and pepper
4 whole cloves
2 dried chillies
12 peppercorns
1 bay leaf
1 blade of mace
60 ml (4 tbsp) malt vinegar
75 ml (5 tbsp) tarragon vinegar
1 shallot, skinned and finely chopped
lemon slices, to garnish
142 ml (5 fl oz) soured cream, to serve

/ 1 / Sprinkle the herring fillets with salt and pepper and roll up each one from the head end, skin side outermost.

/ 2 / Arrange in a casserole and add the cloves, chillies, peppercorns, bay leaf and mace. Cover with the vinegars and 150 ml (¼ pint) water and sprinkle the shallot on top.

/ 3 / Cover and cook in the oven on combination at 200°C/MEDIUM LOW for 10-12 minutes or until tender.

/ 4 / Transfer the fish carefully to a serving dish and strain or pour the liquor over. Leave to cool for about 2-3 hours.

/ 5 / Garnish the casserole with lemon slices and serve cold with soured cream.

SWEDISH HERRINGS

Although they are eaten fresh just as any other oily fish, herrings are immensely popular pickled or soused, especially in northern Europe and Scandinavian countries where they are a favourite starter. Such herrings are easy to obtain from delicatessens and supermarkets, either loose or in jars (rollmops are a kind of soused herring), but it is much nicer to make your own using fresh herring fillets. For a neat appearance to the finished dish, try to get fillets which are all of an even size and thickness.

STUFFED TROUT WITH GINGER AND PEAR
In this recipe the fish is boned before stuffing as it makes eating much easier, and boning instructions are included. You will find it is very simple to do if you follow the instructions carefully. Serve these well-flavoured fish with sauté potatoes and a fresh green vegetable.

SWEDISH HERRINGS

Sprinkle the herring fillets with salt and pepper and roll up from the head end, skin side outermost.

Transfer the cooked fish to a serving dish and strain or pour the liquor over the fish. Leave to cool for about 2-3 hours.

Swedish Herrings make an excellent cold dish for a summer luncheon served with fresh French bread and butter and a selection of salads. Alternatively, halve the quantities given in the recipe and serve as a starter.

Swedish Herrings

Fish in Filo Parcels

FISH IN FILO PARCELS

SERVES 4

25 g (1 oz) butter
30 ml (2 tbsp) vegetable oil
450 g (1 lb) monkfish fillets, skinned and finely diced
100 g (4 oz) cooked peeled prawns, thawed and thoroughly dried if frozen
pinch of saffron powder or saffron threads
15 ml (1 tbsp) finely sliced stem or preserved ginger, with the syrup
8 sheets of frozen filo pastry, thawed
melted butter, for brushing
30 ml (2 tbsp) plain flour
10 ml (2 tsp) ground coriander
150 ml (¼ pint) ginger ale
salt and pepper
90 ml (6 tbsp) single cream
unpeeled prawns, lime twists and sliced stem ginger, to garnish

/ 1 / Put the butter and oil in a large bowl and microwave on HIGH for 30 seconds. Add the monkfish and microwave on HIGH for 3 minutes, stirring occasionally. Add the prawns, saffron and half of the ginger and microwave on HIGH for a further 2 minutes until the fish is tender. Remove with a slotted spoon and set aside, reserving the juices.

/ 2 / Cut 1 sheet of pastry to measure 40.5×20.5 cm (16×8 inches). Brush half of the sheet with a little melted butter, then fold the plain half over to make a 20 cm (8 inch) square. Preheat the oven on convection at 250°C for 5 minutes.

/ 3 / Put one-eighth of the fish mixture in the centre of the square and fold over the opposite corners of the pastry to make an envelope-shaped parcel. Seal with melted butter.

/ 4 / Place the parcel seam side down on a lightly greased pyrex dish. Repeat with the remaining pastry and fish mixture to make 8 parcels altogether. Brush the parcels with melted butter. Cook 4 at a time on combination at 200°C/MEDIUM LOW for 10-15 minutes or until golden brown and crisp. Keep warm.

/ 5 / Make the sauce: whisk the flour, coriander and ginger ale into the reserved cooking juices. Microwave on HIGH for 3-4 minutes or until thick, whisking frequently. Season.

/ 6 / Stir in the cream and remaining stem ginger and microwave on HIGH for 30 seconds or until hot. Do not boil.

/ 7 / Serve the filo parcels hot on individual plates, with the sauce poured around them. Garnish with unpeeled prawns, lime twists and stem ginger, if liked.

PASTA WITH COURGETTES AND SMOKED TROUT

SERVES 2

2 medium courgettes
15 ml (1 tbsp) olive oil
pinch of saffron
225 g (8 oz) fresh spinach pasta, such as tagliatelle
salt and pepper
1 smoked trout, weighing about 225 g (8 oz)
150 ml (¼ pint) crème fraîche or double cream
30 ml (2 tbsp) black lumpfish roe
fresh herb sprigs, to garnish

/ 1 / Cut the courgettes into very thin diagonal slices. Cut each slice in half. Put the courgettes, oil and saffron in a medium bowl and microwave on HIGH for 1 minute, stirring once.

/ 2 / Put the spinach pasta and salt to taste in a large bowl. Pour over enough boiling water to cover by about 2.5 cm (1 inch). Cover and microwave on HIGH for 3-4 minutes or until almost tender. Leave to stand, covered, while finishing the sauce. Do not drain.

/ 3 / To finish the sauce, flake the trout flesh, discarding the skin and bones. Stir into the courgettes with the crème fraîche or cream and salt and pepper to taste. Microwave on HIGH for 2 minutes until hot and slightly thickened.

/ 4 / Drain the pasta and return to the large bowl. Pour over the sauce and toss together to mix. If necessary, reheat the sauce and pasta together on HIGH for about 2 minutes. Transfer the pasta to 2 plates, top each with a spoonful of lumpfish roe and garnish with a herb sprig.

FISH IN FILO PARCELS
These pretty parcels of filo pastry stuffed with monkfish and prawns make a lovely light lunch dish or they could be served as a luxurious starter for a dinner party meal.

Frozen filo pastry is excellent but take care to buy it from a shop with a fast turnover. If the pastry has been stored for too long, it will be brittle and therefore crack easily. Cracking is often a problem when handling filo. Once the pastry is exposed to the air, it quickly dries out and becomes difficult to handle. For this reason, thaw for the time recommended on the packet, use immediately and always keep the pastry wrapped in a damp cloth as your work.

PASTA WITH COURGETTES AND SMOKED TROUT
Crème fraîche is double cream which has been fermented under controlled conditions long enough to have a lactic taste which is neither sweet nor sour.

Instead of using smoked trout for this recipe, try using smoked salmon, cut into thin strips. Toss together with the pasta in step 4.

SWEET COOKED CLAMS

SERVES 2

450 g (1 lb) venus clams in the shell
2.5 cm (1 inch) piece of fresh root ginger, peeled and grated
60 ml (4 tbsp) sake or dry sherry
15 ml (1 tbsp) caster sugar
45 ml (3 tbsp) soy sauce
10 ml (2 tsp) cornflour
2.5 cm (1 inch) piece of cucumber
1 spring onion, trimmed

/ 1 / Thoroughly scrub the clams. Put the ginger, sake or sherry, sugar and soy sauce into a large bowl and microwave on HIGH for 2-3 minutes or until hot. Stir until the sugar has completely dissolved.

/ 2 / Blend the cornflour with 60 ml (4 tbsp) water and stir into the sauce. Microwave on HIGH for 2 minutes or until boiling and thickened, stirring once.

/ 3 / Add the clams and stir to coat in the sauce. Microwave on HIGH for 4-5 minutes or until the clams have opened, stirring occasionally. Discard any clams which do not open.

/ 4 / Meanwhile, cut the cucumber and onion into very thin strips. Spoon the clams and sauce on to 2 plates. Sprinkle with the cucumber and spring onion and serve immediately.

STUFFED MUSSELS

SERVES 4

30 ml (2 tbsp) olive oil
1 large onion, skinned and finely chopped
50 g (2 oz) long-grain rice
5 ml (1 tsp) ground allspice
cayenne pepper
salt and pepper
150 ml (¼ pint) boiling water
50 g (2 oz) pine nuts
50 g (2 oz) raisins
30 ml (2 tbsp) chopped fresh parsley or coriander
150 ml (¼ pint) dry white wine
2.5 ml (½ tsp) ground turmeric
700 g (1½ lb) fresh mussels, cleaned (see Gratin of Mussels and Spinach, page 40)
30 ml (2 tbsp) Greek strained yogurt
parsley or coriander sprigs, to garnish

/ 1 / Make the stuffing: put the oil, onion, rice, allspice and cayenne pepper to taste into a medium bowl and microwave on HIGH for 2 minutes, stirring once. Add salt to taste and pour over the boiling water. Cover and microwave on HIGH for 10-12 minutes until the water is absorbed and the rice is tender.

/ 2 / Stir in the pine nuts, raisins and the 30 ml (2 tbsp) parsley or coriander and season to taste with pepper and more salt if necessary. Cool.

/ 3 / Put the wine and turmeric into a large bowl and microwave on HIGH for 1 minute. Add the mussels, cover and cook on HIGH for 3-5 minutes or until all of the mussels have opened, removing the mussels on the top as they open and shaking the bowl occasionally.

/ 4 / Drain the mussels in a sieve, reserving the cooking liquid. Return the cooking liquid to the large bowl and microwave on HIGH for 8-10 minutes until reduced by half. Stir in the yogurt and season with salt and pepper. Cool.

/ 5 / Meanwhile, reserve 4 mussels for the garnish, then discard 1 half of the shell from the remainder. Fill shells with stuffing.

/ 6 / To serve: arrange the mussels on 4 plates, then pour the sauce around them. Garnish with the reserved mussels and sprigs of parsley or coriander.

SWEET COOKED CLAMS
There are many different species of clam, varying considerably in size. The venus clams for this recipe have a shiny pinkish shell which looks as if it has been varnished. They grow up to about 7.5 cm (3 inches).

This recipe makes a delicious light lunch or an unusual starter. Make sure that you use venus clams, not the much larger varieties.

STUFFED MUSSELS
Don't be put off at the thought of spending hours stuffing mussels. It won't take as long as you think and is well worth the effort. As they are served cold, they can be made in advance. Serve for an informal lunch or supper, or as a starter for a dinner party.

Sweet Cooked Clams

Lemon and Mustard Mackerel

LEMON AND MUSTARD MACKEREL

C   S E R V E S   4

175 g (6 oz) butter
1 large onion, skinned and finely chopped
175 g (6 oz) fresh breadcrumbs
60 ml (4 tbsp) whole mustard seeds
finely grated rind and juice of 2 lemons
30 ml (2 tbsp) French mustard
1 egg, lightly beaten
salt and pepper
4 mackerel, weighing about 350 g (12 oz) each, cleaned and gutted
about 60 ml (4 tbsp) plain flour
fresh coriander, to garnish

/ 1 / Dice 75 g (3 oz) of the butter into a medium bowl, microwave on HIGH for 1 minute. Add the onion and microwave on HIGH for 4-5 minutes or until the onion is soft but not coloured.

/ 2 / Add the breadcrumbs, mustard seeds, lemon rind, mustard, egg and salt and pepper to taste and mix well.

/ 3 / Cut the head off the mackerel and split open along the underside. If the inside is very black, rub with salt to remove and rinse well under cold running water.

/ 4 / With the cut side down, press firmly along the back of the fish to loosen the backbone.

/ 5 / Open out the fish and cut the bone at the base of the tail. Gently pull the bone away from the flesh.

/ 6 / With a little of the remaining butter, grease a shallow ovenproof dish just large enough to hold the mackerel.

/ 7 / Press the breadcrumb mixture well into the cavity of the fish and place in the dish. Make deep slashes along the fish.

/ 8 / Dust the mackerel lightly with flour and pour over the lemon juice. Dot with the remaining butter. Cook, uncovered, on combination at 200°C/MEDIUM LOW for 12-15 minutes. Baste frequently during cooking time. Serve hot, garnished with coriander.

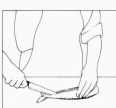

Cut the head off the mackerel and split open along the underside. If the inside is very black, rub with salt to remove, then rinse well under cold running water.

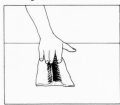

With the cut side down, press firmly along the back of the fish to loosen the backbone.

SOLE AND SPINACH ROULADES

SERVES 4

| 12 sole fillets, each weighing about 75 g (3 oz), skinned |
| 5 ml (1 tsp) fennel seeds, crushed |
| salt and pepper |
| 12 spinach or sorrel leaves, washed |
| 15 ml (1 tbsp) dry white wine |
| 45 ml (3 tbsp) Greek strained yogurt |
| pinch of ground turmeric |
| spinach or sorrel leaves, to garnish |

/ 1 / Place the sole fillets, skinned side up, on a chopping board. Sprinkle with the fennel seeds and season to taste with salt and pepper.

/ 2 / Lay a spinach or sorrel leaf, vein side up on top of each fillet, then roll up and secure with a wooden cocktail stick.

/ 3 / Arrange the fish in a circle around the edge of a large shallow dish and pour over the wine. Cover and microwave on HIGH for 6-7 minutes until tender. Using a slotted spoon, transfer the fish to a serving plate.

/ 3 / Gradually stir the yogurt and turmeric into the cooking liquid. Season to taste with salt and pepper and microwave on HIGH for 1-2 minutes until slightly thickened, stirring occasionally. Serve the roulades with a little of the sauce poured over, garnished with spinach or sorrel leaves.

TROUT IN CREAM

ⓒ SERVES 2

| 2 trout, cleaned and thawed if frozen |
| juice of 1 lemon |
| chopped fresh herbs, such as chives, parsley, chervil or tarragon |
| 150 ml (¼ pint) double cream |
| salt and pepper |
| fresh herbs, to garnish |

/ 1 / Lay the fish in a shallow dish, sprinkle with the lemon juice and herbs, and add the cream. Cover loosely with greaseproof paper.

/ 2 / Stand the dish on the wire rack and cook on combination at 180°C/MEDIUM LOW for 8-10 minutes or until the trout flakes easily when tested with a fork. Season to taste with salt and pepper. Serve immediately, garnished with fresh herbs.

SALMON EN PAPILLOTE

ⓒ SERVES 2

| 5 cm (2 inch) piece of cucumber |
| 2 salmon steaks, each weighing about 175 g (6 oz) |
| 15 ml (1 tbsp) chopped fresh dill |
| 2.5 ml (½ tsp) fennel seeds |
| 30 ml (2 tbsp) lemon juice |
| salt and pepper |
| 15 g (½ oz) butter or margarine |
| dill sprigs, to garnish |

/ 1 / Cut the cucumber into very thin slices. Cut two 30.5 cm (12 inch) squares from a double sheet of greaseproof paper and place 1 salmon steak on top of each.

/ 2 / Sprinkle the cucumber slices, chopped dill, fennel seeds and lemon juice over the salmon steaks. Season to taste with salt and pepper and dot the salmon steaks with butter or margarine.

/ 3 / Fold the greaseproof paper around the salmon steaks to enclose them completely and make 2 neat parcels.

/ 4 / Place the parcels in a shallow ovenproof dish, stand on the wire rack and cook on combination at 200°C/MEDIUM LOW for 10-15 minutes or until the fish flakes easily when tested with a fork. Serve the salmon steaks in their parcels garnished with sprigs of dill.

VARIATION

Other types of fish steaks or cutlets or small whole fish, such as mullet or trout, can be used instead of salmon.

SOLE AND SPINACH ROULADES
There are several varieties of sorrel, but the main ones are wild sorrel and French sorrel. Sorrel is not widely available commercially, but is easily grown in a garden. It should be picked when young before it flowers.

SALMON EN PAPILLOTE
Fish cooked in a paper parcel is a current trend in restaurants across the country. This is not really surprising since this method of cooking has many advantages. Not only is it quick and easy but it saves on washing-up and looks and tastes good too.

TROUT IN CREAM
Farmed trout are now available virtually all year round. Even if you cannot get fresh, frozen trout are nearly always available, usually sold in boxes of 2. Frozen trout should be thawed before cooking. Simply unwrap, place in a large shallow dish and thaw according to the chart on page 86.

Salmon en Papillote

MONKFISH IN WHITE WINE

SERVES 4

25 g (1 oz) butter or margarine
1 large onion, skinned and chopped
1 garlic clove, skinned and crushed
450 g (1 lb) courgettes, trimmed and sliced
30 ml (2 tbsp) plain flour
15 ml (1 tbsp) paprika
150 ml (¼ pint) dry white wine
150 ml (¼ pint) fish or chicken stock
225 g (8 oz) tomatoes, skinned, seeded and chopped
15 ml (1 tbsp) fresh basil or 5 ml (1 tsp) dried
salt and pepper
900 g (2 lb) monkfish, skinned, boned and cut into 5 cm (2 inch) pieces

MONKFISH IN WHITE WINE
Most good fishmongers stock monkfish nowadays, although it hasn't always been a popular fish because of its ugly appearance when whole. For this reason it is almost always displayed without the head, which is its ugliest part, and many fishmongers also skin and fillet it before offering it for sale. Monkfish fillets and steaks taste very like lobster and scampi, however, at a fraction of the price.

/ 1 / Put the butter or margarine in a large bowl and microwave on HIGH for 45 seconds or until the butter melts. Add the onion and garlic and microwave on HIGH for 5-7 minutes or until the onion has softened, stirring once. Add the courgettes, cover and microwave the vegetables on HIGH for 2 minutes.

/ 2 / Stir in the flour, paprika, wine, stock, tomatoes, basil and salt and pepper. Microwave on HIGH for 5 minutes or until the liquid is boiling, then continue to microwave on HIGH for a further 5 minutes.

/ 3 / Add the fish, cover and microwave on HIGH for 10 minutes or until the fish is tender, stirring once.

HADDOCK MOUSSE

SERVES 4

450 g (1 lb) haddock fillet
15 ml (1 tbsp) gelatine
50 ml (2 fl oz) white wine vinegar
225 ml (8 fl oz) hot water
4 hard-boiled eggs
450 ml (¾ pint) mayonnaise
10 ml (2 tsp) tomato purée
5 ml (1 tsp) anchovy essence
salt and pepper
2 egg whites
1 small bunch watercress, trimmed and finely chopped
dill sprig, to garnish

HADDOCK MOUSSE
To use powdered gelatine, always add the gelatine to the liquid. Place the required amount of water or liquid in a heatproof cup or bowl. Leave to soften before heating in the microwave until the gelatine has dissolved.

/ 1 / Arrange the fish in a single layer in a shallow dish. Cover and microwave on HIGH for 6 minutes or until tender. Flake the fish, discarding skin and bones.

/ 2 / Sprinkle the gelatine over the vinegar in a small bowl. Leave to soften slightly, then add the hot water. Microwave on HIGH for 30 seconds or until the gelatine has dissolved.

Monkfish in White Wine; Haddock Mousse

/ 3 / Place the hard-boiled eggs, 150 ml (¼ pint) mayonnaise, tomato purée, anchovy essence, salt and pepper and fish in a blender or food processor and liquidise until smooth. Gradually stir in the gelatine. Tip into a bowl and refrigerate just until the mixture is thick enough to coat the back of a spoon.

/ 4 / Whisk the egg whites until stiff and fold into the fish mixture. Spoon into a 1.7-2.3 litre (3-4 pint) ring mould and refrigerate for about 2 hours until set.

/ 5 / Beat the finely chopped watercress into the remaining mayonnaise and set aside.

/ 6 / To serve, quickly dip the mould into hot water to loosen the mousse, then turn out on to a serving plate. Spoon over a little of the green mayonnaise and garnish with the dill sprig. Serve the remaining mayonnaise separately.

RICH SEAFOOD GRATIN

[C] S E R V E S 6

1 celery stick
1 green pepper, cored and seeded
25 g (1 oz) butter
225 g (8 oz) button mushrooms
1 bay leaf
30 ml (2 tbsp) dry white wine
450 g (1 lb) haddock fillet, skinned
2 small plaice, filleted and skinned
100 g (4 oz) seedless white grapes
100 g (4 oz) cooked peeled prawns
150 ml (¼ pint) double cream
salt and pepper
60 ml (4 tbsp) breadcrumbs

/ 1 / Cut the celery and pepper into thin 5 cm (2 inch) long strips. Place in a large ovenproof serving dish with the butter, mushrooms, bay leaf and wine. Cover and microwave on HIGH for 7-10 minutes or until the vegetables are softened but still crisp.

/ 2 / Meanwhile, cut the haddock and plaice into large chunks.

/ 3 / Add the fish, grapes, prawns and cream to the softened vegetables, season to taste with salt and pepper and mix gently together. Sprinkle with the breadcrumbs.

/ 4 / Stand the dish on the wire rack and cook on combination at 200°C/MEDIUM LOW for 12-18 minutes or until the fish flakes easily when tested with a fork and the breadcrumbs are lightly browned.

SEAFOOD KEBABS

[C] S E R V E S 4

450 g (1 lb) thick firm white fish fillets, such as hake, monkfish or halibut
350 g (12 oz) salmon fillet
4 cooked jumbo prawns in the shell
60 ml (4 tbsp) vegetable oil
juice of 2 limes
30 ml (2 tbsp) chopped fresh chervil
salt and pepper
fresh chervil, to garnish

/ 1 / Skin the fish and cut into 2.5 cm (1 inch) cubes. Thread on to 4 bamboo skewers, alternating the white fish with the salmon. Thread a prawn on to the end of each kebab. Place the kebabs in a large shallow ovenproof dish.

/ 2 / Whisk together the oil, lime juice and chervil, adding salt and pepper to taste. Pour over the kebabs.

/ 3 / Stand the dish on the wire rack and cook on combination at 200°C/MEDIUM LOW for 10-15 minutes or until the fish is tender, basting occasionally. Garnish with chervil and serve immediately with a little of the cooking juices spooned over the kebabs.

BUCKWHEAT SPAGHETTI WITH SMOKED SALMON

S E R V E S 3

225 g (8 oz) buckwheat spaghetti
1.1 litres (2 pints) boiling water
75 g (3 oz) smoked salmon trimmings
finely grated rind and juice of ½ small lemon
75 ml (3 fl oz) buttermilk
30 ml (2 tbsp) snipped fresh chives
1 egg, beaten
pepper
fresh chives, to garnish

/ 1 / Break the spaghetti in half and put into a large bowl. Pour over the boiling water and stir. Cover and microwave on HIGH for 5-6 minutes until almost tender. Leave to stand, covered, while making the sauce. Do not drain.

/ 2 / Cut the salmon into neat pieces and put into an ovenproof serving bowl with the remaining ingredients, except the garnish, adding pepper to taste. Microwave on HIGH for 1 minute or until slightly warmed, stirring once during cooking.

/ 3 / Drain the pasta and rinse with boiling water. Quickly stir into the sauce and toss together to mix. Garnish with chives and serve immediately while piping hot.

Ceylon Prawn Curry

CEYLON PRAWN CURRY

SERVES 4

50 g (2 oz) butter or margarine
1 large onion, skinned and finely chopped
1 garlic clove, skinned and crushed
15 ml (1 tbsp) plain flour
10 ml (2 tsp) ground turmeric
2.5 ml (½ tsp) ground cloves
5 ml (1 tsp) ground cinnamon
5 ml (1 tsp) salt
5 ml (1 tsp) sugar
50 g (2 oz) creamed coconut
450 ml (¾ pint) chicken stock
450 g (1 lb) peeled prawns or 12 Dublin Bay prawns, peeled
5 ml (1 tsp) lemon juice
coriander sprigs, to garnish
cooked rice and chutney, to serve

/ 1 / Put the butter or margarine in a shallow ovenproof dish and microwave on HIGH for 1 minute until melted; stir in the onion and garlic. Cover and microwave on HIGH for 5-7 minutes until the onion softens.

/ 2 / Stir the flour, spices, salt and sugar into the onion. Microwave on HIGH for 2 minutes. Stir in the creamed coconut and stock. Microwave on HIGH for 6-8 minutes until boiling, stirring frequently.

/ 3 / Add the prawns and lemon juice to the sauce and adjust the seasoning. Microwave on HIGH for 1-2 minutes until the prawns are heated through. Garnish with the coriander. Serve with rice and chutney.

Creamed coconut is sold in blocks in larger supermarkets, ethnic stores and delicatessens. It is convenient to use and less expensive than fresh coconut for making coconut milk.

To make coconut milk: break a 198 g (7 oz) packet of creamed coconut into a bowl. Add 450 ml (¾ pint) warm water and stir until the coconut has dissolved. This will make a thick milk. Strain through muslin or a fine sieve before use. For a thinner milk, stir in an extra 150 ml (¼ pint) water.

111

Tandoori-style Halibut

TANDOORI-STYLE HALIBUT

C   SERVES 4

4 halibut or haddock steaks, each weighing about 225 g (8 oz)
75 ml (5 tbsp) natural yogurt
30 ml (2 tbsp) white wine vinegar
2 garlic cloves, skinned
1 medium onion, skinned and roughly chopped
15 ml (1 tbsp) paprika
5 ml (1 tsp) garam masala
2.5 ml (½ tsp) ground turmeric
1 cm (½ inch) piece of fresh root ginger, peeled and finely grated
juice of 1 lemon
lime wedges and fresh coriander sprigs, to garnish

To make a quick Indian style pickle to serve with this dish, finely chop a few ripe tomatoes, ½ a cucumber, a large onion and lots of fresh coriander. Mix together and season with salt, paprika and lemon juice. Cover and leave to stand to allow the flavours to develop while the fish is marinating. Nan bread (bought from your local Indian takeaway) also makes a good accompaniment to Tandoori-Style Halibut.

/1/ Put the halibut or haddock steaks in a shallow ovenproof dish large enough to hold them in a single layer.

/2/ Put all the remaining ingredients, except the garnish, into a blender or food processor and purée until smooth. Pour over the fish. Cover and leave to marinate in the refrigerator for 2-3 hours or overnight, turning occasionally during this time.

/3/ When ready to cook, preheat the oven on convection at 250°C for 10 minutes.

/4/ Uncover the dish, stand it on the wire rack and cook on combination at 200°C/ MEDIUM LOW for 10 minutes or until the fish flakes easily when tested with a fork. Serve the fish garnished with lime wedges and a few sprigs of coriander.

LEAF-WRAPPED MULLET

SERVES 4

4 red mullet, each weighing about 275 g (10 oz), cleaned and scaled
3-4 garlic cloves, skinned
45 ml (3 tbsp) olive oil
30 ml (2 tbsp) white wine vinegar
salt and pepper
8 large Swiss chard or spinach leaves, trimmed

/ 1 / Using a sharp knife, slash the mullet 3 times on each side. Roughly chop the garlic and sprinkle into the slashes. Whisk the oil and vinegar together and season to taste with salt and pepper.

/ 2 / Put the fish into a shallow dish and pour over the oil and vinegar. Leave in a cool place for 30 minutes to marinate.

/ 3 / Remove the fish from the marinade and wrap each of them in 2 of the chard or spinach leaves. Return the wrapped fish to the dish containing the marinade.

/ 4 / Cover and microwave on HIGH for 6-8 minutes or until the fish is tender, rearranging once and basting with the marinade several times during cooking.

/ 5 / Serve the fish in their leaf parcels, with a little of the marinade spooned over.

LIME AND HAKE KEBABS WITH TABOULEH

SERVES 4

175 g (6 oz) bulgar wheat
300 ml (½ pint) boiling water
700 g (1½ lb) hake fillets, skinned
2 limes
60 ml (4 tbsp) chopped fresh parsley
60 ml (4 tbsp) chopped fresh mint
finely grated rind and juice of 1 lemon
2 small red onions, skinned and very finely chopped
45 ml (3 tbsp) olive oil
salt and pepper

Leaf-wrapped Mullet; Lime and Hake Kebabs with Tabouleh

/ 1 / Put the bulgar wheat into a bowl and pour over the boiling water. Leave to soak for 10-15 minutes until all the water is absorbed.

/ 2 / Meanwhile, cut the hake into 2.5 cm (1 inch) cubes. Thinly slice 1½ limes. Thread the lime slices and the hake on to 4 bamboo skewers. Arrange the kebabs in a single layer in a large shallow dish. Squeeze the juice from the remaining half lime over the kebabs.

/ 3 / Put the bulgar into a bowl and mix with the parsley, mint, lemon rind and juice, onions and oil. Season generously with salt and pepper. Arrange on 4 plates.

/ 4 / Cover the kebabs and microwave on HIGH for 4-5 minutes or until the fish is cooked, repositioning once during cooking. Arrange the kebabs on top of the tabouleh and serve.

LEAF-WRAPPED MULLET
No relation to the grey mullet, red mullet is smaller, crimson in colour with a unique and delicate flavour. The liver is a delicacy and should not be discarded – leave it in the fish for this recipe.

LIME AND HAKE KEBABS WITH TABOULEH
Bulgar wheat, or burghul, is available at health food shops – it is whole wheat grain which has been boiled and baked, then cracked so it does not need cooking, simply soak in boiling water for 10-15 minutes or in cold water for 30 minutes.

ONION AND ANCHOVY PIE

C   SERVES 6 - 8

DOUGH
275 g (10 oz) strong plain white flour
5 ml (1 tsp) salt
7.5 ml (1½ tsp) easy blend dried yeast
about 300 ml (½ pint) tepid water

FILLING
50 g (2 oz) can anchovy fillets
15 ml (1 tbsp) olive oil
2 large onions, skinned and thinly sliced
2 garlic cloves, skinned and crushed
15 ml (1 tbsp) sweet paprika
450 g (1 lb) ripe tomatoes, chopped
50 g (2 oz) sultanas
2 hard-boiled eggs, chopped
pepper

/ 1 / Make the dough: put the flour, salt and yeast in a bowl and mix together. Stir in enough tepid water to make a soft dough.

/ 2 / Turn the dough out on to a lightly floured surface and knead for about 10 minutes or until the dough is no longer sticky. Place in a bowl, cover with a clean tea-towel and leave in a warm place for about 1 hour or until the dough has doubled in size.

/ 3 / Meanwhile, make the filling. Drain the oil from the can of anchovies into a large bowl. Add the olive oil, onions, garlic and paprika, cover and microwave on HIGH for 20 minutes or until the onions are very soft. Meanwhile, chop the anchovies.

/ 4 / Add the tomatoes, sultanas, eggs and anchovies to the onions and season to taste with pepper. Microwave on HIGH for 5 minutes or until the tomatoes are softened. Leave to cool while the dough is rising.

/ 5 / When the dough is doubled in size in the bowl, preheat the oven on convection at 250°C for 10 minutes.

/ 6 / Meanwhile, knead the dough lightly and roll half of it out to a 28 cm (11 inch) circle. Place in a large greased shallow ovenproof dish. Using a slotted spoon, spoon the filling on top of the dough.

/ 7 / Roll out the remaining dough to a circle the same size and place on top. Twist the edges together to seal and sprinkle the top of the dough with a little flour.

/ 8 / Stand the dish on the wire rack and cook on combination at 200°C/MEDIUM LOW for 10 minutes or until firm to the touch. Cook on convection at 250°C for a further 5-6 minutes or until golden brown. Serve warm.

BAKED BASS CHINESE STYLE

C   SERVES 3 - 4

700 g (1½ lb) sea bass, cleaned and scaled
1 red, green or yellow pepper, cored, seeded and cut into matchstick strips
1 medium carrot, cut into matchstick strips
1 garlic clove, skinned and chopped
1 cm (½ inch) piece of fresh root ginger, peeled and chopped
30 ml (2 tbsp) soy sauce
30 ml (2 tbsp) hoisin sauce
30 ml (2 tbsp) sherry

/ 1 / Put the fish in a large ovenproof serving dish. Mix together the pepper, carrot, garlic and ginger and sprinkle over the fish.

/ 2 / Mix the soy sauce, hoisin sauce and sherry together and pour over the fish. Cover, stand on the wire rack and cook on combination at 200°C/MEDIUM LOW for 12-15 minutes or until the fish flakes easily. Serve hot.

SARDINES WITH GARLIC AND PARSLEY

C   SERVES 4

900 g (2 lb) sardines, cleaned and scaled
30 ml (2 tbsp) olive oil
2 garlic cloves, skinned and crushed
finely grated rind and juice of 1 large lemon
salt and pepper
45 ml (3 tbsp) chopped fresh parsley
25 g (1 oz) fresh breadcrumbs

/ 1 / Arrange the sardines in a single layer in a large shallow ovenproof dish.

/ 2 / Mix together the oil, garlic, lemon rind and juice and season to taste with salt and pepper. Pour over the sardines and sprinkle with the parsley and breadcrumbs.

/ 3 / Stand the dish on the wire rack and cook on combination at 200°C/MEDIUM LOW for 20 minutes or until the fish flakes easily when tested with a fork. Serve hot.

S E A F O O D C A S S E R O L E

☐   S E R V E S   6

450 g (1 lb) monkfish tail
450 g (1 lb) haddock fillet
3 large courgettes, sliced
450 g (1 lb) ripe tomatoes, chopped
1 red pepper, cored, seeded and chopped
100 g (4 oz) black olives
150 ml (¼ pint) dry white wine
2 garlic cloves, skinned and chopped
30 ml (2 tbsp) chopped fresh parsley
450 g (1 lb) mussels
2 egg yolks
10 ml (2 tsp) cornflour
175 g (6 oz) Gruyère cheese, grated
salt and pepper
chopped fresh parsley, to garnish

/ 1 / Remove the thin, skin-like membrane from the monkfish and discard. Cut down the length of the fish on either side of the central bone, then cut the fish into 2.5 cm (1 inch) chunks. Skin the haddock and cut into 2.5 cm (1 inch) chunks.

/ 2 / Put the monkfish, haddock, courgettes, tomatoes, pepper, olives, wine, garlic and parsley in a large ovenproof serving dish. Cover and cook on combination at 200°C/ MEDIUM LOW for 15-25 minutes or until the vegetables are softened and the fish is tender.

/ 3 / Meanwhile, scrub the mussels and, using a sharp knife, scrape off any seaweed or barnacles and remove the 'beards'. Discard any mussels that do not close when tapped.

Seafood Casserole

/ 4 / Mix the egg yolks with the cornflour and gradually stir into the casserole with the cheese. Stir thoroughly but be careful not to break up the fish. Season the casserole to taste with salt and pepper.

/ 5 / Add the mussels, re-cover and microwave on HIGH for 3-5 minutes or until the mussels are open. Discard any which do not open during cooking. Sprinkle generously with parsley and serve hot.

SEAFOOD CASSEROLE
This is a very filling main course and needs no accompaniment other than crusty bread and chilled dry white wine. Serve after a light salad starter and finish the meal with Peach and Walnut Crisps (see page 159).

When buying scallops, look for shells that are tightly closed. If slightly open, tap the shells sharply and, if fresh, they will close up instantly. Do not buy any that do not close.

To prepare scallops: scrub shells under cold running water. Place on a baking sheet with the rounded side uppermost. Cook in the oven at 150°C (300°F) mark 2 for about 10 minutes, or until the shells open, then set aside until cold. Using your fingers, push the shells slightly apart until there is a gap into which a knife blade can be slipped. Slide the blade through the opening against the rounded upper shell, then ease the scallop away from the top shell. Prise apart the top and bottom shells by pushing the shell backwards until the hinge at the back snaps.

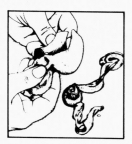

Cut away the grey fringe surrounding the scallop. Slide the point of a small knife under the black thread on the side of the scallop. Ease this up and gently pull it off, with the attached intestinal bag. Ease the scallop away from the bottom shell and wash in cold water.

Warm Salad of Salmon and Scallops is quick to make, but must be served immediately while the fish and dressing are still hot, and before the heat of the fish wilts the salad leaves.

WARM SALAD OF SALMON AND SCALLOPS

SERVES 4

225 g (8 oz) salmon steak or cutlet
8 large shelled scallops
selection of salad leaves such as curly endive, Webb's wonder lettuce, radicchio and watercress
2 stale bridge rolls
45 ml (3 tbsp) olive or nut oil
45 ml (3 tbsp) crème fraîche or soured cream
10 ml (2 tsp) wholegrain mustard
15 ml (1 tbsp) lemon juice
salt and pepper
a few chopped fresh herbs, such as parsley, chives, dill and tarragon

/ 1 / Skin the salmon and remove the bone, if necessary. Cut across the grain into very thin strips. If necessary, remove and discard from each scallop the tough white 'muscle' which is found opposite the coral. Separate the corals from the scallops. Slice the scallops into 3 or 4 pieces vertically. Cut the corals in half if they are large, otherwise leave whole.

/ 2 / Heat a browning dish on HIGH for 5-8 minutes or according to the manufacturer's instructions for your particular type.

/ 3 / Meanwhile, tear the salad leaves into small pieces, if necessary, and arrange on 4 plates. Cut the rolls into thin slices.

/ 4 / Add 30 ml (2 tbsp) of the oil to the browning dish and swirl to coat the bottom of the dish. Quickly add the sliced rolls and microwave on HIGH for 2 minutes. Turn over and microwave on HIGH for a further 1 minute or until crisp. Remove the bridge rolls from the dish and set aside.

/ 5 / Add the remaining oil and the scallops, corals and salmon to the dish and microwave on HIGH for 1½ minutes or until the fish looks opaque, stirring once.

/ 6 / Using a slotted spoon, remove the fish from the dish, and arrange on top of the salad leaves on the individual plates.

/ 7 / Put the crème fraîche or soured cream, mustard, lemon juice and salt and pepper to taste into the browning dish and microwave on HIGH for 1-2 minutes or until hot. Stir thoroughly and pour over the fish. Sprinkle with the croûtons and herbs and serve the salad immediately while warm.

Warm Salad of Salmon and Scallops

Egg Noodles with Squid and Shrimps

E G G   N O O D L E S
W I T H   S Q U I D
A N D   S H R I M P S

S E R V E S   4 - 6

250 g (9 oz) packet thin egg noodles
about 1.7 litres (3 pints) boiling water
45 ml (3 tbsp) hoisin sauce
15 ml (1 tbsp) lemon juice
30 ml (2 tbsp) soy sauce
15 ml (1 tbsp) sweet chilli sauce
45 ml (3 tbsp) sesame oil
30 ml (2 tbsp) vegetable oil
1 garlic clove, skinned and crushed
450 g (1 lb) squid, cleaned
50 g (2 oz) blanched almonds
100 g (4 oz) cooked peeled shrimps or prawns
100 g (4 oz) beansprouts
3 spring onions, trimmed and roughly chopped
black pepper
shredded lettuce and lemon wedges, to garnish

/ 1 / Put the noodles into a large bowl and pour over the boiling water or enough water to cover the noodles. Cover and cook on HIGH for 2 minutes. Leave the noodles to stand while cooking the fish.

/ 2 / Put the hoisin sauce, lemon juice, soy sauce, chilli sauce, oils and garlic into a large bowl. Cut the squid into small pieces or rings and mix into the sauce with the almonds. Microwave on HIGH for 5 minutes or until the squid just looks opaque, stirring once.

/ 3 / Add the shrimps or prawns, beansprouts and drained noodles and mix thoroughly together. Cover and microwave on HIGH for 2-3 minutes or until hot, stirring once. Stir the spring onions into the noodle mixture. Season to taste with black pepper.

/ 4 / To serve, spoon on to plates and top each portion with a pile of shredded lettuce and a lemon wedge. Serve immediately.

To prepare squid: rinse, then pull back the edge of the body pouch to expose the translucent quill. Pull it free and discard. Separate the head and tentacles from the body pouch. Holding the body pouch, pull out the head and tentacles. Cut through the head just above the eyes. Discard eyes and ink sac and reserve the tentacles. Wash under cold water, rub off the purplish skin and cut the tentacles into small pieces. Rub off and discard the skin on the body pouch.

117

Pufftop Scallops with Mushrooms

PUFFTOP SCALLOPS WITH MUSHROOMS

Ⓒ SERVES 2

4 scallops, with their shells
175 g (6 oz) button mushrooms
25 g (1 oz) butter, diced
50 ml (2 fl oz) dry cider
30 ml (2 tbsp) plain flour
150 ml (¼ pint) double cream
10 ml (2 tsp) chopped fresh tarragon or 5 ml (1 tsp) dried
2.5 ml (½ tsp) mustard powder
salt and pepper
200 g (7 oz) packet frozen puff pastry, thawed
1 egg, beaten

/ 1 / Chop the scallops roughly, including the coral. Slice the mushrooms finely.

/ 2 / Put the butter in a medium bowl and microwave on HIGH for 30 seconds. Add the mushrooms and stir to coat in the butter. Cover and microwave on HIGH for 3-4 minutes until soft, stirring occasionally. Add the scallops, microwave on HIGH for 2 minutes, stirring frequently, then pour in the cider and microwave on HIGH for 3 minutes.

/ 3 / Remove the scallops with a slotted spoon and set aside with the mushrooms. Add the flour and cream to the cider and microwave on HIGH for 2 minutes, whisking occasionally.

/ 4 / Add the sauce to the scallops and mushrooms with the tarragon, mustard and salt and pepper to taste. Fold gently to mix. Cool.

/ 5 / Preheat the oven on convection at 250°C for 5 minutes. Meanwhile, roll out the pastry on a lightly floured surface and cut out 4 'lids' to fit the scallop shells.

/ 6 / Divide the cold filling equally between the scallop shells. Brush the edges of the shells with beaten egg, then place the pastry lids on top and press firmly to seal. Brush all over the pastry with beaten egg. Decorate, if liked, then brush with more beaten egg.

/ 7 / Cook on combination at 200°C/MEDIUM LOW for 10-12 minutes or until the pastry is puffed up and golden. Serve hot.

SMOKED HADDOCK SOUFFLÉ

Ⓒ SERVES 4

900 g (2 lb) smoked haddock fillet
about 300 ml (½ pint) milk
40 g (1½ oz) butter or margarine
40 g (1½ oz) plain flour
4 eggs, separated
salt and pepper

/ 1 / Thoroughly grease a 1.4 litre (2½ pint) soufflé dish. Put the fish in a single layer in a large shallow dish with 60 ml (4 tbsp) milk. Cover and microwave on HIGH for 8-10 minutes or until the fish flakes easily when tested with a fork.

/ 2 / Strain the cooking liquid into a measuring jug, make up to 300 ml (½ pint) with milk and set aside. Remove and discard the skin and bones from the fish. Flake the fish and reserve.

/ 3 / Make the sauce: put the milk mixture, butter or margarine and flour into a medium bowl and microwave on HIGH for 4-5 minutes or until boiling and thickened, whisking frequently. Fold in the fish, then leave to cool slightly. Meanwhile, preheat the oven on convection at 250°C for 10 minutes.

/ 4 / Beat the egg yolks into the sauce and season to taste with salt and pepper. Whisk the egg whites until stiff but not dry and fold into the sauce. Pour into the prepared soufflé dish.

/ 5 / Stand the dish on the wire rack and cook on combination at 180°C/MEDIUM LOW for 15-20 minutes or until well risen, firm to the touch and golden brown. Serve immediately.

SMOKED HADDOCK SOUFFLÉ
Although they do not rise quite as much as when cooked conventionally, soufflés cooked in a combination oven, on a combined setting, rise and set very quickly. It's important to get your microwave setting right for this (see page 9).

PUFFTOP SCALLOPS WITH MUSHROOMS

Roll out the pastry on a lightly floured surface and cut out 4 'lids' to fit the scallop shells.

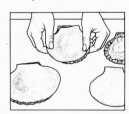

Divide the cold filling equally between the scallop shells. Brush the edges of the shells with beaten egg, then place the pastry lids on top and press firmly to seal. Brush all over the pastry with beaten egg.

Pufftop Scallops with Mushrooms make a very pretty main course for 2 people, or you can serve them as a starter for a dinner party – in which case they will serve 4.

WHITE FISH TERRINE WITH PRAWNS

40 g (1½ oz) butter or margarine
40 g (1½ oz) plain flour
300 ml (½ pint) milk
700 g (1½ lb) white fish fillet, such as cod, haddock or whiting, skinned
150 ml (¼ pint) natural yogurt
150 ml (¼ pint) double cream
3 eggs
salt and pepper
175 g (6 oz) cooked peeled prawns
30 ml (2 tbsp) chopped mixed fresh herbs, such as chervil, chives, tarragon, dill and parsley
whole cooked prawns and fresh herbs, to garnish

/ 1 / Grease a 1.7 litre (3 pint) loaf dish (not tin) and line the base with greaseproof paper.

/ 2 / Put the butter or margarine, flour and milk in a bowl and microwave on HIGH for 4-5 minutes or until boiling and thickened, whisking frequently during cooking.

/ 3 / Chop the fish and put it in a blender or food processor with the natural yogurt, double cream and eggs.

/ 4 / When the sauce is cooked, pour it into the blender or food processor on top of the fish, yogurt, cream and eggs; purée the mixture until smooth. Season to taste with salt and pepper.

/ 5 / Spoon half of the fish mixture into the base of the loaf dish and level the surface. Sprinkle with the prawns and herbs and spoon the remaining fish mixture on top. Level the surface and cover with a double piece of grease-proof paper.

/ 6 / Stand the dish on the wire rack and cook on combination at 200°C/MEDIUM LOW for 15-18 minutes or until firm to the touch and slightly risen. Leave to stand for 5 minutes, then unmould on to a serving plate. Serve hot or cold, cut into slices and garnished with prawns and fresh herbs.

PLAIT OF SALMON AND COURGETTES

150 ml (¼ pint) dry white vermouth
large pinch of saffron strands
75 g (3 oz) butter or margarine
150 ml (¼ pint) double cream
3 large long courgettes
900 g (2 lb) piece of fresh salmon, cut from the middle
salt and pepper

/ 1 / Put the vermouth and saffron into a medium bowl and microwave on HIGH for 2-3 minutes until just boiling. Add 50 g (2 oz) of the butter or margarine and the cream and microwave on HIGH for 4-5 minutes until slightly thickened. Set aside.

/ 2 / Top and tail the courgettes, then cut lengthways into 0.5 cm (¼ inch) slices. Cut the green outer slices into thin strips and add to the sauce. You will need 12 middle slices to make the plaits. If you have more, cut them into thin strips and add to the sauce.

/ 3 / Cut the salmon either side of the central bone to make 2 pieces. To remove the skin, put the fish, skin side down on a flat board. Starting at one corner of the thinner end insert a sharp knife between the skin and the flesh. Using a sawing action, carefully remove the skin, keeping the flesh in 1 piece. Repeat with the second piece of salmon. Discard the skin and bone.

/ 4 / Cut the salmon against the grain into 12 neat strips about 1.5 cm (¾ inch) wide. Cut the 4 thickest strips in half horizontally to make 16 equal-sized strips.

/ 5 / Remove the turntable from the cooker and cover with a double sheet of greaseproof paper. (If your cooker does not have a turntable, use a microwave baking sheet or a very large flat plate.)

/ 6 / Lay 4 of the salmon strips close together on the paper to make a square. Working at right angles to the salmon, take 1 courgette slice and weave it under and over the strips of salmon. Repeat with 2 more courgette slices to make a neat, plaited square.

WHITE FISH TERRINE WITH PRAWNS
Fish terrines are simple to make and never fail to impress, particularly when they have a middle layer of contrasting colour. Inexperienced cooks look on amazed as the terrine is sliced to reveal this layer and wonder how difficult it was to achieve. In this recipe it couldn't be simpler.

Serve White Fish Terrine with Prawns with a cucumber and lime flavoured mayonnaise made by stirring chopped cucumber and finely grated lime rind into home-made or shop-bought mayonnaise.

If preferred, omit the prawns from White Fish Terrine with Prawns. Stir the herbs into the first half of the mixture, then colour the second half pink with 5-10 ml (1-2 tsp) tomato purée.

PLAIT OF SALMON AND COURGETTES
It is essential to buy a piece of salmon cut from the thickest part so that you can cut strips of even thickness, and you must use large, or long, courgettes to get long strips for plaiting. Don't be put off by the long recipe. It can be prepared in advance up to step 8. The finished result makes a stunning dinner party main course.

Plait of Salmon and Courgettes

/ 7 / Repeat with the remaining salmon and courgette to make 4 squares of plaited salmon and courgette, arranged side by side on the turntable or baking sheet.

/ 8 / Dot with remaining butter and cover with a sheet of greaseproof paper, folding the edges together to completely enclose the salmon in the paper.

/ 9 / Microwave on HIGH for about 5 minutes or until the fish is just cooked. Carefully remove from the cooker and arrange on 4 flat plates.

/ 10 / Meanwhile, microwave the sauce on HIGH for 2-3 minutes or until hot. Season to taste with salt and pepper, then spoon around the salmon and courgette plaits. Serve the salmon immediately while piping hot.

Vegetables

All vegetables benefit from microwave cooking. They cook in a fraction of the conventional time and in a minimum amount of water, so retaining their bright colour and crisp texture, as well as their vitamins and minerals. Many popular vegetarian dishes include a pastry or gratin top to add contrasting crunch and texture to the dish and such dishes cook extremely well, and also in a very short time, on a combination setting.

Wherever possible cut vegetables into even-sized pieces to that they cook at the same rate, and always pierce whole vegetables with skins, such as potatoes, to prevent them bursting. Arrange vegetables like cauliflower and broccoli with the thick stems towards the edge of the dish so they will receive more of the microwave energy. If cooking vegetables on their own, do not add salt directly on to them until after they have been cooked as it toughens them.

Many of the recipes in this chapter are good as accompaniments, adding colour, interest and flavour to main course dishes, but some can be served as a light meal or a course on their own.

Tofu and Bean Burgers

COOKING FRESH VEGETABLES IN THE MICROWAVE

When using this chart add 60 ml (4 tbsp) water unless otherwise stated. The vegetables can be cooked in boil-in-the-bags, plastic containers and polythene bags – pierce the bag before cooking to make sure there is a space for steam to escape.

Prepare vegetables in the normal way. It is most important that food is cut to an even size and stems are of the same length. Vegetables with skins, such as aubergines, need to be pierced before cooking to prevent bursting. Season vegetables with salt after cooking if required. Salt distorts the microwave patterns and dries the vegetables.

Vegetable	Quantity	Time on High Setting	Microwave Cooking Technique(s)
Artichoke, globe	1 2 3 4	5-6 minutes 7-8 minutes 11-12 minutes 12-13 minutes	Place upright in covered dish.
Asparagus	450 g (1 lb)	7-8 minutes	Place stalks towards the outside of the dish. Re-position during cooking.
Aubergine	450 g (1 lb) 0.5 cm (¼ inch) slices	5-6 minutes	Stir or shake after 4 minutes.
Beans, broad	450 g (1 lb)	6-8 minutes	Stir or shake after 3 minutes and test after 5 minutes.
Beans, green	450 g (1 lb) sliced into 2.5 cm (1 inch) lengths	10-13 minutes	Stir or shake during the cooking period. Time will vary with age.
Beetroot, whole	4 medium	14-16 minutes	Pierce skin with a fork. Re-position during cooking.
Broccoli	450 g (1 lb) small florets	7-8 minutes	Re-position during cooking. Place stalks towards the outside of the dish.
Brussels sprouts	225 g (8 oz) 450 g (1 lb)	4-6 minutes 7-10 minutes	Stir or shake during cooking.
Cabbage	450 g (1 lb) quartered 450 g (1 lb) shredded	8 minutes 8-10 minutes	Stir or shake during cooking.
Carrots	450 g (1 lb) small whole 450 g (1 lb) 0.5 cm (¼ inch) slices	8-10 minutes 9-12 minutes	Stir or shake during cooking.
Cauliflower	whole 450 g (1 lb) 225 g (8 oz) florets 450 g (1 lb) florets	9-12 minutes 5-6 minutes 7-8 minutes	Stir or shake during cooking.
Celery	450 g (1 lb) sliced into 2.5 cm (1 inch) lengths	8-10 minutes	Stir or shake during cooking.
Corn-on-the-cob	2 cobs 450 g (1 lb)	6-7 minutes	Wrap individually in greased greaseproof paper. Do not add water. Turn over after 3 minutes.

Vegetable	Quantity	Time on High Setting	Microwave Cooking Technique(s)
Courgettes	450 g (1 lb) 2.5 cm (1 inch) slices	5-7 minutes	Do not add more than 30 ml (2 tbsp) water. Stir or shake gently twice during cooking. Stand for 2 minutes before draining.
Fennel	450 g (1 lb) 0.5 cm (¼ inch) slices	7-9 minutes	Stir or shake during cooking.
Leeks	450 g (1 lb) 2.5 cm (1 inch) slices	6-8 minutes	Stir or shake during cooking.
Mange tout	450 g (1 lb)	7-9 minutes	Stir or shake during cooking.
Mushrooms	225 g (8 oz) whole 450 g (1 lb) whole	2-3 minutes 5 minutes	Do not add water. Add 25 g (1 oz) butter or alternative fat and a squeeze of lemon juice. Stir or shake gently during cooking.
Onions	225 g (8 oz) thinly sliced 450 g (1 lb) small whole	7-8 minutes 9-11 minutes	Stir or shake sliced onions. Add only 60 ml (4 tbsp) water to whole onions. Re-position whole onions during cooking.
Okra	450 g (1 lb) whole	6-8 minutes	Stir or shake during cooking.
Parsnips	450 g (1 lb) halved	10-16 minutes	Place thinner parts towards the centre. Add a knob of butter and 15 ml (1 tbsp) lemon juice with 150 ml (¼ pint) water. Turn dish during cooking and re-position.
Peas	450 g (1 lb)	9-11 minutes	Stir or shake during cooking.
Potatoes, baked jacket	1×175 g (6 oz) potato 2×175 g (6 oz) potatoes 4×175 g (6 oz) potatoes	4-6 minutes 6-8 minutes 12-14 minutes	Wash and prick the skin with a fork. Place on absorbent kitchen paper or napkin. When cooking more than 2 at a time arrange in a circle. Turn over halfway through cooking.
Potatoes, boiled (old) halved	450 g (1 lb)	7-10 minutes	Add 60 ml (4 tbsp) water. Stir or shake during cooking.
Potatoes, boiled (new) whole	450 g (1 lb)	6-9 minutes	Add 60 ml (4 tbsp) water. Do not overcook or new potatoes become spongy.
Sweet	450 g (1 lb)	5 minutes	Wash and prick the skin with a fork. Place on absorbent kitchen paper. Turn over halfway through cooking time.
Spinach	450 g (1 lb) chopped	5-6 minutes	Do not add water. Best cooked in roasting bag, sealed with non-metal fastening. Stir or shake during cooking.
Swede	450 g (1 lb) 2 cm (¾ inch) dice	11-13 minutes	Stir or shake during cooking.
Turnip	450 g (1 lb) 2 cm (¾ inch) dice	9-11 minutes	Add 60 ml (4 tbsp) water and stir or shake during cooking.

COOKING FROZEN VEGETABLES IN THE MICROWAVE

Frozen vegetables may be cooked straight from the freezer. Many may be cooked in their original plastic packaging, as long as it is first slit to allow steam to escape, and then placed on a plate. Alternatively, transfer to a bowl.

Vegetable	Quantity	Time on High Setting	Microwave Cooking Technique(s)
Asparagus	275 g (10 oz)	7-9 minutes	Separate and re-arrange after 3 minutes.
Beans, broad	225 g (8 oz)	7-8 minutes	Stir or shake during cooking period.
Beans, green cut	225 g (8 oz)	6-8 minutes	Stir or shake during cooking period.
Broccoli	275 g (10 oz)	7-9 minutes	Re-arrange spears after 3 minutes.
Brussels sprouts	225 g (8 oz)	6-8 minutes	Stir or shake during cooking period.
Cauliflower florets	275 g (10 oz)	7-9 minutes	Stir or shake during cooking period.
Carrots	225 g (8 oz)	6-7 minutes	Stir or shake during cooking period.
Corn-on-the-cob	1 2	3-4 minutes 6-7 minutes	Do not add water. Dot with butter, wrap in greaseproof paper.
Mixed vegetables	225 g (8 oz)	5-6 minutes	Stir or shake during cooking period.
Peas	225 g (8 oz)	5-6 minutes	Stir or shake during cooking period.
Peas and carrots	225 g (8 oz)	7-8 minutes	Stir or shake during cooking period.
Spinach, leaf or chopped	275 g (10 oz)	7-9 minutes	Do not add water. Stir or shake during cooking period.
Swede and Turnip, diced	225 g (8 oz)	6-7 minutes	Stir or shake during cooking period. Mash with butter after standing time.
Sweetcorn	225 g (8 oz)	4-6 minutes	Stir or shake during cooking period.

Broad Beans with Bacon; Courgettes Tossed in Cheese

BROAD BEANS WITH
BACON

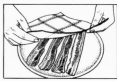

This method of cooking
bacon is the best way to
cook it unless your
combination oven has a
grill. Microwave for 2-2½
minutes for 2 rashers,
4-4½ minutes for 4 rashers,
5-6 minutes for 6 rashers.

Choose only young, small,
tender pods for this recipe.
Old large beans should be
cooked, then made into
soup or puréed.

BROAD BEANS
WITH BACON

SERVES 4 - 6

| 6 streaky bacon rashers |
| 1.1 kg (2½ lb) small young broad beans |
| 25 g (1 oz) butter or margarine |
| salt and pepper |

/ 1 / Arrange the bacon on a plate, cover with a
sheet of absorbent kitchen paper and microwave on HIGH for 5-6 minutes. Quickly remove
the paper to prevent it sticking.

/ 2 / Shell the beans and put in a large bowl
with 60 ml (4 tbsp) water. Cover and microwave on HIGH for 6-10 minutes or until the
beans are just tender, stirring occasionally.
(The exact cooking time will depend on the
age of the beans.)

/ 3 / Meanwhile, chop the bacon and cut the
butter or margarine into small pieces.

/ 4 / Drain the beans. Add the bacon and butter or margarine and toss together so that the
butter melts. Season to taste with salt and pepper. Microwave on HIGH for 1-2 minutes to reheat if necessary, and serve immediately.

COURGETTES
TOSSED IN
CHEESE

SERVES 4

| 450 g (1 lb) courgettes, trimmed |
| 15 ml (1 tbsp) olive oil |
| 1-2 garlic cloves, skinned and crushed |
| salt and pepper |
| 25 g (1 oz) Parmesan cheese, freshly grated |

/ 1 / Cut the courgettes into 0.5 cm (¼ inch)
slices. Put the oil and garlic in a medium bowl
and microwave on HIGH for 2-3 minutes until
the garlic is lightly browned, stirring occasionally during cooking.

/ 2 / Add the courgettes and toss to coat in the
oil. Microwave on HIGH for 4-6 minutes until
the courgettes are just tender, stirring frequently to ensure even cooking.

/ 3 / Season to taste with salt and pepper and
sprinkle in the Parmesan cheese. Toss together
until mixed, then serve hot.

COURGETTES TOSSED
IN CHEESE
Parmesan is possibly the
most famous of the Italian
cheeses, and is certainly the
most expensive, mainly
because it takes the longest
time to mature – at least 2
years. Always buy fresh
Parmesan cheese for
grating; the types sold
ready-grated in drums and
packets cannot compare for
flavour with Parmesan cut
fresh from a large piece.
Look for cheese which is
pale buff-yellow in colour,
and not too crumbly in
texture.

CREAM BAKED CELERY

C   S E R V E S   4

1 head of celery
300 ml (½ pint) double cream
salt and pepper
freshly grated nutmeg
50 g (2 oz) fresh breadcrumbs
15 g (½ oz) butter or margarine

/ 1 / Trim the celery and cut into 5 cm (2 inch) pieces. Wash thoroughly. Finely chop a few of the green celery leaves and discard the remainder (or save for garnishing another dish).

/ 2 / Arrange the celery in a single layer in an ovenproof dish. Sprinkle with the chopped leaves and pour over the cream. Season to taste with salt, pepper and nutmeg.

/ 3 / Sprinkle the breadcrumbs over the celery and cream and dot with the butter or margarine. Stand the dish on the wire rack and cook on combination at 200°C/MEDIUM LOW for 20-25 minutes or until the celery is tender. Serve the celery hot.

BEANS WITH COCONUT

S E R V E S   4

30 ml (2 tbsp) light sesame or vegetable oil
2.5 ml (½ tsp) sesame seeds
2 medium onions, skinned and thickly sliced
450 g (1 lb) fresh or frozen green beans, trimmed
50 (2 oz) fresh grated or desiccated coconut
5 ml (1 tsp) paprika
2.5 ml (½ tsp) ground coriander
1.25 ml (¼ tsp) cayenne pepper
15 ml (1 tbsp) finely chopped fresh coriander leaves
salt and pepper

/ 1 / Put the oil in a shallow casserole dish and microwave on HIGH for 2 minutes or until the oil is hot, then sprinkle in the sesame seeds and stir in the onions.

/ 2 / Cover and microwave the onions on HIGH for 5-7 minutes or until they are softened, then stir in the beans, half the coconut and all remaining ingredients, except the seasoning.

/ 3 / Cover the dish with a lid. Microwave on HIGH for 10-13 minutes (13 minutes for frozen beans) or until the beans are tender, stirring 2 or 3 times during the cooking time. Season with salt and pepper. Sprinkle remaining coconut over the top and serve hot.

──── V A R I A T I O N ────

OKRA WITH COCONUT
Substitute 450 g (1 lb) okra, trimmed at the stalk end, for the green beans. If preferred, all the coconut can be stirred into the mixture before cooking.

MINTED CARROTS AND SPROUTS

S E R V E S   4

450 g (1 lb) Brussels sprouts, trimmed
225 g (8 oz) carrots, peeled and quartered
50 g (2 oz) butter or margarine
30 ml (2 tbsp) chopped fresh mint
salt and pepper

/ 1 / Put the sprouts and carrots in a large casserole. Add 45 ml (3 tbsp) water and cover. Microwave on HIGH for 9-12 minutes or until tender. Shake the casserole once during the cooking time.

/ 2 / Drain the sprouts and carrots and return them to the casserole.

/ 3 / Place the butter or margarine and mint in a small measuring jug and microwave on HIGH for 1 minute or until the butter is melted and foaming. Pour the butter over the vegetables and toss until well coated.

/ 4 / Microwave on HIGH for 1 minute to reheat if necessary. Season to taste with salt and pepper and serve immediately.

CREAM BAKED CELERY
Celery is a neglected vegetable, usually only seen chopped up in salads or used as a flavouring for stocks and stews. Here, generous chunks of celery are baked until tender in a creamy nutmeg custard, topped with golden breadcrumbs. It is delicious served with poached or baked fish.

MINTED CARROTS AND SPROUTS
Choose small round sprouts with tightly packed heads and no wilted leaves. Do not cut a cross in them for this recipe.
   When new baby carrots are in season they may be substituted in this recipe. Leave very small carrots whole; quarter any larger ones.

OKRA WITH COCONUT
Okra or ladies' fingers are a long thin vegetable, used extensively in Indian cooking. When trimming the ends take care not to cut the flesh or a sticky substance will be released during cooking.

128

Minted Carrots and Sprouts; Beans with Coconut

Katie's Potatoes

KATIE'S POTATOES
New potatoes should have skins that can be rubbed off easily. Buy them in small quantities and use up quickly. Suitable varieties for this recipe are Arran Comet, Home Guard, Maris Peer, Pentland Javelin, Red Craigs Royal, Ulster Sceptre, and Wilja.

SOUFFLÉED PARSNIPS
Parsnips are usually roasted or baked. For a change, here they are puréed, mixed with cheese, eggs and milk and baked like a soufflé. Don't expect the mixture to rise as much as a soufflé, but it will rise slightly and taste light and airy. To serve as a vegetarian main meal, add an extra 50 g (2 oz) cheese.

KATIE'S POTATOES

C S E R V E S 6

| 700 g (1½ lb) small new potatoes |
| 50 g (2 oz) butter |
| 2 garlic cloves, skinned and crushed |
| 15 ml (1 tbsp) chopped fresh tarragon |
| salt and pepper |

/ 1 / Wash the potatoes thoroughly and prick each one with the point of a knife. Place the potatoes in an ovenproof dish, dot with the butter and scatter the garlic and tarragon on top. Season to taste with salt and pepper.

/ 2 / Cover the dish, stand on the wire rack and cook on combination at 200°C/MEDIUM LOW for 20-25 minutes or until tender. Serve hot.

SOUFFLÉED PARSNIPS

C S E R V E S 4 - 6

| 900 g (2 lb) parsnips, peeled and thinly sliced |
| 2 eggs, separated |
| 300 ml (½ pint) milk |
| 100 g (4 oz) Cheddar cheese, grated |
| salt and pepper |

/ 1 / Put the parsnips and 150 ml (¼ pint) water in a large bowl. Cover and microwave on HIGH for 10-12 minutes or until tender. Drain well and leave to cool slightly.

/ 2 / Preheat the oven on convection at 250°C for 10 minutes. Meanwhile, place the parsnips in a blender or food processor with the egg yolks and milk and purée until smooth. Transfer to a bowl, stir in 75 g (3 oz) of the cheese and season to taste with salt and pepper.

/ 3 / Grease a deep 1.7 litre (3 pint) ovenproof dish. Whisk the egg whites until stiff and fold into the purée.

/ 4 / Turn the soufflé mixture into the prepared dish and sprinkle with the remaining cheese. Stand on the wire rack and cook on combination at 200°C/MEDIUM LOW for 20-25 minutes or until just firm to the touch, risen and golden brown. Serve the souffléed parsnips immediately.

GRATIN OF VEGETABLES WITH CHÈVRE

C

SERVES 4 - 6
AS A MAIN COURSE

1.4 kg (3 lb) prepared mixed vegetables, such as parsnips, celery, leeks, carrots and onions, cut into chunks
300 ml (½ pint) vegetable stock
1 bay leaf
15 ml (1 tbsp) potato flour
TOPPING
100 g (4 oz) firm Chèvre, rinded and finely chopped
100 g (4 oz) chopped mixed nuts
75 g (3 oz) rolled oats
30 ml (2 tbsp) chopped fresh parsley
salt and pepper
25 g (1 oz) butter or margarine

/ 1 / Place all the vegetables in a large bowl with the stock and bay leaf, cover and microwave on HIGH for 15-20 minutes or until the vegetables are just tender, stirring occasionally. Sprinkle in the potato flour and stir thoroughly until dissolved into the stock.

/ 2 / Preheat the oven on convection at 250°C for 10 minutes. Meanwhile, transfer the vegetables to a large gratin dish.

/ 3 / Make the topping: place the Chèvre in a bowl and mix with the nuts, oats and parsley. Season to taste with salt and pepper. Sprinkle on top of the vegetable mixture and dot with the butter or margarine.

/ 4 / Stand the gratin on the wire rack and cook on combination at 250°C/MEDIUM LOW for 10-15 minutes or until the topping is crisp and golden. Serve hot.

OATMEAL ROASTED VEGETABLES

C

SERVES 4 - 6

450 g (1 lb) parsnips, cut into chunks
450 g (1 lb) onions, skinned and cut into quarters
225 g (8 oz) carrots, cut into chunks
75 ml (5 tbsp) vegetable oil
100 g (4 oz) medium oatmeal
salt and pepper

/ 1 / Toss the vegetables in the oil and then in the oatmeal until completely coated.

/ 2 / Tip the vegetables into a large shallow ovenproof dish. Stand on the wire rack and cook on combination at 250°C/MEDIUM LOW for 20-25 minutes or until the vegetables are cooked through and browned. Season to taste with salt and pepper and serve immediately.

——— VARIATION ———

For extra flavour and colour, toss the roasted vegetables with a few herbs or chilli powder.

GRATIN OF VEGETABLES WITH CHÈVRE
This is a delicious mixture of vegetables with a Chèvre (French goat's cheese), nut and oat topping. Potato flour is used to thicken the vegetable mixture. It's a dried potato product that can be sprinkled directly on to hot liquids with no fear of it going lumpy. It thickens almost immediately on contact with the hot food so it does not need to be cooked. Potato flour is sold in most healthfood shops but if you find it difficult to obtain, use 22.5 ml (1½ level tbsp) cornflour instead. Simply mix the cornflour to a smooth paste with a little cold water, blend into the vegetable mixture and then microwave on HIGH for 2-3 minutes or until boiling and thickened, stirring frequently.

Oatmeal Roasted Vegetables

COURGETTES À LA PROVENÇALE

C SERVES 6

45 ml (3 tbsp) olive oil
1 medium onion, skinned and finely chopped
1 garlic clove, skinned and chopped
700 g (1½ lb) courgettes, thickly sliced
450 g (1 lb) tomatoes, sliced
30 ml (2 tbsp) chopped fresh oregano, chervil, tarragon or parsley or 5 ml (1 tsp) dried Herbes de Provence
salt and pepper

/ 1 / Put the oil, onion and garlic in a large ovenproof dish. Cover and microwave on HIGH for 5-7 minutes or until softened.

/ 2 / Add the courgettes, tomatoes and herbs and season to taste with salt and pepper. Stand the dish on the wire rack and cook on combination at 200°C/MEDIUM LOW for 18-25 minutes, or until the courgettes are done to your liking, stirring occasionally. Serve the vegetables immediately.

TOMATOES WITH PINE NUT AND BASIL DRESSING

SERVES 2

15 ml (1 tbsp) olive or vegetable oil
25 g (1 oz) pine nuts
2.5 ml (½ tsp) Dijon mustard
2.5 ml (½ tsp) brown sugar
salt and pepper
2.5 ml (½ tsp) white wine vinegar
225 g (8 oz) cherry tomatoes, cut in halves
15 ml (1 tbsp) chopped fresh basil
basil sprigs, to garnish

/ 1 / Put the oil and the nuts in a medium bowl and microwave on HIGH for 2-3 minutes, stirring frequently.

/ 2 / Stir in the mustard, sugar, salt and pepper and whisk with a fork. Whisk in the vinegar.

/ 3 / Add the tomatoes and microwave on HIGH for 30 seconds or until the tomatoes are just warm. Stir in the basil and serve immediately, garnished with basil sprigs.

POTATO AND LEEK RAMEKINS

SERVES 2

1 large potato, weighing about 225 g (8 oz)
1 small leek
45 ml (3 tbsp) milk
salt and pepper
freshly grated nutmeg
1 egg yolk
15 g (½ oz) butter or margarine
5 ml (1 tsp) poppy seeds

/ 1 / Grease and line the bases of two 150 ml (¼ pint) ramekin dishes with greaseproof paper.

/ 2 / Prick the potato all over with a fork, place on absorbent kitchen paper and microwave on HIGH for 5-6 minutes or until soft, turning over halfway through cooking.

/ 3 / Meanwhile, finely chop the white part of the leek and slice the green part into very thin 4 cm (1½ inch) long strips. Wash separately and drain well.

/ 4 / Put the white leek in a medium bowl with the milk, cover and microwave on HIGH for 2-3 minutes or until very soft, stirring occasionally during cooking.

/ 5 / Cut the potato in half, scoop out the flesh and stir into the cooked leek and milk. Mash well together and season with salt, pepper and nutmeg. Stir in the egg yolk.

/ 6 / Spoon the mixture into the prepared ramekin dishes. Microwave on HIGH for 2-2½ minutes or until the vegetable ramekins are firm to the touch. Leave to stand.

/ 7 / Meanwhile, put the butter or margarine into a small bowl with the strips of green leek and the poppy seeds. Cover and microwave on HIGH for 2-3 minutes or until tender, stirring occasionally. Season with salt and pepper.

/ 8 / Turn the ramekins out on to a serving plate and spoon over the leek mixture. Microwave on HIGH for 1-2 minutes to heat through. Serve immediately.

TRICOLOUR PÂTÉ TRIO

SERVES 3 - 4

1 large red pepper
175 g (6 oz) cauliflower florets
300 ml (½ pint) natural yogurt
300 ml (½ pint) single cream
salt and pepper
1 ripe avocado
15 ml (1 tbsp) lemon juice
fresh herbs and black olives, to garnish
Melba toast, to serve

/ 1 / Cut the pepper in half lengthways and remove the core and seeds. Place, cut side down, on a double sheet of absorbent kitchen paper and microwave on HIGH for 5-6 minutes or until the pepper is soft.

/ 2 / While the pepper is cooking, cut the cauliflower into very small florets and put into a large bowl with 15 ml (1 tbsp) water.

/ 3 / When the pepper is cooked, microwave the cauliflower on HIGH for 6-7 minutes or until very tender, stirring occasionally.

/ 4 / Meanwhile, carefully peel the skin from the pepper and discard. Put the pepper, a third of the yogurt and a third of the cream in a blender or food processor and purée until smooth. Season to taste with salt and pepper.

/ 5 / Drain the cauliflower and put into the rinsed-out bowl of the blender or food processor with half of the remaining yogurt and half of the remaining cream; purée until smooth. Season to taste with salt and pepper.

/ 6 / Halve the avocado and discard the skin and the stone. Put into the rinsed-out bowl of the blender or food processor with the remaining yogurt, cream and the lemon juice. Purée until smooth. Season to taste with salt and pepper. Leave all pâtés to cool before serving.

/ 7 / To serve: put a large spoonful of each pâté side by side in 6 individual serving bowls. Shake each bowl gently from side to side, allowing the pâtés to merge into one another but leaving 3 distinctive sections of colour. Sprinkle with a few fresh herbs and black olives. Serve immediately with Melba toast.

BAKED BEETROOT

Ⓒ ### SERVES 6

6 raw beetroots, each weighing about 175 g (6 oz)
vegetable oil
90 ml (6 tbsp) soured cream or Greek yogurt
salt and pepper
parsley sprigs, to garnish

/ 1 / Wash the beetroots well, but do not trim. Brush the skins with a little oil and place in a shallow ovenproof dish. Stand the dish on the wire rack and cook on combination at 200°C/ MEDIUM LOW for 40-45 minutes or until tender.

/ 2 / While still warm, cut the beetroots almost through into quarters from the top, then carefully peel back the skin. Top each with a tablespoonful of soured cream or Greek yogurt. Season to taste with a little salt and pepper and garnish with sprigs of parsley before serving.

LENTIL, AUBERGINE AND POTATO PIE

SERVES 4
AS A MAIN COURSE

3 medium potatoes, each weighing about 225 g (8 oz), scrubbed
100 g (4 oz) split red lentils
1 medium onion, skinned and finely chopped
1 bay leaf
5 ml (1 tsp) dried thyme
15 ml (1 tbsp) tomato purée
1 small aubergine, roughly chopped
450 ml (¾ pint) boiling vegetable stock
100 g (4 oz) French beans, trimmed and cut into 2.5 cm (1 inch) lengths
60 ml (4 tbsp) milk
salt and pepper
25 g (1 oz) Parmesan cheese, freshly grated

/ 1 / Prick the potatoes all over with a fork and arrange in a circle on a sheet of absorbent kitchen paper. Microwave on HIGH for 10-15 minutes or until soft, turning over halfway through cooking. Set aside to cool slightly.

TRICOLOUR PÂTÉ TRIO
This is a stunning dish for an informal light lunch, or it could serve 6 as a starter. It is a simple idea, consisting of 3 pâtés each with a distinctive colour – red, white and green. But the secret lies in the presentation, all 3 are served in the same dish but merge together as one. It is not as difficult as it looks and is achieved by making the pâtés quite soft, spooning each into the dish separately and then shaking gently from side to side so that they merge into one.

BAKED BEETROOT
Much of the beetroot available in shops or supermarkets is already cooked and stored in vinegar or brine. For this recipe you need raw beetroots. Look out for small firm beetroots as larger ones are often fibrous. The older the beetroots, the more indigestible they become. Generally beetroot is cooked and served cold in salads, but it is equally delicious served hot as an accompaniment topped with soured cream or Greek yogurt.

LENTIL, AUBERGINE AND POTATO PIE
If preferred, this pie can be cooked on combination. Follow the instructions in step 4 of Cheese Potato Pie on page 155.
    For a different topping, omit the milk and mash the potatoes with 75 g (3 oz) low- or full-fat soft cheese with garlic and herbs and 30 ml (2 tbsp) chopped fresh chives. Omit the Parmesan cheese and sprinkle the top of the pie with a little sweet paprika.

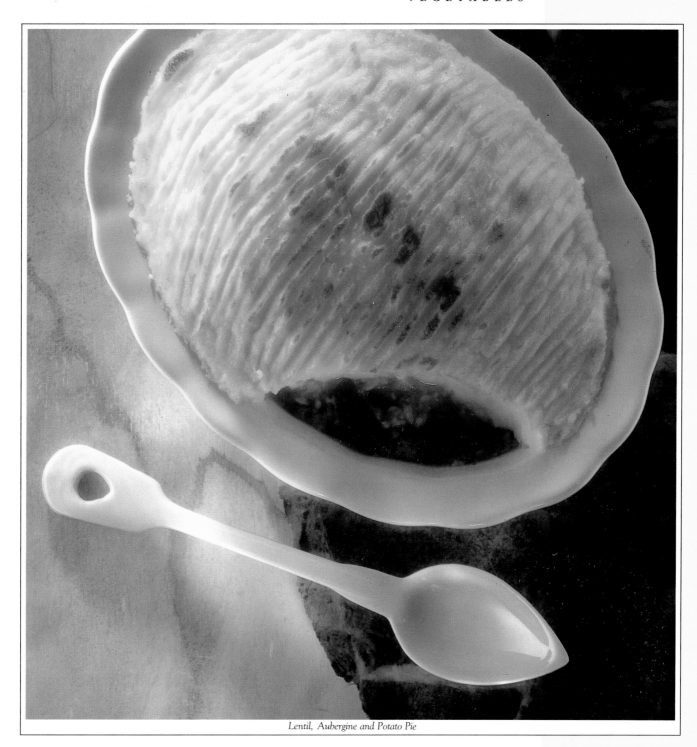

Lentil, Aubergine and Potato Pie

/ 2 / While the potatoes are cooling, put the lentils, onion, bay leaf, thyme, tomato purée, aubergine and vegetable stock in a large bowl and mix well together.

/ 3 / Cover the bowl and then microwave on HIGH for 20-25 minutes or until the lentils and aubergine are tender and most of the liquid is absorbed. Add the beans and microwave on HIGH for 2 minutes.

/ 4 / Meanwhile, cut the potatoes in half and scoop out the flesh into a bowl. Mash with the milk and season to taste with salt and pepper.

/ 5 / Spoon the lentil and aubergine mixture into a flameproof serving dish. Spoon over the mashed potato and sprinkle with the cheese. Microwave on HIGH for 1-2 minutes or until heated through, then brown under a hot grill, if liked. Serve hot.

TOFU AND BEAN BURGERS

SERVES 6

275 g (10 oz) silken tofu
397 g (14 oz) can red kidney beans, drained and rinsed
2.5 ml (½ tsp) miso
2.5 ml (½ tsp) yeast extract
30 ml (2 tbsp) hot water
5 ml (1 tsp) dried mixed herbs
1 medium onion, skinned and grated
2 medium courgettes, grated
25 g (1 oz) wholemeal breadcrumbs
a few drops of chilli sauce
1 egg, beaten
15 ml (1 tbsp) lemon juice
grated rind of 1 small lemon
pepper

/ 1 / Put the tofu and kidney beans in a bowl and mash together using a potato masher or a fork. Dissolve the miso and yeast extract in the hot water and stir in with the remaining ingredients. Beat well together.

/ 2 / Shape the mixture into 6 burgers, about 2 cm (¾ inch) thick.

/ 3 / Arrange the burgers in a circle around the edge of a large flat ovenproof plate. Microwave on HIGH for 8 minutes. Carefully turn them over and microwave on HIGH for a further 8 minutes. Serve hot.

CARROT AND COURGETTE TIMBALES

SERVES 4

350 g (12 oz) courgettes, finely grated
350 g (12 oz) carrots, finely grated
1 egg
salt and pepper

/ 1 / Mix the courgettes and carrots with the egg and season to taste with salt and pepper.

/ 2 / Lightly grease 4 ramekin dishes and fill with the mixture, packing it in tightly.

/ 3 / Preheat the oven on convection at 250°C for 10 minutes. Stand the timbales on the wire rack and cook on combination at 200°C/ MEDIUM LOW for 10 minutes.

VEGETABLE AND CHICK-PEA CASSEROLE

SERVES 6
AS A MAIN COURSE

4 medium courgettes, trimmed and cut into 1 cm (½ inch) lengths
1 red pepper, cored, seeded and chopped
1 green pepper, cored, seeded and chopped
2 medium onions, skinned and coarsely chopped
2 medium carrots, peeled and thinly sliced
225 g (8 oz) turnips, peeled and thinly sliced
1 small cauliflower, trimmed and cut into florets
4 large tomatoes, skinned, seeded and chopped
100 g (4 oz) dried apricots, cut into quarters
2 garlic cloves, skinned and and crushed
425 g (15 oz) can chick-peas, drained
25 g (1 oz) almonds, blanched
5 ml (1 tsp) ground turmeric
10 ml (2 tsp) paprika
2.5 ml (½ tsp) ground coriander
salt and pepper
600 ml (1 pint) vegetable stock
chopped fresh coriander or parsley, to garnish

/ 1 / Place all of the prepared vegetables, tomatoes, apricots, garlic, chick-peas and almonds in a large casserole dish and stir in the spices, the salt, pepper and stock.

/ 2 / Cover and microwave on HIGH for 8-10 minutes or until the vegetables come to the boil, then microwave for a further 30-40 minutes until the vegetables are well cooked. Stir 2 or 3 times during cooking. Serve garnished with coriander or parsley.

VEGETABLE AND CHICK-PEA CASSEROLE Make sure that you use a large casserole dish for this recipe. The size of dishes is important when cooking foods in the microwave. Foods cooked in shallow dishes cook more quickly than those in deep dishes. Choose cooking dishes that are large enough to hold the quantity of food and avoid overfilling – this not only results in spillages but also prevents even cooking.

TOFU AND BEAN BURGERS Tofu, also known as bean curd, is made from a soya bean and water mixture which is strained and pressed to form white blocks. It is high in protein and very low in fat, making it a nutritious substitute for meat, fish and dairy produce. Used extensively in Chinese cooking, tofu is bland in flavour so always marinate before cooking or use in a well-flavoured dish.

CARROT AND COURGETTE TIMBALES This is a pretty and easy way of serving ordinary vegetables. Grated finely and shaped into small moulds, they are then turned out to serve. Don't be tempted to use a food processor to grate vegetables – it makes them too mushy and watery.

Try other combinations of vegetables for these timbales. Try swede and apple with herbs for colour and cook for 15 minutes; potato and onion with chives and cook for 15 minutes; or parsnip and pear with fresh coriander and cook for 15 minutes.

Picture opposite: Vegetable and Chick-pea Casserole

137

STRIPED VEGETABLE TERRINE WITH SEAWEED

SERVES 4 - 6
AS A MAIN COURSE

450 g (1 lb) carrots
450 g (1 lb) parsnips
300 ml (½ pint) double cream or Greek strained yogurt
2 eggs
salt and pepper
3 sheets of nori, each measuring about 20.5×20.5 cm (8×8 inches)
WATERCRESS VINAIGRETTE
½ bunch of watercress
150 ml (¼ pint) vegetable oil
30 ml (2 tbsp) white wine vinegar
5 ml (1 tsp) clear honey

/ 1 / Roughly chop the carrots and put into a roasting bag with 15 ml (1 tbsp) water. Peel and chop the parsnips and put in a roasting bag with 15 ml (1 tbsp) water. Loosely seal the bags and microwave them both at once on HIGH for 12 minutes or until the vegetables are tender.

/ 2 / Put the carrots, half the cream or yogurt and 1 egg in a blender or food processor and purée until smooth. Turn into a bowl and season to taste with salt and pepper.

/ 3 / Put the parsnips into the rinsed-out bowl of the blender or food processor with the remaining cream or yogurt and egg. Purée until smooth and season the purée to taste.

/ 4 / Grease a 1.4 litre (2½ pint) loaf dish and line the base with greaseproof paper. Spoon in half the carrot purée and level the surface. Fold 1 of the sheets of nori in half lengthways and lay on top of the purée.

/ 5 / Spoon half of the parsnip purée on top of the nori and level the surface. Fold a second sheet of nori in half lengthways and lay on top. Repeat the layers, ending with another layer of parsnip purée.

/ 6 / Stand on a roasting rack, cover with absorbent kitchen paper and microwave on MEDIUM for 12-15 minutes or until just firm to the touch. Leave to cool in the dish, then turn out on to a serving plate.

/ 7 / Make the watercress vinaigrette: trim the watercress, reserve a few sprigs to garnish, and put the remainder into a blender or food processor with the oil, vinegar and honey and process until the watercress is finely chopped. Season to taste with salt and pepper.

/ 8 / Serve the terrine hot or cold, arranged on individual plates in a pool of vinaigrette, garnished with reserved watercress.

VEGETARIAN MOUSSAKA

C
SERVES 6
AS A MAIN COURSE

900 g (2 lb) aubergines
olive oil
900 g (2 lb) prepared vegetables, thinly sliced
2 garlic cloves, skinned and crushed
1 bay leaf
30 ml (2 tbsp) chopped fresh oregano or 5 ml (1 tsp) dried
397 g (14 oz) can chopped tomatoes
salt and pepper
CUSTARD TOPPING
3 eggs
450 ml (¾ pint) Greek yogurt
freshly grated nutmeg

/ 1 / Prick the aubergines all over with a fork and brush with a little oil. Place on a large plate and microwave on HIGH for 5-7 minutes or until slightly softened. Leave to cool.

/ 2 / Put the vegetables, garlic, bay leaf, oregano and tomatoes in a large bowl and season to taste with salt and pepper. Cover and microwave on HIGH for 15-20 minutes or until softened, stirring occasionally.

/ 3 / Pour the vegetable mixture into a large gratin dish. Thinly slice the aubergines and arrange on top of the vegetables to cover.

/ 4 / Make the topping: beat the eggs and yogurt together and season to taste with nutmeg and salt and pepper. Pour on top of the aubergines and spread out to cover completely.

/ 5 / Stand the dish on the wire rack and cook on combination at 200°C/MEDIUM LOW for 15-20 minutes or until the yogurt topping is set. Serve the moussaka hot.

STRIPED VEGETABLE TERRINE WITH SEAWEED
The seaweed used in this terrine is called nori; it is sold compressed into large thin sheets and is available from health food stores. Once sliced, this terrine is most attractive and can be served nouvelle cuisine style, in a pool of vinaigrette. Serve as a lunch dish, or as a dinner party starter.

VEGETARIAN MOUSSAKA
It is a good idea to cook aubergines whole on a microwave setting before slicing and including in a moussaka, as it not only saves time and effort but also reduces the fat content. They should be cooked just until they give a litle when gently squeezed. Don't overcook or they will be cooked to a mush. Obviously if you have several small aubergines, they will cook much more quickly than a large one, so cook for 5 minutes, do the squeeze test, then continue to cook if necessary. For the remaining vegetables in the moussaka, use any you have.

Vegetarian Moussaka

Spicy Cauliflower with Yogurt

SPICY CAULIFLOWER WITH YOGURT

SERVES 4 - 6

30 ml (2 tbsp) vegetable oil
5 ml (1 tsp) medium curry powder
2.5 ml (½ tsp) mustard powder
2.5 ml (½ tsp) ground turmeric
pinch of cayenne pepper
1 medium onion, skinned and finely chopped
1 large cauliflower, trimmed and broken into tiny florets
1 cooking apple, peeled, cored and chopped
100 g (4 oz) frozen peas
150 ml (¼ pint) natural yogurt
10 ml (2 tsp) cornflour
salt and pepper

/ 1 / Place the oil, curry powder, mustard, turmeric, cayenne pepper and onion in a large bowl and microwave on HIGH for 5-7 minutes until onion is soft, stirring occasionally.

/ 2 / Add the cauliflower and apple, cover and microwave on HIGH for 10-12 minutes until the vegetable and fruit are just tender.

/ 3 / Stir in the peas. Then gradually blend the yogurt into the cornflour and stir into the cauliflower mixture.

/ 4 / Microwave on HIGH for 2 minutes until the vegetables are heated through. Season well with salt and pepper.

CREAMED BROCCOLI RING

C   SERVES 6 - 8

700 g (1½ lb) broccoli
1 medium onion, skinned and sliced
1 garlic clove, skinned and thinly sliced
150 ml (¼ pint) vegetable stock or water
100 g (4 oz) full- or low-fat soft cheese
3 eggs
50 g (2 oz) fresh brown breadcrumbs
salt and pepper

/ 1 / Thinly slice the broccoli stalks and divide the heads into small even-sized pieces. Put the broccoli, onion, garlic and stock or water in a large bowl. Cover and microwave on HIGH for 10-12 minutes or until the broccoli is tender. Cool slightly.

/ 2 / Put the broccoli mixture and the cheese in a blender or food processor and purée until smooth. Transfer to a bowl, stir in the eggs and breadcrumbs and season the mixture to taste with salt and pepper.

/ 3 / Lightly grease a 1.7 litre (3 pint) ring mould. Spoon the broccoli mixture into the mould and level the surface. Stand on the wire rack and cook on combination at 180°C/ MEDIUM LOW for 20-25 minutes or until slightly risen and just firm to the touch.

/ 4 / Leave to stand for 5 minutes, then carefully loosen around the edges of the mould. Turn the ring out on to a serving plate and cut into slices or wedges to serve.

SPICY CAULIFLOWER
WITH YOGURT
To make your own curry powder: grind in a small electric mill or with a pestle and mortar 30 ml (2 tbsp) cumin seeds, 30 ml (2 tbsp) fenugreek seeds, 7.5 ml (1½ tsp) mustard seeds, 15 ml (1 tbsp) black peppercorns, 120 ml (8 tbsp) coriander seeds, 15 ml (1 tbsp) poppy seeds, 15 ml (1 tbsp) ground ginger, 5 ml (1 tsp) chilli powder and 60 ml (4 tbsp) turmeric. Store in an airtight container for up to 3 months.

CREAMED BROCCOLI
RING
This ring of lightly set broccoli purée makes an unusual vegetable accompaniment. When preparing the broccoli, cut the stalks and divide the heads into equal-sized pieces to ensure even cooking in the microwave. Serve the broccoli ring thinly sliced or in wedges.

BABY CARROTS WITH WATERCRESS

SERVES 4

1 bunch of watercress
450 g (1 lb) whole new carrots, scrubbed
15 g (½ oz) butter or margarine
60 ml (4 tbsp) orange juice
salt and pepper

/ 1 / Wash the watercress and reserve a few sprigs for garnish. Cut away any coarse stalks. Chop the leaves and remaining stalks.

/ 2 / Put the watercress and carrots in a shallow dish. Dot with the butter and spoon over the orange juice. Season to taste.

/ 3 / Cover and microwave on HIGH for 10-12 minutes or until tender. Serve garnished with the reserved sprigs of watercress.

CABBAGE WITH APPLES AND CIDER

C   SERVES 4 - 6

225 g (8 oz) red cabbage, finely shredded
225 g (8 oz) green cabbage, finely shredded
1 large onion, skinned and thinly sliced
2 eating apples, cored and sliced
200 ml (7 fl oz) dry cider
salt and pepper

/ 1 / Place the cabbage and onion in a large ovenproof dish with the apples and cider and season to taste with salt and pepper.

/ 2 / Cover the dish, stand on the wire rack and cook on combination at 180°C/MEDIUM LOW for 15-20 minutes or until tender, stirring occasionally. Serve hot.

BABY CARROTS WITH WATERCRESS

Wash the watercress and reserve a few sprigs for garnishing. Cut away any coarse stalks. Chop the leaves and remaining stalks.

Orange and watercress, both rich in vitamin C, are a perfect combination with sweet, baby carrots. Watercress is also a good source of iron.
   When baby carrots are not in season, use old carrots cut into chunky finger shapes.
   Serve with either fish or chicken dishes.

CABBAGE WITH APPLES AND CIDER
Cabbage and apple is such a good combination that it seems wrong to change a favourite recipe just in the hope of making something new, so here we stick to tradition but add extra apple flavour in the form of cider, just for good measure. This tastes particularly good with cold roast pork or thick slices of York ham.

Cabbage with Apples and Cider

141

CUCUMBER WITH ONION AND TARRAGON

SERVES 4

1 cucumber
salt and pepper
15 g (½ oz) butter or margarine
30 ml (2 tbsp) chopped fresh tarragon
1 bunch of spring onions, trimmed and sliced
fresh tarragon sprigs, to garnish

/ 1 / Remove thin strips of skin evenly from all round the cucumber. Quarter the cucumber lengthways and cut into 5 cm (2 inch) chunks. Sprinkle with salt. Leave for 20 minutes, then drain and pat dry.

/ 2 / Put the cucumber, butter or margarine, chopped tarragon and pepper to taste into a large bowl and cover. Microwave on HIGH for 1 minute, then add the spring onions and microwave on HIGH for 2 minutes or until tender. Season with pepper, then serve garnished with tarragon sprigs.

VEGETABLE DAL WITH ALMONDS

C
SERVES 4 - 6
AS A MAIN COURSE

25 g (1 oz) flaked almonds
1 small onion, skinned and sliced
15 ml (1 tbsp) vegetable oil
2 garlic cloves, skinned and crushed
15 ml (1 tbsp) coriander seeds, crushed
15 ml (1 tbsp) black poppy seeds
100 g (4 oz) split red lentils
450 g (1 lb) turnips, peeled and cut into chunks
1 medium aubergine, cut into chunks
50 g (2 oz) creamed coconut
900 ml (1½ pints) boiling water
salt and pepper
15 ml (1 tbsp) chopped fresh coriander or parsley

/ 1 / Spread the almonds on an ovenproof plate, stand on the wire rack and cook on convection at 250°C for 3-5 minutes or until lightly browned. Set aside.

/ 2 / Put the onion, oil, garlic and coriander seeds in a large ovenproof bowl, cover and microwave on HIGH for 5-7 minutes or until softened. Add the poppy seeds, lentils, turnips and aubergine.

/ 3 / Put the coconut in a jug, pour over the boiling water and stir until dissolved. Pour over the vegetable mixture and mix thoroughly. Season with salt and pepper.

/ 4/ Cover the bowl, stand on the wire rack and cook on combination at 200°C/MEDIUM LOW for 30-35 minutes or until the vegetables are tender, stirring occasionally. Sprinkle with the toasted almonds and the coriander or parsley and serve hot.

GLAZED VEGETABLES PROVENÇAL

SERVES 4

½ red pepper
½ yellow pepper
½ green pepper
1 courgette, trimmed
1 large tomato
30 ml (2 tbsp) vegetable oil
1 garlic clove, skinned and crushed
50 g (2 oz) mange-tout, trimmed
60 ml (4 tbsp) dry white wine
salt and pepper
fresh basil, to garnish

/ 1 / Remove the core and seeds from the peppers, then cut the flesh into thin strips. Thinly slice the courgette. Skin, seed and cut the flesh of the tomato into strips.

/ 2 / Heat a browning dish on HIGH for 5-8 minutes or according to manufacturer's instructions. Add the oil and garlic for the last 30 seconds of the heating time.

/ 3 / Add the vegetables and stir. Microwave on HIGH for 2-3 minutes or until the vegetables are slightly softened.

/ 4 / Stir in the white wine and season to taste with salt and pepper. Microwave on HIGH for 1 minute. Transfer to a serving dish and garnish with fresh basil.

COOKING PULSES IN THE MICROWAVE

The following pulses will cook successfully in the microwave cooker, making considerable time savings on conventional cooking.

However, pulses with very tough skins, such as red-kidney beans, black beans, butter beans, cannellini beans, haricot beans and soya beans will not cook in less time and are better if cooked conventionally. Large quantities of all pulses are best cooked conventionally.

All pulses double in weight when cooked, so if a recipe states 225 g (8 oz) cooked beans, you will need to start with 100 g (4 oz) dried weight.

Soak beans overnight, then drain and cover with enough boiling water to come about 2.5 cm (1 inch) above the level of the beans. Cover and microwave on HIGH for the time stated below, stirring occasionally.

Type 225 g (8 oz) quantity	Time on High Setting	Microwave Cooking Technique
Aduki beans	30-35 minutes	Stand for 5 minutes. Do not drain.
Black-eye beans	25-30 minutes	Stand for 5 minutes. Do not drain.
Chick-peas	50-55 minutes	Stand for 5 minutes. Do not drain.
Flageolet beans	40-45 minutes	Stand for 5 minutes. Do not drain.
Mung beans	30-35 minutes	Stand for 5 minutes. Do not drain.
Split peas/lentils (do not need overnight soaking)	25-30 minutes	Stand for 5 minutes. Do not drain.

Dietary fibre, known as roughage, is found only in plant foods, where it gives structure to plant cell walls. It is indigestible and, although of no nutritional value, plays a vital role in keeping the body healthy. It prevents constipation and may also prevent certain diseases of the intestine, such as diverticulosis, cancer of the large bowel and possibly other disorders like varicose veins and heart disease, although this has yet to be proved.

Dietary fibre works by holding a lot of water. The more fibre is eaten, the more moisture is absorbed and it becomes easy for the intestine to push the soft, bulky waste matter along without pressure or straining. It means that any potentially harmful substances are diluted and eliminated quickly from the body, spending little time in contact with the wall of the intestine.

Good sources of fibre are pulses, whole grain cereals (including wholemeal bread), wholewheat pasta, brown rice, fruit and vegetables.

MUSHROOM, COURGETTE AND BEAN STEW

SERVES 4
AS A MAIN COURSE

25 g (1 oz) butter or margarine

1 medium onion, skinned and chopped

25 g (1 oz) wholemeal flour

450 ml (¾ pint) vegetable stock

15 ml (1 tbsp) mild wholegrain mustard

450 g (1 lb) cooked beans such as flageolet, red kidney, borlotti, or black-eye beans (see chart), or two 425 g (15 oz) cans beans, drained and rinsed

225 g (8 oz) mushrooms

450 g (1 lb) courgettes

45 ml (3 tbsp) chopped fresh mixed herbs

salt and pepper

brown rice or Herb, Cheese and Olive Bread (see page 191)

/1/ Put the butter or margarine and the onion in a large bowl. Cover and microwave on HIGH for 2-3 minutes or until slightly softened. Stir in the flour and microwave on HIGH for 1 minute, then gradually stir in the stock.

/2/ Microwave on HIGH for 4-5 minutes or until the stock is boiling and thickened, stirring frequently.

/3/ Add the mustard, beans and the mushrooms (cut in half if large) and microwave on HIGH for 2-3 minutes.

/4/ Meanwhile, cut the courgettes into 1 cm (½ inch) slices. Stir the courgettes and half of the herbs into the stew. Cover and microwave on HIGH for 5-6 minutes or until the courgettes are just cooked. Season to taste with salt and pepper and stir in the remaining herbs. Serve the stew with brown rice or chunks of Herb, Cheese and Olive Bread.

144

Mushroom, Courgette and Bean Stew

SPICY NUT BURGERS WITH RAITA

SERVES 2

45 ml (3 tbsp) vegetable oil
1 small onion, skinned and chopped
1 medium carrot, peeled and finely grated
1 garlic clove, skinned and crushed
1 cm (½ inch) piece fresh root ginger, peeled and chopped
2.5 ml (½ tsp) coriander seeds, finely crushed
2.5 ml (½ tsp) cumin seeds
100 g (4 oz) mixed nuts, finely chopped
25 g (1 oz) Cheddar cheese, finely grated
50 g (2 oz) brown breadcrumbs
salt and pepper
1 egg, size 6, beaten
30 ml (2 tbsp) chopped fresh coriander
150 ml (¼ pint) natural yogurt
lemon wedges and fresh coriander, to garnish

/ 1 / Put 15 ml (1 tbsp) of the oil, the onion, carrot, garlic and ginger in a medium bowl. Cover and microwave on HIGH for 5-7 minutes or until the vegetables have softened, stirring occasionally during cooking.

/ 2 / Stir in the coriander and cumin seeds and microwave on HIGH for 1 minute, stirring occasionally. Stir in the nuts and microwave on HIGH for 2 minutes, stirring once.

/ 3 / Stir in the cheese and breadcrumbs and season with salt and pepper. Mix thoroughly and bind together with the egg.

/ 4 / Preheat a browning dish to maximum, according to the manufacturer's instructions.

/ 5 / Meanwhile, divide the mixture into 6 and shape into burgers. When the browning dish is hot, add the remaining oil and microwave on HIGH for 30 seconds.

/ 6 / Quickly put the burgers in the dish and microwave on HIGH for 1½ minutes, then turn over and microwave on HIGH for a further minute or until browned. Leave to stand for 1 minute while making the raita.

/ 7 / To make the raita: beat the chopped coriander into the yogurt and season to taste with salt and pepper.

/ 8 / Garnish the burgers with lemon wedges and sprigs of coriander and serve piping hot with the coriander raita.

CAULIFLOWER CHEESE

C

SERVES 4 - 6
AS AN
ACCOMPANIMENT

700 g (1½ lb) cauliflower florets
50 g (2 oz) plain flour
50 g (2 oz) butter or margarine
568 ml (1 pint) milk
5 ml (1 tsp) Dijon mustard
175 g (6 oz) Double Gloucester cheese
salt and pepper
50 g (2 oz) fresh breadcrumbs

/ 1 / Place the cauliflower florets in a large bowl with 75 ml (5 tbsp) water. Cover and microwave on HIGH for 10-15 minutes or until the cauliflower is just tender. Drain and arrange in a gratin dish.

/ 2 / Put the flour, butter or margarine, milk and mustard in a bowl and microwave on HIGH for 8-10 minutes or until boiling and thickened, whisking frequently. Stir in 100 g (4 oz) of the cheese and season to taste with salt and pepper.

/ 3 / Pour the sauce over the cauliflower and sprinkle with the remaining cheese and the breadcrumbs. Stand the dish on the wire rack and cook on convection at 250°C for 15-20 minutes or until the topping is golden brown. Serve immediately.

—CAULIFLOWER CHEESE—

When making sauces such as this cheese sauce in the microwave, always use a container large enough to prevent the sauce from boiling over. Whisk sauces frequently during cooking to prevent lumps forming. When making sauces thickened with cornflour or arrowroot, make sure the thickening agent is completely dissolved in cold liquid before adding a hot one.

SPICY NUT BURGERS WITH RAITA
These spicy burgers make a good lunch, supper or snack meal. Use any chopped nuts of your choice – almonds, Brazil nuts, cashews, hazelnuts, pistachio nuts or walnuts are all suitable.

CAULIFLOWER CHEESE
Recently, Cauliflower Cheese has become popular as a main dish, served with chunks of warmed French bread or garlic bread. It makes a wonderfully filling lunch or supper dish, but it is equally good as a vegetable accompaniment to roast poultry or meat served with a green vegetable such as beans.

Picture opposite:
Spicy Nut Burgers with Raita

SPICED VEGETABLE AND CHEESE PIE

[C]

SERVES 6
AS A MAIN COURSE

100 g (4 oz) butter or margarine
15 ml (1 tbsp) ground cumin
2 medium onions, skinned and thinly sliced
2 large carrots, sliced
2 medium leeks, thickly sliced
6 medium courgettes, thickly sliced
65 g (2½ oz) plain flour
450 ml (¾ pint) milk
100 g (4 oz) Cheddar cheese, grated
beaten egg yolk, to glaze
30 ml (2 tbsp) freshly grated Parmesan cheese
paprika
PASTRY
175 g (6 oz) plain wholemeal flour
pinch of salt
75 g (3 oz) butter or margarine

/ 1 / Put the butter or margarine in a large bowl and microwave on HIGH for 1-2 minutes or until melted. Add the cumin and onions, cover and microwave on HIGH for 5-7 minutes or until soft.

/ 2 / Add all the remaining vegetables to the bowl, re-cover and microwave on HIGH for 5-7 minutes or until the vegetables have just softened slightly.

/ 3 / Stir in the flour and microwave, uncovered, on HIGH for 1 minute. Gradually stir in the milk and microwave on HIGH for 5-7 minutes or until boiling and thickened, stirring frequently. Stir in the cheese. Spoon into a 1.7 litre (3 pint) pie dish.

/ 4 / Make the pastry: mix the flour and salt together in a bowl. Rub in the butter or margarine until the mixture resembles fine breadcrumbs, then stir in about 45 ml (3 tbsp) water, adding just enough to mix to a firm dough.

/ 5 / Knead the pastry lightly, then roll out on a lightly floured surface to an oval about 5 cm (2 inches) wider all round than the pie dish.

/ 6 / Cut a 2.5 cm (1 inch) strip from the edge of the pastry to form a collar. Dampen the rim of the pie dish with water and press the pastry collar firmly in place.

/ 7 / Dampen the pastry collar with water, then place the pastry lid on top. Press down firmly, then trim and knock up the edges. Use the trimmings to decorate the top of the pie. Brush the top of the pie with egg yolk. Chill for 10 minutes. Meanwhile, preheat the oven on convection at 250°C.

/ 8 / Stand the pie on the wire rack and cook on combination at 200°C/MEDIUM LOW for 20-25 minutes or until lightly browned. Sprinkle with the grated Parmesan cheese and a little paprika before serving.

VEGETABLE LASAGNE

[C]

SERVES 4-6
AS A MAIN COURSE

900 g (2 lb) prepared mixed vegetables, finely chopped
397 g (14 oz) can tomatoes
60 ml (4 tbsp) tomato purée
1 garlic clove, skinned and crushed
salt and pepper
150 ml (¼ pint) boiling vegetable stock
50 g (2 oz) plain flour
50 g (2 oz) butter
568 ml (1 pint) milk
12 sheets wholewheat no-need-to-precook lasagne
30 ml (2 tbsp) freshly grated Parmesan cheese

/ 1 / Put the vegetables, tomatoes with their juice, tomato purée and garlic in a large bowl and season to taste. Cover and microwave on HIGH for 10-15 minutes until tender. Stir in the boiling stock.

/ 2 / Put the flour, butter and milk in a bowl and microwave on HIGH for 8-10 minutes or until boiling and thickened, whisking frequently. Season to taste with salt and pepper.

/ 3 / Put a layer of the vegetable sauce in the bottom of a rectangular ovenproof dish. Top with 4 sheets of lasagne. Repeat the layers of sauce and lasagne twice more, ending with a layer of lasagne. Pour over the white sauce and spread out to cover the top completely. Sprinkle with the Parmesan cheese.

/ 4 / Stand the dish on the wire rack and cook on combination at 200°C/MEDIUM LOW for 25-35 minutes or until the top is golden brown and the pasta is tender. Serve hot.

SPICED VEGETABLE PIE
In this pie the chunky vegetable filling is spiced with cumin, a spice vital to Indian and Middle Eastern cooking, but much neglected in this country. It is sold as cumin seeds, which must be crushed before cooking, or in ground form. The seeds have a much stronger flavour, so here ground cumin is used to give a subtle, spicy flavour.

The pastry for Spiced Vegetable Pie can be made with half wholemeal and half plain flour, or all plain flour, if preferred. Alternatively, make a really quick pastry using oil. Put 40 ml (8 tsp) vegetable oil in a bowl with 15 ml (1 tbsp) chilled water. Beat well with a fork to form an emulsion. Mix 100 g (4 oz) flour and a pinch of salt together and gradually add to the oil to make a smooth dough. Roll out on a floured surface or between pieces of greaseproof paper.

VEGETABLE LASAGNE
Use whatever vegetables you have to hand to make the vegetable sauce for this lasagne, including a good mixture for maximum flavour. In this recipe quick-cook lasagne is used to save time and effort.

Vegetable Lasagne

SPICED VEGETABLES WITH COUSCOUS

C

SERVES 6
AS A MAIN COURSE

225 g (8 oz) couscous
30 ml (2 tbsp) coriander seeds
5 ml (1 tsp) mustard seeds
5 ml (1 tsp) cumin seeds
1 cinnamon stick
8 green cardamon pods
3 cloves
30 ml (2 tbsp) vegetable oil
1 small onion, skinned and chopped
2 garlic cloves, skinned and crushed
450 g (1 lb) tomatoes, chopped
225 g (8 oz) small okra, trimmed
pared rind and juice of 1 lemon
100 g (4 oz) button mushrooms
150 ml (¼ pint) vegetable stock
425 g (15 oz) can chick-peas, drained and rinsed
salt and pepper
30 ml (2 tbsp) chopped fresh coriander

/ 1 / Put the couscous in a large ovenproof serving dish and pour over enough boiling water to cover by 2.5 cm (1 inch). Stir with a fork, then leave to soak for 10-12 minutes or until the water has been absorbed.

/ 2 / Meanwhile, crush the spices in a pestle and mortar. Put the crushed spices, oil, onion and garlic in a large bowl and microwave on HIGH for 2-3 minutes or until the spices are sizzling in the oil.

/ 3 / Add the tomatoes, okra, lemon rind and juice, mushrooms and stock and mix together well. Microwave on HIGH for 5 minutes or until the vegetables are slightly softened, stirring once. Stir in the chick-peas and season to taste with salt and pepper.

/ 4 / Spoon the vegetable mixture on top of the couscous. Cover the bowl, stand on the wire rack and cook on combination at 200°C/MEDIUM LOW for 15-20 minutes or until the vegetables are tender. Carefully fluff up the couscous with a fork, sprinkle with the coriander and serve immediately.

SALAD OF OYSTER MUSHROOMS

SERVES 4
AS A MAIN COURSE

25 g (1 oz) butter or margarine
30 ml (2 tbsp) vegetable oil
15 ml (1 tbsp) lemon juice
450 g (1 lb) oyster mushrooms
mixed salad leaves such as frisée, radicchio, mâche
15 ml (1 tbsp) white wine vinegar
salt and pepper
1 small red onion, skinned and finely chopped
45 ml (3 tbsp) chopped fresh mixed herbs

/ 1 / Put the butter or margarine, oil and lemon juice in a large shallow dish and microwave on HIGH for 1 minute or until the butter or margarine melts. Add the mushrooms, cover and microwave on HIGH for 2-3 minutes or until the mushrooms are tender.

/ 2 / Meanwhile, arrange the salad leaves on 4 plates. When the mushrooms are cooked, remove them with a slotted spoon and arrange on top of the salad.

/ 3 / Quickly add the vinegar to the liquid remaining in the dish and microwave on HIGH for 1 minute. Season to taste with salt and pepper. Pour over the mushrooms and sprinkle with the onion and the herbs. Serve immediately.

SALAD OF OYSTER MUSHROOMS

Serve this warm mushroom salad with crisp Melba toast which you can make in the microwave. Toast the bread on both sides, then using a sharp knife, slice the bread in half horizontally (to make 2 very thin slices). Place, untoasted side up, on a large plate or straight on the cooker base and microwave on HIGH for 30-40 seconds until dry and crisp.

SALAD OF OYSTER MUSHROOMS
Oyster mushrooms grow on dead or dying tree trunks. They are much larger than the everyday button mushrooms and are oyster-like in shape. They are now more widely available in larger supermarkets and are worth trying as they have a delicious flavour. If you cannot find them, use flat black or cup mushrooms instead, but do not use button mushrooms as the flavour is not as good.
   Serve Salad of Oyster Mushrooms as a lunch dish. Alternatively, it could be served as a starter.

SPICED VEGETABLES WITH COUSCOUS
It's important to soak the couscous in a really large heatproof serving dish in step 1. Not only does it expand during cooking, but the rest of the ingredients will be added to this dish too. Select a dish with a wide circumference for faster cooking. Check that the dish can revolve in the oven before you start.

Spiced Vegetables with Couscous tastes particularly good served with a fiery hot sauce called Harissa. To make Harissa Sauce: put 15 ml (1 tbsp) vegetable oil, 1 large red pepper, seeded and chopped, 2 red chillies, seeded and chopped, 2 garlic cloves, skinned and crushed, 15 ml (1 tbsp) ground coriander and 5 ml (1 tsp) ground caraway into a medium bowl and mix well together. Cover and cook on HIGH for 8-10 minutes or until the pepper is really soft. Add 300 ml (½ pint) water, re-cover and cook on HIGH for 3-4 minutes or until the water is boiling. Push through a sieve or purée in a blender or food processor until smooth. Season to taste with salt and pepper. reheat on HIGH for 2-3 minutes or serve cold.

Picture opposite: Spiced Vegetables with Couscous

Gratin de Pommes à la Dauphinoise

LENTIL, MINT AND YOGURT SALAD

SERVES 2

100 g (4 oz) green lentils, washed
900 ml (1½ pints) boiling water
bouquet garni
60 ml (4 tbsp) olive or vegetable oil
30 ml (2 tbsp) lemon juice
large pinch of ground allspice
salt and pepper
45 ml (3 tbsp) chopped fresh mint
4 spring onions
3 large tomatoes
30 ml (2 tbsp) Greek strained yogurt
lemon wedges and mint sprigs, to garnish

/ 1 / Put the lentils in a large bowl and pour over the boiling water. Add the bouquet garni, cover and microwave on HIGH for 10-12 minutes or until the lentils are just tender.

/ 2 / Meanwhile, mix together the olive or vegetable oil and lemon juice and season with allspice, salt and pepper. Stir in the mint.

/ 3 / Drain the lentils and stir in the dressing whilst they are still hot so that they absorb the flavour of the dressing. Chill in the refrigerator for at least 30 minutes.

/ 4 / Meanwhile, trim and chop the spring onions finely and cut the tomatoes into small wedges, using a sharp knife.

/ 5 / Stir into the chilled lentils and mix together well. Stir in the yogurt. Season if necessary. Serve chilled, garnished with lemon wedges and mint sprigs.

———— VARIATIONS ————

LENTIL AND GARLIC SALAD
Omit mint and add 2 garlic cloves, skinned and crushed.

LENTIL AND FRESH HERB SALAD
Omit mint and add 45 ml (3 tbsp) chopped fresh parsley.

LENTIL, MINT AND YOGURT SALAD.

Mix together the olive oil and lemon juice and season with allspice, salt and pepper. Stir in the chopped mint.

Instead of measuring the water for cooking the lentils, an alternative method is to pour enough boiling water over the lentils to cover them by about 2.5 cm (1 inch). Always boil the water in a kettle because large quantities are slow to heat up in the microwave cooker.

GRATIN DE POMMES À LA DAUPHINOISE

[C] SERVES 4

900 (2 lb) old potatoes, peeled and very thinly sliced
salt and pepper
1 garlic clove, skinned and crushed
freshly grated nutmeg
225 ml (8 fl oz) single cream
15 g (½ oz) butter or margarine
50 g (2 oz) Gruyère cheese, grated

/ 1 / Arrange the potatoes in overlapping layers in a greased 1.1 litre (2 pint) ovenproof dish. Season each layer with salt and pepper.

/ 2 / Stir the garlic and nutmeg into the cream, pour over the potatoes and dot the surface with the butter or margarine.

/ 3 / Stand the dish on the wire rack and cook on combination at 200°C/MEDIUM LOW for 15 minutes. Sprinkle with the cheese and continue to cook for a further 15-20 minutes or until the potatoes are tender. Serve while still hot and bubbling.

Lentil, Mint and Yogurt Salad

Bean Goulash

OKRA WITH BABY ONIONS AND CORIANDER

SERVES 4 - 6

450 g (1 lb) okra
15 ml (1 tbsp) olive oil
15 ml (1 tbsp) coriander seeds, crushed
1 garlic clove, skinned and crushed
225 g (8 oz) baby onions, skinned and halved
60 ml (4 tbsp) vegetable stock
salt and pepper

/ 1 / Trim off the tops and tails of the okra. Put the oil, coriander and garlic in a serving bowl. Microwave on HIGH for 2 minutes.

/ 2 / Add the onions, okra and stock and mix well together. Cover and microwave on HIGH for 5-7 minutes or until the onions and okra are tender, stirring occasionally. Season to taste with salt and pepper and serve hot.

CHEESE POTATO PIE

C   SERVES 4

700 g (1½ lb) prepared mixed vegetables, such as peppers, courgettes, onions, leeks, carrots and mushrooms
75 g (3 oz) butter or margarine
700 g (1½ lb) potatoes
175 g (6 oz) Cheddar cheese, grated
300 ml (½ pint) milk
salt and pepper
25 g (1 oz) plain flour
mixed salad, to serve

/ 1 / Cut the mixed vegetables into bite-sized chunks and place in a large bowl with 50 g (2 oz) of the butter or margarine. Cover and microwave on HIGH for 10-15 minutes or until softened, stirring occasionally during the cooking time.

/ 2 / Meanwhile, peel the potatoes, cut into chunks and cook conventionally in boiling salted water until tender. Drain and mash with the remaining butter, half the grated cheese and a little of the milk. Season to taste with salt and pepper.

/ 3 / When the vegetables are softened, stir in the flour and microwave on HIGH for 1 minute. Stir in the remaining milk and microwave on HIGH for 3-5 minutes or until boiling and thickened. Pour into a large pie dish. Preheat the oven on convection at 250°C for 5 minutes.

/ 4 / Spoon the cheesy potato on top to cover completely, mark the surface with a fork and sprinkle with the remaining cheese. Stand the pie dish on a plate on the wire rack. Cook on combination at 200°C/MEDIUM LOW for 18-23 minutes or until hot. Serve with salad.

BEAN GOULASH

SERVES 4 - 6 AS A MAIN COURSE

100 g (4 oz) black-eye beans, soaked overnight
100 g (4 oz) aduki beans, soaked overnight
15 ml (1 tbsp) vegetable oil
1 garlic clove, skinned and crushed
1 yellow pepper, cored, seeded and roughly chopped
10 ml (2 tsp) caraway seeds, lightly crushed
15 ml (1 tbsp) paprika
397 g (14 oz) can chopped tomatoes
175 g (6 oz) mushrooms, thickly sliced
60 ml (4 tbsp) natural yogurt
salt and pepper
chopped fresh parsley, to garnish
brown rice, to serve

/ 1 / Drain the beans, rinse well under cold running water and put in a large bowl. Pour over enough boiling water to cover by about 2.5 cm (1 inch). Cover and microwave on HIGH for 25-30 minutes or until tender. Leave to stand, covered. Do not drain.

/ 2 / Meanwhile, put the oil, garlic, yellow pepper, caraway seeds and paprika in a large serving bowl. Cover and microwave on HIGH for 2 minutes, stirring once.

/ 3 / Drain the beans, rinse with boiling water and add to the pepper with the tomatoes and mushrooms. Re-cover and microwave on HIGH for 8-10 minutes, stirring once.

/ 4 / Stir in 30 ml (2 tbsp) of the yogurt and season to taste with salt and pepper. Drizzle the remaining yogurt on top and sprinkle with the parsley. Serve hot with brown rice.

OKRA WITH BABY ONIONS AND CORIANDER

Trim off the tops and tails of the okra, taking care not to cut the flesh.

CHEESE POTATO PIE
This can be made in advance, left to cool and stored in the refrigerator until required. If cooking straight from the refrigerator allow an extra 10 minutes cooking time. The mashed potatoes are cooked on the hob here, while the vegetables are cooked in the microwave. If you have not got a hob, or prefer to use the microwave, follow the method for Lentil, Aubergine and Potato Pie (see page 134).

BEAN GOULASH
This makes a good main course for a vegetarian meal. Pulses play an important part in a vegetarian diet. They are very versatile ingredients and can be used in savoury dishes of all kinds. Nutritionally they are an excellent food: they contain plenty of dietary fibre, protein, B group vitamins, iron and potassium. They have virtually no fat and are best eaten with a cereal such as bread, rice or pasta.

Desserts

A hot dessert makes a good end to a meal and, as you might expect, pies, flans, cakes and custards all cook beautifully in the combination oven in a fraction of the normal time. Many of the recipes in this chapter are so quick to cook that they can be prepared in advance and then put into the oven to cook while you eat the main course.

As well as cooking, the microwave is useful during the preparation of desserts. Chocolate can be melted and gelatine dissolved in a matter of seconds. Fresh fruit can be quickly and simply cooked in the microwave for an easy dessert on its own served with cream or yogurt, or to use as the base of desserts like crumbles, which can then be cooked on combination to achieve crisp toppings.

Fresh Fruit Tartlets

Orange and Blackcurrant Upside-down Pudding

PEACH AND WALNUT CRISPS

C   MAKES 6

50 g (2 oz) walnut halves
50 g (2 oz) plain wholemeal flour
50 g (2 oz) plain white flour
25 g (1 oz) semolina
25 g (1 oz) light soft brown sugar
75 g (3 oz) butter or margarine
1 egg yolk, beaten
60 ml (4 tbsp) apricot jam
30 ml (2 tbsp) almond-flavoured liqueur
15 ml (1 tbsp) lemon juice
3 ripe peaches, stoned and sliced
a few walnut halves, to decorate

/ 1 / Grease a large shallow ovenproof dish or plate. Put the 50 g (2 oz) walnuts in a blender or food processor and process until finely ground. Mix with the flours, semolina and sugar in a bowl.

/ 2 / Rub in the butter or margarine until the mixture resembles fine breadcrumbs. Add the egg yolk and 15 ml (1 tbsp) water and bind to form a firm dough. Knead together gently until the dough is smooth.

/ 3 / Roll out the dough on a lightly floured surface to a thickness of 0.5 cm (¼ inch). Using a 9 cm (3½ inch) fluted cutter, cut out 12 rounds. Cut 6 of the rounds in half. Chill in the refrigerator for 30 minutes.

/ 4 / Arrange half of the biscuits on the prepared dish or plate and prick with a fork. Stand on the wire rack and cook on combination at 200°C/MEDIUM LOW for 5-10 minutes or until firm to the touch and lightly browned. Transfer to a wire rack and leave to cool. Repeat with the remaining biscuits.

/ 5 / Mix the apricot jam, almond liqueur and lemon juice together and use to brush one side of each of the 6 round biscuits. Arrange the sliced peaches on top and brush with the glaze.

/ 6 / Brush the half-biscuits with the glaze and arrange 2 on top of each round, sticking them in between the sliced peaches at an angle to the base. Decorate each with a walnut half.

ORANGE AND BLACKCURRANT UPSIDE-DOWN PUDDING

C   SERVES 6

75 g (3 oz) butter or margarine
100 g (4 oz) light soft brown sugar
225 g (8 oz) fresh blackcurrants
2 eggs
50 g (2 oz) caster sugar
finely grated rind and juice of 1 large orange
175 g (6 oz) self-raising flour

/ 1 / Cream the butter or margarine and brown sugar together until pale and fluffy. Spread 60 ml (4 tbsp) of the creamed mixture in the base of a 20.5 cm (8 inch) dish and sprinkle the blackcurrants on top.

/ 2 / Add all the remaining ingredients to the remaining creamed mixture and beat until it is completely smooth.

/ 3 / Carefully pour the mixture on top of the blackcurrants and level the surface. Stand the dish on the wire rack and cook on combination at 200°C/MEDIUM LOW for 12-15 minutes or until the cake begins to shrink away from the sides of the dish and is firm to the touch.

/ 4 / Leave to stand for 5 minutes, then turn out so that the blackcurrants are on top of the cake. Serve warm.

─────── VARIATION ───────

The flavour of this upside-down pudding is particularly good when it is made with blackcurrants, but, if preferred, or if blackcurrants are not available, you can use other currants or berries instead.

ORANGE AND BLACKCURRANT UPSIDE-DOWN PUDDING
Dark purple blackcurrants make a stunning contrast to the pale sponge in this upside down pudding. If, when you turn the pudding out, it is not quite cooked on the bottom, simply return it to the oven (blackcurrant side up) and microwave on HIGH for 1-2 minutes. It is best served warm with lots of creamy Greek yogurt.

PEACH AND WALNUT CRISPS
Peach and Walnut Crisps are individual walnut shortbread biscuits topped with sliced peaches. When peaches are out of season, use grapes, strawberries or tangerines instead.

The biscuits for Peach and Walnut Crisps can be made in advance and stored in an airtight tin for up to 3 days. They can also be frozen, if wished.

GLAZED FRUIT FLAN

C   SERVES 6

PASTRY
175 g (6 oz) plain flour
salt
100 g (4 oz) butter or margarine
15 ml (1 tbsp) caster sugar
1 egg, beaten
FILLING
2 egg yolks
50 g (2 oz) caster sugar
30 ml (2 tbsp) plain flour
30 ml (2 tbsp) cornflour
225 ml (8 fl oz) milk
75 ml (5 tbsp) apricot jam
150 ml (¼ pint) natural yogurt
15 ml (1 tbsp) rum
prepared fresh fruit, to decorate

/ 1 / Make the pastry: mix the flour and salt together in a bowl. Add the butter or margarine and rub in until the mixture resembles fine breadcrumbs. Stir in the sugar and mix in the egg, using a round-bladed knife. Knead together lightly to form a firm smooth dough.

/ 2 / Turn the dough on to a lighty floured surface and roll out thinly. Use to line a 23 cm (9 inch) fluted flan dish. Prick the pastry all over with a fork and chill for 10 minutes while preheating the oven on convection at 250°C.

/ 3 / Line the pastry with a piece of greaseproof paper weighted down with baking beans, stand the dish on the wire rack and bake blind on combination at 200°C/MEDIUM LOW for 8-10 minutes or until just lightly set. Lift out the paper and beans and return the pastry to the oven for 3 minutes or until just firm.

/ 4 / Make the filling: put the egg yolks in a bowl with the sugar. Whisk until pale in colour. Mix the flour and cornflour with a little of the cold milk and beat until smooth. Stir into the egg mixture.

/ 5 / Put the remaining milk in a medium bowl and microwave on HIGH for 1-2 minutes or until hot but not boiling. Gradually pour on to the egg mixture, stirring continuously. Microwave on HIGH for 2-3 minutes or until thickened, stirring frequently. Cover closely with damp greaseproof paper and cool.

/ 6 / Put the apricot jam and 30 ml (2 tbsp) water in a small bowl and microwave on HIGH for 1-1½ minutes or until boiling, stirring occasionally. Sieve and leave to cool slightly.

/ 7 / Beat the yogurt and rum into the custard and spoon into the cooled flan case. Arrange the fruit on top and brush with the apricot glaze. Leave to set.

— VARIATION —

Use double cream in place of yogurt, and a liqueur of your choice. Try and match the liqueur with the fruit e.g. cherries with Kirsch, oranges or tangerines with Cointreau, apricots with Amaretto and bananas with Tia Maria (dip the banana slices in lemon juice to prevent discoloration). You could also use fruit brandies such as peach brandy with peaches or apricot brandy with apricots.

APPLE AND BLACKCURRANT CRUMBLE

SERVES 3 - 4

75 g (3 oz) butter or margarine
75 g (3 oz) plain wholemeal flour
25 g (1 oz) rolled oats
25 g (1 oz) sunflower seeds (optional)
15 g (½ oz) desiccated coconut
25 g (1 oz) chopped mixed nuts (optional)
25 g (1 oz) light soft brown sugar
5 ml (1 tsp) ground cinnamon (optional)
2.5 ml (½ tsp) ground mixed spice (optional)
225 g (8 oz) eating apples
225 g (8 oz) blackcurrants
yogurt, cream or custard, to serve

/ 1 / Put the butter or margarine and flour into a bowl and rub in until the mixture resembles fine breadcrumbs. Stir in the dry ingredients and mix thoroughly together.

/ 2 / Peel, quarter, core and slice the apples. Put in a 1.1 litre (2 pint) deep ovenproof dish with the blackcurrants. Spoon the crumble mixture evenly over the fruit and press down lightly. Microwave on HIGH for 11-12 minutes or until the fruit is tender. Serve hot or cold with yogurt, cream or custard.

GLAZED FRUIT FLAN
Choose a colourful mixture of fresh fruit such as strawberries, oranges and grapes to arrange in this flan.

APPLE AND BLACKCURRANT CRUMBLE

Peel, quarter, core and slice the eating apples.

Apple and Blackcurrant Crumble has a rich, nutty texture and is far healthier than the conventional crumble as it contains little added sugar but gets most of its sweetness from coconut, nuts and sunflower seeds.

Apple and Blackcurrant Crumble

FRESH FRUIT TARTLETS

Mix 175 g (6 oz) of the plain flour, the wholemeal flour, 25 g (1 oz) of the sugar, the hazelnuts and salt in a bowl. Rub in the fat until the mixture resembles fine breadcrumbs. Add 1 egg and enough water to make a dough.

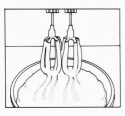

To make the filling: put the remaining eggs and sugar in a large bowl and whisk until pale and creamy and the mixture leaves a trail when the whisk is lifted. Sift in the remaining flour and the cornflour, then beat well. Put the milk in a bowl and microwave on HIGH for 2-2½ minutes until just boiling. Gradually pour on the egg mixture, stirring all the time. Add the vanilla flavouring.

The pastry cases for the Fresh Fruit Tartlets are cooked on microwave only for speed, but they could also be cooked on combination. Roll out the pastry thinly and use to line the base and sides of the glass dishes – don't invert. Line with greaseproof paper and fill with non-metallic baking beans. Chill. Preheat the oven on convection at 250°C for 10 minutes. Bake the tartlets on combination at 200°C/MEDIUM LOW for 8-10 minutes or until set. Remove the beans and paper and cook for a further 3 minutes or until the pastry is light brown.

Picture opposite:
Walnut and Honey Tart

FRESH FRUIT TARTLETS

MAKES 8

200 g (7 oz) plain white flour
25 g (1 oz) plain wholemeal flour
75 g (3 oz) caster sugar
25 g (1 oz) hazelnuts, toasted and ground
pinch of salt
50 g (2 oz) butter or margarine
3 eggs
25 g (1 oz) cornflour
300 ml (½ pint) milk
a few drops of vanilla flavouring
300 ml (½ pint) double cream
prepared fresh fruit, such as figs, strawberries, raspberries, cherries, kiwi fruit, grapes
30 ml (2 tbsp) apricot conserve
5 ml (1 tsp) lemon juice

/ 1 / Mix 175 g (6 oz) of the plain flour, the wholemeal flour, 25 g (1 oz) of the sugar, the hazelnuts and salt in a bowl. Rub in the butter or margarine until the mixture resembles fine breadcrumbs. Add 1 egg and enough water to make a dough.

/ 2 / Turn on to a lightly floured surface and knead for a few seconds until smooth. Wrap in greaseproof paper and chill in the refrigerator for 20-30 minutes until firm.

/ 3 / Cut the pastry in half, then roll out one half very thinly on a lightly floured surface. Use to cover the base and sides of 4 inverted 10 cm (4 inch) shallow glass flan dishes.

/ 4 / Prick all over with a fork and microwave on HIGH, pastry side uppermost, for 2½-3 minutes or until the pastry is firm to the touch. Remove the pastry cases from the dishes and invert on to a wire rack to cool. Repeat with the remaining pastry to make 8 pastry cases.

/ 5 / Make the filling: put the remaining eggs and sugar in a large bowl and whisk until pale and creamy and the mixture leaves a trail when the whisk is lifted. Sift in the remaining flour and the cornflour, then beat well.

/ 6 / Put the milk in a bowl and microwave on HIGH for 2-2½ minutes until just boiling. Gradually pour on the egg mixture, stirring all the time. Add the vanilla flavouring.

/ 7 / Microwave on HIGH for 1½-2 minutes until very thick, stirring frequently. Cover and leave to cool.

/ 8 / When cold, whip the cream until it just holds its shape, then fold into the custard. Fill the pastry cases with the mixture and decorate with the prepared fruit.

/ 9 / Put the apricot conserve and lemon juice in a small bowl and microwave on HIGH for 30 seconds until melted. Carefully brush over the fruit to glaze. Serve as soon as possible.

WALNUT AND HONEY TART

C	SERVES 6

175 g (6 oz) plain wholemeal flour
pinch of salt
75 g (3 oz) butter
finely grated rind and juice of 1 orange
75 ml (5 tbsp) clear honey
100 g (4 oz) fresh wholemeal breadcrumbs
60 ml (4 tbsp) dark soft brown sugar
4 eggs
100 g (4 oz) walnut pieces, roughly chopped
clotted or double cream, to serve

/ 1 / Make the pastry: put the flour and salt in a bowl and rub in the butter until the mixture resembles fine breadcrumbs. Stir in the orange rind and enough orange juice to bind the mixture together. Preheat the oven on convection at 250°C for 5 minutes.

/ 2 / Roll out the pastry on a lightly floured surface and use to line a 20.5 cm (8 inch) fluted flan dish. Stand on the wire rack and bake blind on combination at 200°C/MEDIUM LOW for 8 minutes or until lightly set. Remove the baking beans and paper and cook for a further 2 minutes at 200°C/MEDIUM LOW.

/ 3 / Mix the honey, breadcrumbs and the sugar together. Gradually beat in the eggs, 1 at a time, and any remaining orange juice.

/ 4 / Sprinkle the walnuts in the bottom of the pastry case and pour over the filling. Stand on the wire rack and cook on combination at 200°C/MEDIUM LOW for 10-12 minutes or until set. Cover with greaseproof paper if it browns too quickly. Serve warm or cold with cream.

CHERRY TART

C

SERVES 8

225 g (8 oz) plain white flour
pinch of salt
25 g (1 oz) cornflour
100 g (4 oz), plus 10 ml (2 tsp) icing sugar
100 g (4 oz) butter
1 egg yolk
450 g (1 lb) cherries, stoned
2 eggs
75 g (3 oz) ground almonds
a few drops of almond essence

/ 1 / Sift the flour, salt, cornflour and the 10 ml (2 tsp) icing sugar into a bowl, then rub in the butter until the mixture resembles fine breadcrumbs. Add the egg yolk and 30 ml (2 tbsp) cold water and stir to bind the mixture together. Preheat the oven on convection at 250°C for 5 minutes.

/ 2 / Knead lightly on a lightly floured surface; roll out. Use to line a 23 cm (9 inch) fluted flan dish. Stand on the wire rack and bake blind on combination at 200°C for 8 minutes or until lightly set. Remove the baking beans and paper and cook for a further 2 minutes at 200°C/MEDIUM LOW.

/ 3 / Arrange the cherries in the flan case. Mix 100 g (4 oz) icing sugar, eggs, almonds and essence, and pour over the cherries.

/ 4 / Stand on the wire rack and cook on combination at 200°C/MEDIUM LOW for 10-12 minutes or until the top is firm and golden. Serve hot or cold.

CHERRY TART

Ready ground almonds are the easiest to use for this recipe; you can buy them in small 50 g (2 oz) packets or in larger quantities. Beware of buying too many at once as they tend to loose their flavour once the pack is opened. However, the best flavour comes from nuts that you have ground freshly yourself. Buy them either in the shell or shelled but unblanched. Remove the shells with nut crackers, then soak the kernels in boiling water until the skins will slip off easily. Grind the almonds in a blender or food processor (beware of over-grinding the almonds and turning them to a paste if you use a food processor), or use a nut mill.

KIWI UPSIDE-DOWN PUDDING

SERVES 2

25 g (1 oz) butter or margarine
25 g (1 oz) light soft brown sugar
25 g (1 oz) self-raising wholemeal flour
1.25 ml (¼ tsp) ground mixed spice
1 egg, beaten
2 kiwi fruit, peeled
15 ml (1 tbsp) clear honey
15 ml (1 tbsp) lemon juice

/ 1 / Line the base of a 7.5×11 cm (3×4½ inch) ovenproof dish with greaseproof paper.

Cherry Tart

/ 2 / Put the butter or margarine in a bowl and microwave on HIGH for 10-15 seconds or until just soft enough to beat. Add the sugar, flour, mixed spice and the egg and beat well together, using a wooden spoon, until the mixture is well blended and slightly glossy.

/ 3 / Cut 1 of the kiwi fruit into thin slices and arrange in the base of the prepared dish.

/ 4 / Chop the remaining kiwi fruit and stir into the sponge mixture. Beat well together. Spoon the mixture on top of the kiwi slices in the ovenproof dish and cover with a double thickness of absorbent kitchen paper.

/ 5 / Microwave on MEDIUM for 4-4½ minutes or until slightly shrunk away from the sides of the dish, but the surface still looks slightly moist. Leave to stand covered, for 5 minutes, then turn out on to a serving plate.

/ 6 / Meanwhile, put the honey and lemon juice in a ramekin dish or cup. Microwave on HIGH for 15-30 seconds or until warmed through. Spoon the honey mixture over the pudding and serve warm.

——————— VARIATION ———————

You can use other fruit for this pretty pudding. Try sliced peaches or bananas for a change.

KIWI UPSIDE-DOWN PUDDING
Kiwi fruit, also known as Chinese gooseberries originated in China, but are now grown in New Zealand and in other warm countries. Peel off the thin, hairy brown skin and the entire fruit can be eaten. It is highly decorative – a fresh light green colour with a cluster of dark seeds forming a circle round the soft core – and the flavour is very refreshing. Kiwi fruit have a very high vitamin C content.

Use a small plastic dish from the microwave range to make Kiwi Upside-down Pudding. The recipe makes just enough to serve 2.

Almond Eve's Pudding

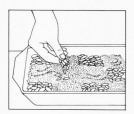

Place the flaked almonds on top of the pudding in 6 squares to form a chequerboard effect.

When the pudding is cooked, dredge icing sugar between the flaked nut squares.

ALMOND EVE'S PUDDING

[C] SERVES 4

| 700 g (1½ lb) cooking apples |
| 5 ml (1 tsp) ground cinnamon |
| 175 g (6 oz) demerara sugar |
| 100 g (4 oz) butter, softened |
| 2 eggs, beaten |
| 100 g (4 oz) self-raising flour |
| 25 g (1 oz) ground almonds |
| 2.5 ml (½ tsp) almond flavouring |
| 30 ml (2 tbsp) milk |
| 25 g (1 oz) flaked almonds |
| icing sugar, to dredge |
| single cream, to serve |

/ 1 / Peel, quarter and core the cooking apples, then slice them thickly into a 1.4 litre (2½ pint) ovenproof dish. Combine the cinnamon with 50 g (2 oz) of the demerara sugar and scatter over the apples. Cover tightly with cling film while preparing the topping.

/ 2 / Beat the butter and remaining sugar, creaming until fluffy. Gradually beat in eggs.

/ 3 / Fold in the flour, ground almonds, flavouring and milk. Remove the cling film and spread the mixture over the cooking apples.

/ 4 / Place the flaked almonds on top in 6 squares to form a chequerboard effect. Preheat the oven on convection at 250°C for 10 minutes. Stand the dish on the wire rack and cook on combination at 200°C/MEDIUM LOW for 12-15 minutes or until the sponge begins to shrink away from the sides and is risen and golden brown.

/ 5 / Dredge icing sugar between the flaked nut squares. Serve with cream.

— VARIATION —

If liked, you can add 50 g (2 oz) sultanas, currants or raisins to the apple mixture in the base of this delicious family pudding. Grated orange or lemon zest added to the sponge topping also adds extra flavour – and goes particularly well with the cinnamon-flavoured apples.

CHRISTMAS PUDDING

SERVES 8

450 g (1 lb) mixed dried fruit
175 g (6 oz) stoned prunes
450 ml (¾ pint) orange juice
100 g (4 oz) plain flour
1.25 ml (¼ tsp) freshly grated nutmeg
1.25 ml (¼ tsp) ground cinnamon
2.5 ml (½ tsp) salt
75 g (3 oz) fresh breadcrumbs
100 g (4 oz) shredded suet
100 g (4 oz) dark soft brown sugar
25 g (1 oz) blanched almonds, chopped
finely grated rind of ½ lemon
30 ml (2 tbsp) sherry
2 eggs, beaten

/ 1 / Line the base of a 1.3 litre (2½ pint) pudding basin with a circle of greaseproof paper.

/ 2 / Put the dried fruit, prunes and orange juice in a large bowl and mix well together. Cover and microwave on HIGH for 20 minutes until the fruit is plump and the liquid absorbed. Leave to cool.

/ 3 / Add the remaining ingredients to the fruit mixture and mix well together. Spoon the mixture into the prepared basin, pushing down well with the back of a spoon.

/ 4 / Cover the basin with a plate and microwave on MEDIUM for 25-30 minutes until the top is only slightly moist.

/ 5 / Leave to stand, covered, for 5 minutes before turning out the cooked pudding on to a warmed serving plate.

To reheat either home-made or shop-bought Christmas puddings

Christmas puddings containing a large quantity of alcohol or Christmas puddings that have previously been flambéed, are unsuitable for reheating in a microwave because of the risk of them catching fire.

/ 1 / Remove all the wrappings and basin from the pudding. Put the pudding on an ovenproof serving plate, cut into the required number of portions and pull apart so that there is a space in the centre.

/ 2 / Place a small tumbler of water in the centre. This introduces steam and helps to keep the pudding moist. Cover the plate with a large upturned bowl.

/ 3 / Microwave on HIGH for 2-3 minutes, depending on the size of the pudding, or until the portions are hot.

/ 4 / Remove the cover and glass and reshape the pudding with the hands. Decorate with a sprig of holly and serve.

/ 5 / To reheat an individual portion of Christmas pudding, put on a plate and microwave, uncovered, for 1-1½ minutes until hot.

SPICED BREAD AND BUTTER PUDDING

SERVES 4

225 g (8 oz) fruity malt loaf
25 g (1 oz) butter, softened
30 ml (2 tbsp) soft brown sugar
75 g (3 oz) sultanas
5 ml (1 tsp) ground cinnamon
finely grated rind of 1 orange
3 eggs
568 ml (1 pint) milk
caster sugar, for dredging

/ 1 / Thoroughly grease a shallow 1.3 litre (2¼ pint) ovenproof dish. Thinly slice the fruit loaf, then spread each slice with a little of the butter. Mix together the brown sugar, sultanas, cinnamon and orange rind.

/ 2 / Arrange a few slices of the fruit loaf in the prepared dish. Sprinkle over the sugar mixture, then add another layer of fruit loaf.

/ 3 / Whisk together the eggs and milk, pour over the pudding and dot the surface with the remaining butter.

/ 4 / Stand the dish on the wire rack and cook on combination at 200°C/MEDIUM LOW for 15-22 minutes or until just firm to the touch in the middle and golden brown. Leave to stand for 5 minutes, then sprinkle with caster sugar before serving warm.

CHRISTMAS PUDDING
Because the traditional Christmas pudding recipe contains a high proportion of sugar, dried fruits, fat and alcohol, all of which attract microwave energy and quickly reach a high temperature, it means great care must be taken not to overcook and possibly burn the pudding. As this may be potentially dangerous, Christmas pudding should be watched during cooking. However, a Christmas pudding can be cooked in only 45 minutes in the microwave instead of 6-8 hours by conventional cooking, and you do not need a saucepan of boiling water that has to be continually replenished. If, therefore, you are adapting your favourite Christmas pudding recipe, only add 30 ml (2 tbsp) of the alcohol suggested and replace the remaining liquid with milk or orange juice. Additional liquid should also be added to keep the pudding moist: allow an extra 15 ml (1 tbsp) milk for each egg added. Because a pudding cooked in the microwave does not have long, slow cooking, it will not keep like the traditional cooked pudding and should be eaten soon after making. Store for 2-3 weeks in a cool place.

SPICED BREAD AND BUTTER PUDDING
Instead of ordinary bread, this version of bread and butter pudding uses a fruity malt loaf, available in supermarkets and corner shops. Left-over sliced hot cross buns or other fruit breads could be used instead of malt loaf.

LAYERED FRUIT TERRINE

SERVES 6 - 8

100 g (4 oz) self-raising flour
100 g (4 oz) softened butter or soft tub margarine
100 g (4 oz) light soft brown sugar
2 eggs
30 ml (2 tbsp) milk
275 g (10 oz) cream cheese
50 g (2 oz) caster sugar
50 g (2 oz) ground almonds
a few drops of almond essence
300 ml (½ pint) double cream
15 ml (1 tbsp) gelatine
30 ml (2 tbsp) orange juice
3 kiwi fruit
225 g (8 oz) seedless white grapes, halved
225 g (8 oz) strawberries
15 ml (1 tbsp) icing sugar
15 ml (1 tbsp) orange-flavoured liqueur (optional)

/ 1 / Grease a 1.7 litre (3 pint) loaf dish and line the base with greaseproof paper.

/ 2 / Put the flour, butter or margarine, brown sugar, eggs and milk in a bowl and beat until smooth. Pour into the prepared loaf dish. Stand on a roasting rack and microwave on HIGH for 4-5 minutes or until firm to the touch. Turn out and leave to cool on a wire rack.

/ 3 / Meanwhile, beat the cheese, caster sugar and ground almonds together. Flavour with almond essence. Whip the cream until it just holds its shape, then carefully fold it into the cheese mixture.

/ 4 / When the sponge is cold, cut in half horizontally and return half of the sponge to the bottom of the loaf dish.

/ 5 / Put the gelatine and orange juice in a small bowl and microwave on HIGH for 30 seconds-1 minute until dissolved; do not boil.

/ 6 / Stir into the cheese mixture. Spread one-third of the cheese mixture on top of the sponge lining the loaf dish. Peel and slice the kiwi fruit and arrange on top. Top with half of the remaining cheese mixture and then a layer of grapes. Cover the grapes with the remaining cheese mixture.

/ 7 / Level the surface, then press the remaining piece of sponge on top. Chill in the refrigerator for 3-4 hours before serving.

/ 8 / To make the sauce, purée the strawberries in a blender or food processor with the icing sugar and liqueur, if using. Serve the terrine sliced, with the strawberry sauce.

ROLY-POLY PUDDINGS

SERVES 4

175 g (6 oz) self-raising flour
pinch of salt
75 g (3 oz) shredded suet
milk, for brushing
custard, to serve

/ 1 / Mix the flour, salt and suet together in a bowl. Using a round-bladed knife, stir in enough water to give a light, elastic dough. Knead very lightly until smooth.

/ 2 / Roll out the dough to an oblong about 23×28 cm (9×11 inches) and use as required. (See variations below.) Brush the edges with milk and roll up, starting from the short end.

/ 3 / Make a 5 cm (2 inch) pleat across a large sheet of greaseproof paper. Wrap the roll loosely in the paper, allowing room for expansion. Pleat the open edges tightly together. Twist the ends to seal.

/ 4 / Stand the parcel on a roasting rack and microwave on HIGH for 4-5 minutes or until firm to the touch. Serve sliced, with custard.

— VARIATIONS —

JAM ROLY-POLY
Spread the pastry with 60-90 ml (4-6 tbsp) jam.

SYRUP ROLY-POLY
Spread the pastry with 60 ml (4 tbsp) golden syrup mixed with 30-45 ml (2-3 tbsp) fresh white breadcrumbs.

LEMON ROLY-POLY
Add the finely grated rind of 1 lemon to the dough. Roll out and spread with 60-90 ml (4-6 tbsp) lemon curd.

MINCEMEAT ROLY-POLY
Add the finely grated rind of 1 orange to the dough. Roll out and spread with 60-90 ml (4-6 tbsp) mincemeat.

Butterscotch Cream Pie

BUTTERSCOTCH CREAM PIE

Ⓒ   SERVES 6

150 g (5 oz) plain flour	
1.25 ml (¼ tsp) salt	
165 g (5½ oz) butter or block margarine	
10 ml (2 tsp) caster sugar	
5 egg yolks and 1 egg white	
150 ml (¼ pint) milk	
200 ml (7 fl oz) evaporated milk	
50 g (2 oz) dark soft brown sugar	
15 ml (1 tbsp) cornflour	
300 ml (½ pint) double cream	

/ 1 / Put the flour in a bowl with half the salt. Add 100 g (4 oz) of the butter or margarine, cut into pieces, and rub in with the fingertips until the mixture resembles fine breadcrumbs.

If you don't like piping cream, simply spread the cream on top of the pie and mark into swirls with a fork. If liked, decorate with chocolate: using a potato peeler, peel off slices of chocolate from a block to make curls, then sprinkle them on top of the pie.

/ 2 / Stir in the sugar and 1 egg yolk and draw the dough together with your hand to form a smooth ball. Add a few drops of cold water if the dough is too dry.

/ 3 / Press the dough gently into a 20.5 cm (8 inch) fluted flan dish. Leave to chill in the refrigerator for 30 minutes. Preheat the oven on convection at 250°C for 10 minutes.

/ 4 / Prick the base of the pastry case, line with greaseproof paper and fill with non-metallic beans, then bake blind on combination at 200°C/MEDIUM LOW for 8-10 minutes or until lightly set. Remove the paper and beans, brush the pastry with egg white, then return to the oven for a further 3 minutes until crisp and lightly coloured.

/ 5 / Meanwhile, make the filling. Put the milk and evaporated milk in a medium bowl and microwave on HIGH for 2-3 minutes or until boiling. Put the brown sugar, cornflour, remaining butter, egg yolks and salt in a medium bowl and beat together. Pour over the hot milk, whisk well to blend and return to the warm bowl.

/ 6 / Microwave on HIGH for 3-4 minutes, whisking frequently until the custard is thick.

/ 7 / Cool slightly, then pour into the baked pastry case. Cover the surface of the butterscotch cream closely with cling film (to prevent a skin forming) and leave for about 1 hour until completely cold.

/ 8 / To serve, whip the cream until stiff, then pipe on top of the pie. Chill the pie until ready to serve.

APPLE AND PEAR MERINGUE

C   S E R V E S   4

700 g (1½ lb) cooking apples
finely grated rind and juice of 1 small lemon
50 g (2 oz) light soft brown sugar
2 ripe pears
2 egg whites
100 g (4 oz) caster sugar

/ 1 / Grease a 1.7 litre (3 pint) ovenproof dish. Peel, quarter, core and slice the apples very thinly. Place in the dish with the grated lemon rind and juice. Cover and microwave on HIGH for 4-6 minutes or until the apples are very soft.

/ 2 / Mash the apples with a fork and stir in the brown sugar. Peel, quarter and core the pears, cut into chunks and stir into the apple mixture. Allow the mixture to cool slightly while making the meringue.

/ 3 / Whisk the egg whites until stiff but not dry. Add 10 ml (2 tsp) of the caster sugar and whisk again for 1 minute. Carefully fold in the remaining sugar. Spoon on to the apple and pear mixture, covering completely and swirling the top to form soft peaks.

/ 4 / Stand the dish on the wire rack and cook on combination at 200°C/MEDIUM LOW for 4-8 minutes or until lightly set and golden brown. Serve immediately.

SPONGE PUDDING

S E R V E S   3 - 4

50 g (2 oz) soft tub margarine
50 g (2 oz) caster sugar
1 egg, beaten
a few drops of vanilla flavouring
100 g (4 oz) self-raising flour
45-60 ml (3-4 tbsp) milk

/ 1 / Beat the margarine, sugar, egg, vanilla flavouring and flour until smooth. Gradually stir in enough milk to give the mixture a soft dropping consistency.

/ 2 / Spoon into a greased 600 ml (1 pint) pudding basin and level the surface. Microwave on HIGH for 5-7 minutes until the top of the sponge is only slightly moist and a skewer inserted in the centre comes out clean.

/ 3 / Leave to stand for 5 minutes before turning out on to a warmed serving dish. Serve with custard.

——— V A R I A T I O N S ———

ESSEX PUDDING
Spread jam over the sides and base of the greased pudding basin.

APRICOT SPONGE PUDDING
Drain a 411 g (14½ oz) can of apricot halves and arrange them in the base of the greased pudding basin.

SYRUP SPONGE PUDDING
Put 30 ml (2 tbsp) golden syrup into the bottom of the basin before adding the mixture. Flavour the mixture with the grated rind of a lemon.

CHOCOLATE SPONGE PUDDING
Blend 60 ml (4 tbsp) cocoa powder to a smooth cream with 15 ml (1 tbsp) hot water and add to the beaten ingredients.

JAMAICA PUDDING
Add 50-100 g (2-4 oz) chopped stem ginger with the milk.

LEMON OR ORANGE SPONGE PUDDING
Add the grated rind of 1 orange or lemon when beating the ingredients.

SPONGE PUDDING
Sponge puddings are wonderful cooked in a microwave. They are beautifully light and fluffy and quick to make too.

APPLE AND PEAR MERINGUE
Cooking meringue on combination can be a tricky business. If your oven has a fixed, HIGH microwave output (2 currently on the market are fixed at 350 watts), then the meringue will cook quickly by microwave before it has a chance to be browned by the convected heat. Meringue cooked by microwave is not successful as it puffs up like magic and then collapses into a pancake. Here, the meringue is cooked on combination for a short time, just until it is set and lightly tinged with brown, rather like a grilled meringue. Do not overcook or it will be flat! If you prefer a crisp meringue that is cooked right through, or if your oven has a fixed HIGH microwave output, it's best to cook on convection at 250°C for 10 minutes or until brown and crisp.

You can use leftover egg white to make the meringue. Egg whites will keep for 3-4 days in the refrigerator. Cover tightly to prevent them picking up strong flavours from the refrigerator.

LAYERED FRUIT PUDDING

SERVES 6

PASTRY
100 g (4 oz) self-raising white flour
100 g (4 oz) self-raising wholemeal flour
15 ml (1 tbsp) light muscovado sugar
100 g (4 oz) vegetable suet
finely grated rind and juice of ½ lemon

FILLING
225 g (8 oz) eating apples
finely grated rind and juice of 1 lemon
225 g (8 oz) ripe plums
30-60 ml (2-4 tbsp) light muscovado sugar
225 g (8 oz) raspberries or blackberries

/ 1 / Grease a 1.4 litre (2½ pint) pudding basin or bowl and line the base with a circle of greaseproof paper.

/ 2 / Make the pastry: put the flours, sugar, suet and lemon rind in a bowl, then mix with the lemon juice and about 70 ml (6 tbsp) water to make a soft, but not sticky, dough.

/ 3 / Turn the dough out on to a lightly floured surface and shape into a cylinder, wider at one end than the other. Cut into 4 pieces.

/ 4 / Shape the smallest piece of pastry into a round, large enough to fit the bottom of the pudding basin. Press the pastry into the bottom of the basin.

/ 5 / Peel the apples, if liked, and remove the core. Cut into thin slices, then put in the bowl on top of the pastry. Sprinkle with the lemon rind and juice.

/ 6 / Shape the next smallest piece of pastry into a round and place on top of the apples. Halve the plums and remove the stones and place on top of the pastry. Sprinkle with light muscovado sugar to taste.

/ 7 / Shape a third piece of pastry into a round and place on top of the plums. Spoon the raspberries or blackberries on top. Shape the remaining pastry into a round large enough to cover the raspberries and place on top making sure that the pastry fits right to the edges of the pudding basin.

/ 8 / Push the pastry down with your hand to compress the layers slightly and allow space for the pudding to rise during cooking.

/ 9 / Cover and microwave on HIGH for 14-15 minutes or until the top layer of pastry feels firm to the touch. Leave to stand, covered, for 5 minutes, then turn out the pudding and serve immediately.

STRAWBERRY FOOL

SERVES 6

30-40 ml (2-3 tbsp) sugar
20 ml (4 tsp) cornflour
300 ml (½ pint) milk
700 g (1½ lb) strawberries, hulled
300 ml (½ pint) double cream

/ 1 / Blend 15 ml (1 tbsp) of the sugar and the cornflour with a little of the milk in a measuring jug or medium bowl. Stir in the remainder of the milk.

/ 2 / Microwave on HIGH for 3-4 minutes or until the sauce has thickened, stirring every minute. Cover the surface of the sauce closely with cling film and leave until cold.

/ 3 / Reserve a few whole strawberries for decoration. Push the remaining strawberries through a nylon sieve to form a purée or put in a blender or food processor and liquidise until smooth, then push through a nylon sieve to remove the pips.

/ 4 / Stir the cold sauce into the strawberry purée. Mix well and sweeten to taste with the remaining sugar.

/ 5 / Lightly whip the cream and fold into the strawberry mixture. Turn into 6 individual dishes and chill for 1-2 hours.

/ 6 / Thinly slice the reserved strawberries and arrange on top of each portion, to decorate.

LAYERED FRUIT PUDDING
Suet puddings cook very successfully in the microwave because microwave cooking is similar to steaming. Vegetable suet is made from palm oil and can be substituted in any recipe calling for suet. The best covering for suet puddings in the microwave is a plate.

Suet pastry may be used for both sweet and savoury basin puddings. It is quick and easy to make, and should be light and spongy in texture – the correct mixing and quick light handling will achieve this. For a lighter texture, replace 50 g (2 oz) of the flour with 50 g (2 oz) fresh breadcrumbs.

STRAWBERRY FOOL
A true summer fruit, the majority of strawberries available during the summer season are British grown. As with most berries, check the base of the punnet for staining as this will indicate squashed fruit. Strawberries are probably most famous for being eaten raw with cream but are also delicious puréed and chilled. Be sure to buy plump glossy berries with their green hulls still attached. Only wash them just before hulling.

Strawberry Fool

Chocolate Creams

CHOCOLATE CREAMS

SERVES 8

15 ml (1 tbsp) gelatine
30 ml (2 tbsp) rum or strong coffee
100 g (4 oz) plain dessert chocolate
3 eggs, separated
pinch of salt
410 g (14½ oz) can evaporated milk
100 g (4 oz) sugar
300 ml (½ pint) double cream
chocolate curls or rice paper flowers, to decorate

/ 1 / Sprinkle the gelatine over the rum or coffee in a small bowl and leave to soften.

/ 2 / Break the chocolate into a large bowl and microwave on HIGH for 2 minutes or until the chocolate melts. Beat in the gelatine with the rum or coffee, egg yolks, salt, evaporated milk and 50 g (2 oz) of the sugar.

/ 3 / Microwave on MEDIUM for 6 minutes or until the mixture is thick and smooth, stirring several times. Leave to stand at room temperature until cool (do not refrigerate).

/ 4 / Lightly whip the cream and fold half into the chocolate mixture.

/ 5 / Whisk the eggs whites until stiff and fold in the remaining sugar. Gently fold into the chocolate cream.

/ 6 / Spoon into individual serving glasses and chill. Pipe the remaining cream on top of the chocolate creams. Decorate with chocolate curls or rice paper flowers and serve.

BAKED EGG CUSTARDS WITH PASSION FRUIT

SERVES 4

450 ml (¾ pint) milk
2 eggs
30 ml (2 tbsp) caster sugar
4 passion fruit

/ 1 / Put the milk in a medium bowl. Microwave on HIGH for 2-3 minutes or until hot.

/ 2 / Beat together the eggs and sugar, strain in the milk, then return to the medium bowl. Pour into 4 ramekin dishes and microwave on MEDIUM for 4-5 minutes or until just set.

/ 3 / Cut the passion fruit in half, scoop out the seeds and spoon over the egg custard. Serve the custards immediately.

CHOCOLATE AND PEAR CUSTARDS

SERVES 4

2 medium ripe pears
100 g (4 oz) dark chocolate or plain carob bar
5 ml (1 tsp) cocoa or carob powder
15 ml (1 tbsp) dark muscovado sugar
300 ml (½ pint) milk or a mixture of milk and single cream
1 egg
1 egg yolk
TO SERVE
2 medium ripe pears
5 ml (1 tsp) icing sugar
5 ml (1 tsp) cocoa or carob powder

/ 1 / Peel and core the pears, chop roughly and divide between 4 ramekin dishes. Break the chocolate or carob into squares and put 1 square into each dish on top of the pear.

/ 2 / Put the remaining chocolate or carob, cocoa or carob powder, sugar and the milk in a jug or small bowl and microwave on HIGH for 2-3 minutes or until the chocolate or carob has melted, stirring occasionally. Stir in the egg, and egg yolk and beat thoroughly together. Carefully pour the mixture on top of the pears. Arrange the ramekins in a circle in the cooker and microwave on LOW for just 15 minutes or until the custards are just set. Cool, then chill for at least 2 hours before serving.

/ 3 / To serve: peel the remaining pears and cut into neat slices. Arrange the custards on individual plates with the sliced pears. Dust the top of each custard with the icing sugar and the pears with cocoa or carob powder. Serve immediately. These chilled custards are best eaten on the day of making.

CHOCOLATE CREAMS

When whisking the egg whites, start whisking with a slow circular movement and gradually work faster, lifting the eggs high out of the bowl to help incorporate as much air as possible. Whisk until the egg whites stand in stiff peaks when the whisk is lifted from the eggs.

Fold in the egg whites using a metal spoon or a plastic spatula. Use a continuous cutting and lifting movement, scooping right down to the bottom of the bowl. Scoop one way, turning the bowl the other. Stop folding as soon as the mixture is blended. Too much folding and the egg white may start to liquify.

BAKED EGG CUSTARD WITH PASSION FRUIT
Passion fruit are tropical vine fruit that look like large wrinkled plums. The inedible skin is deeply wrinkled when ripe. The yellow flesh is sweet and juicy and pitted with small edible black seeds.

If you have any vanilla sugar, this can be used instead of plain caster sugar. To make vanilla sugar: store a vanilla pod in a jar of caster sugar and leave to flavour the sugar for about 3 weeks. It can be left in the jar while the sugar is in use.

PEARS WITH ALMOND CUSTARD

C

S E R V E S   6

6 Comice pears
C U S T A R D
450 ml (¾ pint) milk
3 eggs
30 ml (2 tbsp) caster sugar
a few drops of almond essence
25 g (1 oz) ground almonds

/ 1 / Core the pears, cutting from the base, so keeping the stalks intact. Place the pears in a large shallow ovenproof dish and microwave on HIGH for 10-12 minutes until tender.

/ 2 / Meanwhile, warm the milk gently but do not boil. Whisk together the eggs, caster sugar and almond essence. Pour on the warm milk, then strain the mixture into a heavy-based saucepan. Stir over a gentle heat until the sauce lightly coats the back of a wooden spoon. Do not boil. Stir in the almonds.

/ 3 / Serve the pears with a little of the custard poured over, and hand the remainder of the custard separately.

BAKED CLEMENTINE CUSTARDS

S E R V E S   2

2 clementines or satsumas
25 ml (1½ tbsp) caster sugar
15 ml (1 tbsp) orange-flavoured liqueur (optional)
200 ml (7 fl oz) milk
1 egg and 1 egg yolk

/ 1 / Finely shred the rind of 1 of the clementines or satsumas. Put half into a heatproof jug with 10 ml (½ tbsp) of the sugar and 75 ml (3 fl oz) water.

/ 2 / Microwave on HIGH for 2 minutes or until boiling, then continue to boil on HIGH for 2 minutes. Leave to cool.

/ 3 / Peel and segment the fruit, remove the pips and stir the fruit into the syrup with the liqueur, if using. Set aside to marinate.

/ 4 / Meanwhile, mix the remaining rind and sugar with the milk, egg and egg yolk. Beat well together, then pour into two 150 ml (¼ pint) ramekin or soufflé dishes. Cover, then microwave on LOW for 8-10 minutes or until the custards are set around the edge but still soft in the centre.

/ 5 / Leave to stand for 20 minutes. When cool, chill for at least 2 hours. To serve, decorate the custards with a few marinated clementine segments.

DRIED FRUIT COMPOTE

S E R V E S   4 - 6

100 g (4 oz) dried prunes
100 g (4 oz) dried apple rings
25 g (1 oz) seedless raisins
300 ml (½ pint) unsweetened apple juice
1 lemon

/ 1 / Put all the dried fruits in a large bowl. Pour over the unsweetened apple juice with 300 ml (½ pint) water.

/ 2 / Using a potato peeler, thinly pare the lemon rind. Squeeze and strain the juice. Stir the rind into the fruit mixture with 30 ml (2 tbsp) lemon juice. Make sure all the fruit is under liquid, adding more water if necessary.

/ 3 / Cover and microwave on HIGH for 10 minutes until the fruits are almost tender, stirring occasionally.

/ 4 / Leave to stand for about 30 minutes before serving warm. Alternatively, leave to cool completely, then chill well before serving.

Baked Clementine Custards

Hot Stuffed Dates

HOT STUFFED DATES

SERVES 2

30 ml (2 tbsp) ground almonds
30 ml (2 tbsp) pistachio nuts, chopped
pinch of ground ginger
large pinch of ground cinnamon
30 ml (2 tbsp) clear honey
6 large fresh dates, stoned
90 ml (6 tbsp) double cream
5 ml (1 tsp) rum

/ 1 / Mix together the almonds, pistachio nuts, ginger and cinnamon. Stir in the honey and mix well together.

/ 2 / Stuff the dates with this mixture and arrange on a small ovenproof plate.

/ 3 / Cover loosely and microwave on HIGH for 1-1½ minutes or until hot. Leave to stand.

/ 4 / Meanwhile, make the sauce. Put the cream and the rum into a heatproof jug. Mix well together and microwave on HIGH for 3 minutes or until the sauce is thickened and reduced. Pour the sauce around the dates and serve immediately.

/ 5 / To serve 4: double all the ingredients, then follow the recipe as above, but in step 3 microwave on HIGH for 2-3 minutes; in step 4 microwave on HIGH for 5-7 minutes.

ALMOND-STUFFED PEACHES

SERVES 4

4 firm ripe peaches
50 g (2 oz) ground almonds
finely grated rind of ½ orange
5 ml (1 tsp) clear honey
150 ml (¼ pint) unsweetened orange juice
15 ml (1 tbsp) Amaretto (optional)
a few mint leaves, to decorate

/ 1 / Cut the peaches in half and carefully ease out the stones with finger and thumb.

/ 2 / Make the hollows in the peaches a little deeper with a teaspoon and reserve the removed flesh.

/ 3 / Finely chop the removed peach flesh and mix with the almonds, orange rind, honey and 15 ml (1 tbsp) of the orange juice.

/ 4 / Use this mixture to stuff the hollows of the peach halves, mounding the filling slightly.

/ 5 / Place the peaches around the edge of a large shallow dish. Mix the remaining orange juice with the Amaretto, if using, and pour around the peaches.

/ 6 / Cover and microwave on HIGH for 3-5 minutes or until the peaches are tender. Leave to stand for 5 minutes, then serve warm with the juices spooned over and decorated with fresh mint leaves.

STUFFED BAKED APPLES

SERVES 4

4 medium cooking apples
clear honey
butter
cream, yogurt or custard, to serve

/ 1 / Make a shallow cut through the skin around the middle of each apple, then core the apples.

/ 2 / Stand the apples in a shallow ovenproof dish. Spoon a little honey into the centre of each apple and top with a knob of butter.

/ 3 / Microwave on HIGH for 5-7 minutes until the apples are tender. Turn the dish once during cooking. Leave to stand for 5 minutes, then serve the apples with cream, yogurt or custard, if liked.

— VARIATIONS —

Omit the honey and stuff the apples with mincemeat or a mixture of dried fruits such as sultanas, currants and mixed peel or chopped dried dates, apricots or prunes, and flavour with grated orange, lemon or lime rind.

ALMOND-STUFFED PEACHES

Cut the peaches in half and carefully ease out the stones with finger and thumb.

Make the hollows in the peaches a little deeper with a teaspoon and reserve the removed flesh.

Stuff the hollows of the peach halves, mounding the filling slightly.

STUFFED BAKED APPLES

Remove the apple cores with an apple corer.

FRUIT AND POLENTA PUDDING

SERVES 6

568 ml (1 pint) milk
100 g (4 oz) cornmeal
100 g (4 oz) raisins
25 g (1 oz) butter or margarine
30 ml (2 tbsp) clear honey
a few drops of vanilla essence
finely grated rind and juice of 1 lemon
fresh fruit, such as star fruit, strawberries, kiwi fruit, raspberries, apricots, mangoes, prepared and sliced
GLAZE
30 ml (2 tbsp) apricot jam
lemon juice

FRUIT AND POLENTA PUDDING
Polenta is usually a savoury dish, flavoured with cheese, but here it is combined successfully with lemon, raisins and honey to make an unusual and nutritious dessert, rather similar to a chilled cheesecake.

/ 1 / Grease a 23 cm (9 inch) square dish and line the base with greaseproof paper.

/ 2 / Put the milk into a large bowl and microwave on HIGH for 4-5 minutes or until hot but not boiling. Gradually stir in the cornmeal and mix thoroughly together. Microwave on HIGH for 5-6 minutes or until the mixture is very thick, stirring frequently.

/ 3 / Stir in the raisins, butter or margarine, honey, vanilla essence, lemon rind and juice and mix well together. Pour into the prepared dish and level the surface. Leave for 2-3 hours or until set.

/ 4 / Turn the polenta out on to a flat surface and cut into 6 pieces. Arrange the fruit attractively on top of the polenta.

/ 5 / Make the glaze: put the jam and a squeeze of lemon juice in a small bowl and microwave on HIGH for 20-30 seconds or until the jam has melted. Brush over the fruit to glaze.

FIG AND HONEY RAMEKINS

SERVES 4

about 20 dried figs
chopped shelled pistachio nuts, to decorate
FILLING
175 g (6 oz) curd cheese
50 g (2 oz) shelled pistachio nuts, finely chopped
50 g (2 oz) no-soak apricots, finely chopped
15 ml (1 tbsp) clear honey
15 ml (1 tbsp) brandy
SAUCE
60 ml (4 tbsp) clear honey
15 ml (1 tbsp) brandy

FIG AND HONEY RAMEKINS
Use the large dried figs that are sold loose, rather than the type compressed into a large block, to make these ramekins as they have a much better shape and texture.

/ 1 / Put the figs in a large bowl and pour over enough boiling water to cover. Cover and microwave on HIGH for 5-7 minutes.

/ 2 / Make the filling: beat the cheese, nuts, apricots, honey and brandy in a bowl.

/ 3 / Grease 4 ramekin dishes. Split the figs down 1 side if necessary, to open them out flat. Use 5 figs to line the base and sides of each ramekin, arranging them skin side outwards. Fill each dish with the cheese mixture. Level the surface, cover and chill for at least 4 hours.

/ 4 / When ready to serve, make the sauce. Put the honey and brandy in a small bowl and microwave on HIGH for 1-1½ minutes or until just hot. To serve: turn out on to 4 plates and sprinkle with chopped pistachio nuts. Serve with the hot brandy sauce.

PEARS EN CHEMISE

PEARS EN CHEMISE

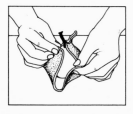

Bring the 4 corners of each pastry square to the top of each pear and press the edges to seal.

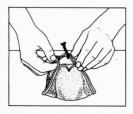

Fold back the 4 points to expose the stalk and allow steam to escape.

SERVES 4

368 g (13 oz) packet frozen shortcrust pastry, thawed
4 large dessert pears, such as Comice or Williams
finely grated rind and juice of 1 lemon
45 ml (9 tsp) redcurrant jelly
1 egg, beaten, to glaze
10 ml (2 tsp) caster sugar
pouring cream, to serve

/ 1 / Cut the pastry into 4 and roll out each piece on a lightly floured work surface to an 18 cm (7 inch) square.

Pears en Chemise

/ 2 / Peel the pears and core them carefully from the bottom. Leave the stalks on. Brush them immediately with lemon juice to prevent the apples from discoloring.

/ 3 / Mix together the lemon rind and half the redcurrant jelly. Put 5 ml (1 tsp) into the cavity of each pear, then stand the pears upright in the centre of each pastry square. Brush the edges of the pastry with water.

/ 4 / Bring the 4 corners of each square to the top of each pear and press the edges to seal.

/ 5 / Fold back the 4 points to expose the stalk and allow steam to escape. Stand the pears on a lightly greased plate and chill in the refrigerator for 30 minutes.

/ 6 / Preheat the oven on convection at 250°C for 10 minutes. Brush the pears all over with beaten egg and sprinkle with the sugar. Cook on combination at 200°C/MEDIUM LOW for 10-15 minutes or until the pastry is crisp and golden in colour.

/ 7 / Warm the remaining redcurrant jelly and brush all over the pastry. Serve warm, with pouring cream.

APRICOT CHEESECAKES

SERVES 2

100 g (4 oz) ricotta or curd cheese
1 egg yolk
30 ml (2 tbsp) ground almonds
30 ml (2 tbsp) caster sugar
finely grated rind of ½ lemon
20 ml (4 tsp) brandy
400 g (14 oz) can apricot halves in natural juice
15 ml (1 tbsp) apricot jam
mint sprigs, to decorate

/ 1 / Put the ricotta or curd cheese and egg yolk in a medium bowl and beat thoroughly together to combine.

/ 2 / Beat in the ground almonds, sugar and grated lemon rind. Gradually stir in 10 ml (2 tsp) of the brandy.

/ 3 / Drain the apricots, reserving the juice. Finely chop 1 apricot half and stir into the cheese mixture.

/ 4 / Spoon into two 150 ml (¼ pint) ramekin dishes and level the surface. Cut 2 of the apricot halves crossways into thin slices and fan out. Press lightly on top of the cheesecakes.

/ 5 / Microwave on LOW for 15 minutes until the cakes are cooked, or until they shrink away slightly from the edges of the dishes. Leave to stand for 10 minutes, then chill.

/ 6 / Meanwhile, liquidise the remaining apricots and 30 ml (2 tbsp) juice in a blender or food processor until smooth. Pour into a small bowl and stir in the remaining brandy.

/ 7 / Microwave on HIGH for 2 minutes or until the liquid is boiling. Leave to cool.

/ 8 / To serve: unmould the cheesecakes and put on to 2 serving plates. Put the apricot jam into a small bowl and microwave on HIGH for 30 seconds or until the jam melts. Brush the cheesecakes with the glaze.

/ 9 / Pour the sauce around the cheesecakes and decorate with the mint.

BAKED STRAWBERRY CHEESECAKE

C SERVES 6

100 g (4 oz) butter or margarine
100 g (4 oz) caster sugar
350 g (12 oz) full-fat soft cheese
2 eggs, separated
50 g (2 oz) ground almonds
50 g (2 oz) semolina
finely grated rind of 1 lemon
30 ml (2 tbsp) lemon juice
450 g (1 lb) firm strawberries
icing sugar, for dusting

/ 1 / Grease a 20.5 cm (8 inch) ovenproof dish and line the base of the dish with greaseproof paper.

/ 2 / Put the butter or margarine and sugar in a bowl and cream together until pale and fluffy. Gradually beat in the cheese and egg yolks. Beat until smooth.

/ 3 / Stir in the ground almonds, semolina, lemon rind and lemon juice. Roughly chop 225 g (8 oz) of the strawberries and fold carefully into the mixture.

/ 4 / Whisk the egg whites until stiff but not dry and fold into the mixture. Spoon into the prepared dish. Stand on the wire rack and cook on combination at 180°C/MEDIUM LOW for 20 minutes or until the cheesecakes are golden brown and just firm to the touch.

/ 5 / Leave to cool in the dish. When cold, turn out, dust with icing sugar and decorate with the remaining strawberries.

VARIATION

Instead of dusting icing sugar on the top, lightly whip 150 ml (¼ pint) double cream and fold in 150 ml (¼ pint) Greek yogurt. Flavour with a little orange rind. Spread on top of the cold cheesecake. Decorate with strawberries.

UNRIPENED CHEESES
Cheesecakes are always made from unripened cheeses. These may be full-fat soft cheese, ricotta, curd cheese or cottage cheese. Curd cheese is made from full milk and has the most pronounced cheesy flavour. Its texture is slightly grainy when compared with the cream-enriched full-fat soft cheese. Cottage cheese is lighter than either, as it is made from skimmed milk. The texture of cottage cheese is lumpy, the flavour mild and there is often a good deal of whey left in the cheese, making it rather moist.

BAKED STRAWBERRY CHEESECAKE
This is a firm, lemon-flavoured cheesecake packed with fresh strawberries. It doesn't have a base, but if you prefer you can make a simple biscuit base by mixing 225 g (8 oz) crushed digestive biscuits with 100 g (4 oz) melted butter. Press into the base of the dish. Baked strawberry cheesecake is best eaten on the day of making: the strawberries tend to 'weep' and make the cheesecake soggy if it is kept overnight.

Picture opposite:
Apricot Cheesecakes

Raspberry Almond Torte

/ 2 / Meanwhile, roll out the pastry on a lightly floured surface and use to line a 20.5 cm (8 inch) loose-bottomed flan dish.

/ 3 / Transfer the cooled dried fruit to a blender or food processor and purée until smooth. Pour into the pastry lined dish.

/ 4 / Put the butter, sugar, almonds, maca-roons, eggs and almond essence in a bowl and beat together until smooth. Carefully spoon on top of the fruit purée and sprinkle with the flaked almonds.

/ 5 / Stand the dish on the wire rack and cook on combination at 200°C/LOW for 25-30 minutes or until well risen and firm to the touch. Cover with greaseproof paper if the tart browns too quickly. Serve warm or cold.

RASPBERRY ALMOND TORTE

C   S E R V E S   6

150 g (5 oz) butter or margarine
150 g (5 oz) caster sugar
150 g (5 oz) ground almonds
150 g (5 oz) plain flour
1 egg
225 g (8 oz) fresh raspberries
icing sugar and a few fresh raspberries, to decorate

/ 1 / Put the butter or margarine, sugar, almonds, flour and egg in a bowl and beat to-gether until well mixed. Spread half the mix-ture in the base of a 20.5 cm (8 inch) loose-bottomed dish. Sprinkle with the raspberries.

/ 2 / Dot the remaining almond mixture over the raspberries so that the crumble almost covers the fruit.

/ 3 / Stand the dish on the wire rack and cook on combination at 200°C/MEDIUM LOW for 15-18 minutes or until golden brown and just firm to the touch. Leave to stand for 10 minutes, then turn out of the dish.

/ 4 / Dust the torte with icing sugar, cut into wedges and serve warm or cold. Decorate each portion with a few raspberries.

APRICOT AND PRUNE MACAROON TART

C   S E R V E S   6 - 8

250 g (9 oz) mixed no-soak dried apricots and stoned prunes
200 g (7 oz) packet frozen puff pastry, thawed
100 g (4 oz) butter
100 g (4 oz) caster sugar
100 g (4 oz) ground almonds
50 g (2 oz) macaroons, finely crushed
2 eggs
2.5 ml (½ tsp) almond essence
25 g (1 oz) flaked almonds

/ 1 / Put the apricots and prunes in a bowl with 300 ml (½ pint) water. Cover and microwave on HIGH for 10 minutes or until the fruit is very soft. Leave to cool slightly.

BLACKBERRY AND APPLE LATTICE

© SERVES 6

275 g (10 oz) plain white flour
pinch of salt
150 g (5 oz) butter or margarine
75 g (3 oz) light soft brown sugar
1 egg, separated
grated rind and juice of 1 small lemon
2.5 ml (½ tsp) ground cinnamon
30 ml (2 tbsp) semolina
700 g (1½ lb) cooking apples
225 g (8 oz) blackberries
caster sugar

/ 1 / Mix the flour and salt together in a bowl and rub in the butter or margarine until the mixture resembles fine breadcrumbs. Stir in 25 g (1 oz) of the brown sugar. Make a well in the centre, add the egg yolk and 45 ml (3 tbsp) water and mix to form a firm dough.

/ 2 / Turn the dough on to a lightly floured surface and knead lightly until smooth. Wrap in cling film and chill while preparing the filling.

/ 3 / In a large bowl, mix together the grated lemon rind and juice, remaining brown sugar, cinnamon and semolina. Peel, core and roughly chop the apples. Stir into the semolina mixture with the blackberries.

/ 4 / Roll out two-thirds of the pastry and use to line a 900 ml (1½ pint) shallow pie dish. Pile the apple mixture into the dish.

/ 5 / Roll out the remaining pastry and cut into thin strips. Use to make a lattice on top of the apple mixture. Pinch the edges of the pastry together to seal.

/ 6 / Brush the pastry with the beaten egg white and sprinkle generously with caster sugar. Stand the dish on the wire rack and cook on combination at 200°C/MEDIUM LOW for 20-25 minutes or until golden brown. Serve the pie warm or cold.

GINGERED APPLE PIE

© SERVES 6

PASTRY
225 g (8 oz) plain white flour
pinch of salt
100 g (4 oz) butter or margarine
25 g (1 oz) caster sugar
1 egg
egg yolk, beaten, and caster sugar, to glaze

FILLING
700 g (1½ lb) cooking apples, peeled, cored and thinly sliced
100 g (4 oz) sultanas
50 g (2 oz) preserved stem ginger, finely chopped
25 g (1 oz) caster sugar
juice of 1 lemon

/ 1 / Make the pastry: mix the flour and salt together in a bowl. Rub in the butter or margarine until the mixture resembles fine breadcrumbs. Stir in the sugar. Mix in the egg and about 15 ml (1 tbsp) water, using a round-bladed knife and adding just enough water to bind the mixture together. Knead lightly to form a smooth dough.

/ 2 / Cut the pastry in half. Roll out half on a lightly floured surface, and use to line a 23 cm (9 inch) pie dish.

/ 3 / Fill the pastry case with the apples, sultanas and ginger, piling the mixture up in the centre. Sprinkle with the sugar, lemon juice and 45 ml (3 tbsp) water. Preheat the oven on convection at 250°C for 5 minutes.

/ 4 / Roll out the remaining pastry to a circle large enough to cover the pie. Dampen the pastry edges, place the lid on top and press the edges together to seal. Trim and crimp the edges. Brush with a little beaten egg yolk and sprinkle generously with sugar.

/ 5 / Stand on the wire rack and cook on combination at 200°C/MEDIUM LOW for 18-22 minutes or until golden brown.

APRICOT AND PRUNE MACAROON TART
This is a delicious variation of that good old English favourite, Bakewell Tart. Instead of jam, this tart is filled with a thick purée of dried fruit. Here a mixture of apricots and prunes is used, but you could experiment with dried peaches, pears or apples. Macaroons are small almond-flavoured biscuits sold in supermarkets and delicatessens. If you cannot find them, use semolina instead.

BLACKBERRY AND APPLE LATTICE
Cut the apples into large chunks so that they retain their shape during cooking and hold the pastry lattice up. Mixing a little semolina into the fruit before cooking is a good tip to remember for all fruit pies. As it cooks, the semolina slightly thickens the fruit juices, preventing the pastry from going soggy, and making a thick sauce to bind the fruit together.
    Serve the pie with thick cream.

Spicy pies were popular in Elizabethan times. Cinnamon was always one of the favourite spices to use with apples, so too were nutmeg and ginger.
    The Elizabethans often added wine to their sweet pies, with lemon or orange zest, and sometimes candied peel. To give your apples a real old-fashioned flavour, add 1 or 2 quinces instead of some of the apples.

GINGERED APPLE PIE
Stem ginger, or Chinese ginger, is the tender young roots which are cleaned and peeled, then simmered in a heavy syrup.

Baking

Recipes in this chapter include breads, scones, tea-breads, cakes and biscuits, some cooked by microwave alone, others on combination. Breads and cakes cook quickly in a combination oven and, unlike microwave cakes, they have the traditional baked brown crust.

Most cakes benefit from cooking in a preheated combination oven, so do this while you are preparing the mixture. Always use non-metal dishes in the combination oven rather than traditional cake tins, since metal reflects microwaves and makes it pointless cooking on combination. You can, of course, cook your favourite cake recipes in your ordinary metal cake tins and containers if you are cooking on a convection setting.

Fruit cakes do not benefit from cooking on combination. They are best cooked slowly on convection to obtain the traditional moist texture and to allow the flavours to develop as they should.

Chocolate Fudge Cake

THAWING BREADS AND CAKES

To absorb the moisture of thawing breads and cakes, place them on absorbent kitchen paper (remove as soon as thawed to prevent sticking). For greater crispness, place baked goods and the paper on a microwave rack to allow the air to circulate underneath.

Type	Quantity	Time on Low or Defrost Setting	Notes
Loaf, whole Loaf, whole	1 large 1 small	6-8 minutes 4-6 minutes	Uncover and place on absorbent kitchen paper. Turn over during thawing. Stand for 5-15 minutes.
Loaf, sliced Loaf, sliced	1 large 1 small	6-8 minutes 4-6 minutes	Thaw in original wrapper but remove any metal tags. Stand for 10-15 minutes.
Slice of bread	25 g (1 oz)	10-15 seconds	Place on absorbent kitchen paper. Time carefully. Stand for 1-2 minutes.
Bread rolls, tea-cakes, scones, crumpets etc.	2 4	15-20 seconds 25-35 seconds	Place on absorbent kitchen paper. Time carefully. Stand for 2-3 minutes.
Cakes	2 small 4 small	30-60 seconds 1-1½ minutes	Place on absorbent kitchen paper. Stand for 5 minutes.
Sponge cake	450 g (1 lb)	1-1½ minutes	Place on absorbent kitchen paper. Test and turn after 1 minute. Stand for 5 minutes.

BASIC BREAD

☐

MAKES 1 LARGE LOAF

450 g (1 lb) strong white flour (or a mixture of white and wholemeal)

5 ml (1 tsp) salt

25 g (1 oz) butter or margarine

1 sachet of easy blend dried yeast

150 ml (¼ pint) milk

/ 1 / Grease a 1.7 litre (3 pint) loaf dish. Mix the flour and salt together in a large bowl and rub in the butter or margarine. Stir in the easy blend yeast.

/ 2 / Put the milk and 150 ml (¼ pint) water in a small bowl and microwave on HIGH for 1 minute or until warm. Add the liquid to the dry ingredients and mix to form a soft dough. (If using half wholemeal flour, you may need a little extra liquid.)

/ 3 / Turn the dough on to a lightly floured surface and knead for 10 minutes or until the dough is smooth and no longer sticky. Form into a loaf shape and place in the prepared dish. Cover with a clean tea-towel and leave to rise in a warm place for about 45 minutes or until doubled in size.

/ 4 / Uncover the loaf, stand on the wire rack and cook on combination at 200°C/MEDIUM LOW for 10-12 minutes or until well risen, golden brown and firm to the touch. When cooked, the bread should sound hollow when tapped underneath.

/ 5 / Leave the loaf to stand for 5 minutes, then turn out and leave to cool on a wire rack.

Many people find it difficult to shape a round 'blob' of dough into a neat loaf shape. The easiest way to do this is to stretch the dough into an oblong the same width as the length of the dish, fold it in 3, then turn it over so that the seam is underneath. Tuck the ends under and place the dough in the dish. It might sound difficult, but once you have the dough and the dish in front of you, you will see that it's quite simple.

HERB, CHEESE AND OLIVE BREAD

MAKES 1 LOAF

225 g (8 oz) self-raising wholemeal flour
5 ml (1 tsp) baking powder
salt and pepper
100 g (4 oz) mature Cheddar cheese, grated
45 ml (3 tbsp) roughly chopped fresh mixed herbs
75 g (3 oz) black olives, quartered
1 egg
30 ml (2 tbsp) olive oil
225 ml (8 fl oz) milk
TOPPING
25 g (1 oz) mature Cheddar cheese, grated
15 ml (1 tbsp) roughly chopped fresh mixed herbs
25 g (1 oz) black olives, roughly chopped

/ 1 / Grease a 1.7 litre (3 pint) loaf dish and line the base with greaseproof paper.

/ 2 / Put the flour, baking powder, salt and pepper, cheese, herbs, black olives, egg, olive oil and milk in a large bowl and beat thoroughly until well mixed.

/ 3 / Spoon the mixture into the prepared dish and level the surface. Sprinkle on the topping ingredients. Stand the container on a roasting rack and microwave on HIGH for 3 minutes, then continue to microwave on MEDIUM for 14 minutes or until firm and well risen.

/ 4 / Leave to cool in the dish. When cold, turn out and serve sliced.

HERBY BAPS

C

MAKES 8

50 g (2 oz) All-bran
450 g (1 lb) strong white flour
5 ml (1 tsp) salt
50 g (2 oz) butter or margarine
1 sachet of easy blend dried yeast
60 ml (4 tbsp) chopped fresh mixed herbs

/ 1 / Grease a shallow 23 cm (9 inch) round ovenproof dish. Put the cereal in a bowl and stir in 150 ml (¼ pint) water. Leave to soak for about 10 minutes or until the liquid has been absorbed by the cereal.

/ 2 / Mix the flour and salt together in a large bowl and rub in the butter or margarine. Stir in the easy blend yeast, chopped herbs and soaked cereal mixture.

/ 3 / Put 225 ml (8 fl oz) water in a jug and microwave on HIGH for 1-2 minutes or until just warm. Pour on to the flour mixture and mix to form a soft dough. Turn out on to a lightly floured surface and knead for 10 minutes or until the dough is smooth and no longer feels sticky.

/ 4 / Using a sharp knife, divide the dough into 8 equal-sized pieces and shape into baps. Arrange in the prepared dish, cover with a clean tea-towel and leave to rise in a warm place for about 45 minutes or until the baps have doubled in size.

/ 5 / Uncover the baps, stand the dish on the wire rack and cook on combination at 200°C/ MEDIUM LOW for 15-17 minutes or until well risen, golden brown and firm to the touch. When cooked, the baps should sound hollow when tapped underneath.

/ 6 / Dust the baps with a little flour, leave to stand for 5 minutes, then turn out and leave to cool on a wire rack.

BRAN MUFFINS

MAKES 8

50 g (2 oz) bran
75 g (3 oz) plain wholemeal flour
7.5 ml (1½ tsp) baking powder
1 egg, beaten
300 ml (½ pint) skimmed milk
30 ml (2 tbsp) clear honey
butter or margarine, for spreading

/ 1 / Put the bran, flour and baking powder in a bowl and mix together. Add the egg, milk and honey and stir until well mixed.

/ 2 / Divide the mixture between an 8-hole bun tray. Microwave on HIGH for 5-6 minutes until firm to the touch.

/ 3 / Leave to stand for 5 minutes. Split each muffin in half horizontally and serve spread lightly with butter or margarine.

HERB, CHEESE AND OLIVE BREAD
This makes a moist, quick bread, delicious served warm or cold with soups or salads. Use a strong Cheddar cheese and juicy black olives packed in olive oil for the best flavour. Fresh herbs such as oregano, marjoram or rosemary complement the flavour of cheese and olives.

HERBY BAPS
All-bran breakfast cereal, soaked until soft, gives these baps a pleasant nutty flavour and a high fibre content. Try to include a good mixture of fresh herbs and don't be tempted to substitute with dried as the flavour will be too harsh. A little chopped garlic or a few chopped, stoned olives added with the herbs tastes good too.

BRAN MUFFINS
These fibre-rich muffins are best served warm straight from the oven. Serve them on their own or to accompany a breakfast dish such as scrambled eggs.

191

CHEESE AND ONION BREAD

CHEESE AND ONION BREAD
This moist, rich bread is baked in a homely round shape reminiscent of soda bread. Serve it while still warm, in generous chunks with home-made soup.

FRUIT SCONES

Sift the flour, salt and baking powder together into a bowl, then rub in the butter or margarine until the mixture resembles fine breadcrumbs. Stir in the sugar and sultanas.

If you leave the scones to stand for about 10 minutes before cooking, they rise much more than normal. In this recipe the oven is preheated after the scones are rolled and cut out to allow for this standing time. If time is short, you can, of course, preheat the oven while making the scones and cook them straight away.

Picture opposite:
Cheese and Onion Bread

MAKES 1 LARGE LOAF

450 g (1 lb) strong white flour
5 ml (1 tsp) salt
pinch of cayenne pepper
50 g (2 oz) butter or margarine
1 sachet of easy blend dried yeast
300 ml (½ pint) milk
1 large onion, skinned and thinly sliced
15 ml (1 tbsp) vegetable oil
1 egg yolk, lightly beaten
25 g (1 oz) matured Cheddar cheese, grated

/ 1 / Grease a large ovenproof plate. Mix the flour, salt and cayenne pepper together in a large bowl and rub in the butter or margarine. Stir in the yeast.

/ 2 / Put the milk in a jug and microwave on HIGH for 1-2 minutes or until warm. Pour on to the flour mixture and mix to form a soft dough. Turn out on to a lightly floured surface and knead for 10 minutes or until the dough is smooth and no longer sticky.

/ 3 / Shape the dough into a flat round, about 18 cm (7 inches) in diameter. Place on the prepared plate and, with a sharp knife, mark the dough into 6 wedges. Cover loosely with a clean tea-towel and leave to rise in a warm place for about 45 minutes or until the dough has doubled in size.

/ 4 / Put the onion and oil in a bowl, cover and microwave on HIGH for 5-7 minutes or until softened. Drain well.

/ 5 / Uncover the dough, brush with the egg yolk and spoon the onion evenly on top. Sprinkle with the grated cheese. Stand the plate on the wire rack and cook on combination at 200°C/MEDIUM LOW for 12-17 minutes or until well risen, golden brown and firm to the touch. When cooked, the bread should sound hollow when tapped underneath.

/ 6 / Leave to stand for 5 minutes, then serve the bread warm in wedges.

FRUIT SCONES

MAKES 8

225 g (8 oz) self-raising flour
2.5 ml (½ tsp) salt
5 ml (1 tsp) baking powder
50 g (2 oz) butter or margarine
25 g (1 oz) caster sugar
50 g (2 oz) sultanas
about 150 ml (¼ pint) milk
beaten egg or milk, to glaze (optional)
butter, for spreading

/ 1 / Lightly grease a large plate. Sift the flour, salt and baking powder together into a bowl, then rub in the butter or margarine until the mixture resembles fine breadcrumbs. Stir in the sugar and sultanas.

/ 2 / Make a well in the centre and, using a round-bladed knife, stir in just enough milk to give a fairly soft dough. Turn out on to a lightly floured surface and knead very lightly. Roll out to about 2 cm (¾ inch) thick.

/ 3 / Cut out 8 rounds with a 6.5 cm (2½ inch) plain cutter, re-rolling the dough as necessary. Place on the prepared plate and brush with beaten egg or milk, if liked. Leave the scones to stand while preheating the oven on convection at 250°C for 10 minutes.

/ 4 / Stand the plate of scones on the wire rack and cook on combination at 200°C/MEDIUM LOW for 8-10 minutes or until well risen and lightly browned. Serve warm, spread with a little butter.

─── VARIATIONS ───

Replace the sultanas with 50 g (2 oz) raisins, currants, chopped dates or a mixture of dried fruits. To make savoury scones, replace the sultanas and sugar with 50 g (2 oz) grated cheese and 15 ml (1 tbsp) chopped fresh herbs.

Griddle Scones

GRIDDLE SCONES

MAKES 8

225 g (8oz) self-raising flour
2.5 ml (½ tsp) salt
15 g (½ oz) butter or margarine
25 g (1 oz) caster sugar
about 150 ml (¼ pint) milk or buttermilk
butter and jam, for serving

/1/ Put the flour and salt in a bowl. Using both hands, rub in the butter or margarine until the mixture resembles fine breadcrumbs, then stir in the sugar. Add enough milk or buttermilk to give a soft but manageable dough.

/2/ With one hand, collect the mixture together and knead lightly for a few seconds to give a firm, smooth dough. Divide in 2 and roll into 2 rounds 0.5 cm (¼ inch) thick. Cut each round into 4.

/3/ Heat a large browning dish, skillet or griddle on HIGH for 4-5 minutes. Do not allow the dish to become too hot or the scones will burn.

/4/ Quickly place 4 quarters on the browning dish and microwave on HIGH for 1½ minutes. Turn the scones over and microwave on HIGH for a further 2 minutes. Repeat with the remaining scones, without reheating the browning dish. Eat the scones while still hot, spread with butter and jam.

GRIDDLE SCONES

A microwave browning dish, skillet or griddle gives perfectly browned scones just like a conventional griddle. They are made of a material which can withstand a very high temperature and are heated empty before the food to be cooked is placed on the hot surface. This immediately sears and browns the food. Manufacturers usually recommend that they are heated on HIGH for 5-8 minutes but for this recipe they should only be heated for 4-5 minutes otherwise they will become too hot and the scones will burn.

SULTANA TEACAKES

MAKES 8

225 g (8 oz) strong white flour
225 g (8 oz) plain wholemeal flour
5 ml (1 tsp) salt
2.5 ml (½ tsp) mixed spiced
50 g (2 oz) butter or margarine
1 sachet of easy blend dried yeast
25 g (1 oz) light soft brown sugar
100 g (4 oz) sultanas
300 ml (½ pint) milk
1 egg white, lightly beaten
caster sugar

/1/ Grease a shallow 23 cm (9 inch) round ovenproof dish. Mix the flours, salt and mixed spice together in a large bowl and rub in the butter or margarine. Stir in the yeast, sugar and sultanas and mix well.

/2/ Put the milk in a jug and microwave on HIGH for 1-2 minutes or until just warm. Pour on to the flour mixture and mix to form a soft dough. Turn out on to a lightly floured surface and knead for 10 minutes or until the dough is smooth and no longer sticky.

/3/ Using a sharp knife, divide the dough into 8 equal-sized pieces and shape into rolls. Arrange in the prepared dish. Cover with a clean tea-towel and leave to rise in a warm place for about 45 minutes or until the rolls have doubled in size.

/4/ Uncover the dough, flatten slightly, then brush with egg white and sprinkle with caster sugar. Stand the dish on the wire rack and cook on combination at 200°C/MEDIUM LOW for 10-15 minutes or until risen, lightly browned and firm to the touch. When cooked, the teacakes should sound hollow when tapped underneath with fingertips.

/5/ Sprinkle with a little extra caster sugar after cooking. Leave to stand for 5 minutes, then turn out and leave to cool on a wire rack.

SULTANA TEACAKES

Turn the dough on to a lightly floured surface and knead for 10 minutes or until the dough is smooth and no longer sticky.

When cooked these spicy Sultana Teacakes join together to form a ring.

GRIDDLE SCONES

Put the flour and salt in a bowl. Using both hands, rub in the butter or margarine until the mixture resembles fine breadcrumbs, then stir in the sugar. Add enough milk or buttermilk to give a soft but manageable dough. With 1 hand, collect the mixture together and knead lightly for a few seconds to give a firm, smooth dough.

FRUITY TEABREAD

◧ MAKES 10-12 SLICES

450 ml (¾ pint) cold tea
175 g (6 oz) seedless raisins
175 g (6 oz) sultanas
100 g (4 oz) chopped mixed peel
100 g (4 oz) plain wholemeal flour
100 g (4 oz) plain white flour
5 ml (1 tsp) baking powder
50 g (2 oz) light soft brown sugar
1 egg, beaten
butter, for spreading

/1/ Mix together the tea, raisins, sultanas and mixed peel and leave to soak for 2-3 hours.

/2/ Grease a 1.7 litre (3 pint) loaf dish and line the base with greaseproof paper.

/3/ Mix the flours, baking powder, sugar and egg into the soaked fruit and beat well together. Spoon into the prepared dish.

/4/ Stand the dish on the wire rack and cook on combination at 200°C/LOW for 23-28 minutes or until well risen and firm to the touch. Leave to stand for 5 minutes, then turn out, remove the lining paper and leave to cool on a wire rack. Serve sliced with butter.

FLAPJACKS

MAKES 16

75 g (3 oz) butter or margarine
50 g (2 oz) light soft brown sugar
30 ml (2 tbsp) golden syrup
175 g (6 oz) porridge oats

/1/ Grease a shallow 12.5 × 23 cm (5×9 inch) dish. Put the butter or margarine, sugar and syrup in a large bowl. Microwave on HIGH for 2 minutes until the sugar has dissolved, stirring once. Stir well, then mix in the oats.

/2/ Press the mixture into the dish. Stand on a roasting rack and microwave on HIGH for 2-3 minutes until firm to the touch.

/3/ Leave to cool slightly, then mark into 16 bars. Allow to cool completely before turning out of the dish.

———FLAPJACKS———

Few biscuits are suitable for cooking in a microwave because they can only be cooked in small batches and often need to be turned over. These delicious crunchy flapjacks, however, are one of the quickest and easiest biscuits to make in the microwave.

WALNUT, BANANA AND ORANGE TEABREAD

MAKES 16 SLICES

225 g (8 oz) self-raising wholemeal flour
100 g (4 oz) light soft brown sugar
100 g (4 oz) butter or margarine
100 g (4 oz) walnut halves, roughly chopped
3 ripe bananas, mashed
1 egg
finely grated rind and juice of 1 large orange
2.5 ml (½ tsp) ground mixed spice
TOPPING
25 g (1 oz) walnut halves
25 g (1 oz) dried banana chips
15 ml (1 tbsp) clear honey

/1/ Grease a 1.7 litre (3 pint) loaf dish. Line with greaseproof paper and grease the paper.

/2/ Put the flour, sugar, butter or margarine, walnuts, bananas, egg, orange rind and juice and mixed spice in a large bowl and beat thoroughly until well mixed.

/3/ Spoon the mixture into the prepared dish and level the surface. Sprinkle with the walnut halves and banana chips for the topping. Stand on a roasting rack and microwave on MEDIUM for 14 minutes until risen and firm to the touch.

/4/ Leave to cool in the dish. When cold turn out and brush with the honey to glaze.

FRUITY TEABREAD
This is a teabread in every sense of the word. Soaking the mixed fruit in tea ensures a deliciously moist result. Use a strong tea, such as Assam, to give a good flavour. You get the best result if this teabread is cooked on a LOW microwave setting, but if you cannot alter the microwave level on your oven, simply cook for slightly less time before checking.

FLAPJACKS

Press the flapjack mixture into the prepared dish. Stand on a roasting rack and microwave on HIGH for 2-3 minutes until firm to the touch.

Leave to cool slightly, then mark into 16 bars. Cool completely before turning out of the dish.

Picture opposite:
Flapjacks; Walnut, Banana and Orange Teabread

WALNUT YOGURT CAKE

MAKES 8 SLICES

150 g (5 oz) walnuts, finely chopped
50 g (2 oz) dark soft brown sugar
10 ml (2 tsp) ground mixed spice
5 ml (1 tsp) ground coriander (optional)
175 g (6 oz) butter or margarine
175 g (6 oz) caster sugar
2 eggs
150 ml (¼ pint) Greek yogurt
175 g (6 oz) plain white flour
50 g (2 oz) plain wholemeal flour
5 ml (1 tsp) baking powder
2.5 ml (½ tsp) bicarbonate of soda
pinch of salt
icing sugar and ground coriander or mixed spice, for dredging

/ 1 / Grease a 1.6 litre (2¾ pint) ring mould. Preheat the oven on convection at 250°C for 10 minutes.

/ 2 / Meanwhile mix the walnuts with the brown sugar, mixed spiced and coriander, if using, and set aside.

/ 3 / Place the butter or margarine and caster sugar in a bowl and cream together until pale and fluffy. Beat the eggs into the yogurt, then gradually mix into the creamed mixture.

/ 4 / Sift the flours, baking powder, bicarbonate of soda and salt together into the bowl and gradually fold into the mixture, then beat thoroughly together. Spoon half of the mixture into the prepared dish. Sprinkle with the nuts and spices, then spoon the remaining cake mixture on top and level the surface.

/ 5 / Stand the dish on the wire rack and cook on combination at 200°C/LOW for 10-15 minutes or until just firm to the touch and shrinking away from the sides of the mould.

/ 6 / Turn the cake out on to a wire rack to cool. When cold, dredge the top of the cake with icing sugar flavoured with a little ground coriander or mixed spice.

CHERRY AND COCONUT CAKE

MAKES 10 SLICES

250 g (9 oz) self-raising white flour
100 g (4 oz) butter or margarine
75 g (3 oz) desiccated coconut
100 g (4 oz) caster sugar
100 g (4 oz) glacé cherries, finely chopped
2 eggs
175 ml (6 fl oz) milk
25 g (1 oz) shredded coconut

/ 1 / Preheat the oven on convection at 250°C for 10 minutes. Meanwhile, grease a deep 20.5 cm (8 inch) round cake dish and line the base with greaseproof paper.

/ 2 / Put the flour into a bowl and rub in the butter or margarine until the mixture resembles fine breadcrumbs. Stir in the desiccated coconut, sugar and cherries.

/ 3 / Put the eggs and milk in a bowl and whisk together. Gradually beat into the dry ingredients. Turn the mixture into the prepared dish, level the top and sprinkle over the shredded coconut.

/ 4 / Stand the dish on the wire rack and cook on combination at 200°C/MEDIUM LOW for 15-20 minutes or until the cake is well risen, golden brown and a skewer inserted into the centre comes out clean. Leave to stand for 5 minutes, then cool on a wire rack.

CHERRY AND COCONUT CAKE
This moist family cake is studded with cherries and flavoured with coconut. Two kinds are used, desiccated and shredded. Although both are forms of dried coconut, the shredded variety seems to have a stronger flavour.

This cake works equally well baked in a 1.4 litre (2½ pint) loaf dish.

WALNUT YOGURT CAKE
This delicious, moist cake is cooked in a ring and filled with a spiced walnut mixture. Serve cold, sliced, as a cake with tea or coffee, or while still warm with Greek yogurt as a dessert.

If you don't have a ring mould, improvise by placing a straight-sided heavy tumbler in the middle of a deep round dish.

Picture opposite:
Walnut Yogurt Cake; Cherry and Coconut Cake

APPLE CAKE

SERVES 6 - 8

225 g (8 oz) cooking apples, peeled, cored and chopped
100 g (4 oz) sultanas
75 ml (3 fl oz) milk
75 g (3 oz) dark soft brown sugar
175 g (6 oz) self-raising flour
10 ml (2 tsp) mixed spice
2.5 ml (½ tsp) ground cinnamon
75 g (3 oz) butter or margarine
1 egg, size 2, beaten
2 apples, quartered and sliced
15 ml (1 tbsp) apricot jam, heated
custard or cream, to serve

/ 1 / Grease a 23 cm (9 inch), 2.3 litre (4 pint) ovenproof glass or microwave ring mould.

/ 2 / Mix the apples, sultanas, milk and sugar together in a bowl. Sift the flour and spices into a mixing bowl and rub in the butter or margarine until the mixture resembles fine breadcrumbs. Add the apple mixture and egg and mix the ingredients together well.

/ 3 / Spoon the cake mixture into the prepared mould and smooth the top. Cover with a double thickness of absorbent kitchen paper and microwave on HIGH for 10 minutes, then uncover and microwave on HIGH for 1-2 minutes until the cake is cooked and a wooden cocktail stick or skewer inserted into the centre of the cake comes out clean.

/ 4 / Leave the cake to stand in its mould for 5 minutes before carefully turning it out. Arrange the sliced apple on top of the cake and brush with the apricot jam. Serve the apple cake warm with custard or cream.

———————— A P P L E C A K E ————————

Covering cakes with a plate during cooking keeps them moist but they are then similar in texture to a sponge pudding. A light covering is therefore the answer; the best thing to use when a covering is called for is a double thickness of absorbent kitchen paper.

CARROT CAKE

SERVES 6 - 8

100 g (4 oz) butter or margarine
100 g (4 oz) dark soft brown sugar
2 eggs, size 2
grated rind and juice of 1 lemon
5 ml (1 tsp) ground cinnamon
2.5 ml (½ tsp) grated nutmeg
2.5 ml (½ tsp) ground cloves
15 g (½ oz) shredded coconut
100 g (4 oz) carrots, peeled and finely grated
40 g (1½ oz) ground almonds
100 g (4 oz) self-raising wholemeal flour
caster sugar, for dredging

/ 1 / Grease an 18 cm (7 inch) diameter ovenproof ring mould. Cream the butter or margarine and sugar together until they are very soft, pale and fluffy. Beat in the eggs 1 at a time, beating well between each addition.

/ 2 / Beat in the lemon rind and juice, spices, coconut and carrots. Fold in the ground almonds and the wholemeal flour.

/ 3 / Spoon the mixture into the prepared mould, smooth the top and dredge it with a thin layer of caster sugar.

/ 4 / Cover with a double thickness of absorbent kitchen paper and microwave on HIGH for 10 minutes or until the cake is cooked, when it will shrink slightly away from the sides of the mould. Give the cake a quarter turn 4 times during the cooking time.

/ 5 / Uncover and leave the cake to stand for 10-15 minutes before turning it out on to a rack to cool.

———————— C A R R O T C A K E ————————

The carrots add texture and moisture to this cake. They must be grated by hand rather than in a food processor as the latter gives a 'wet' result that prevents the cake from rising properly.

Ring moulds are ideal for cooking cakes as the microwaves can reach the food from the inside as well as the outside.

Cakes baked in a plastic container will not need greasing unless the mixture you are using contains only a small amount of fat. Other containers, however, should be greased and the base of larger containers lined with greaseproof paper. Avoid flouring dishes as this will produce an unpalatable coating on the cake.

Cake mixtures should be a softer consistency than when baked conventionally. As a rule, they need an extra 15 ml (1 tbsp) milk for each egg used.

Apple Cake

ENGLISH MADELEINES

Spread the coconut out on a large plate. Spear a cake on a skewer or fork, brush with jam and then roll in the coconut until evenly coated. Repeat with the remaining cakes.

Top each cake with half a glacé cherry and small pieces of angelica.

The continental cousin of the English Madeleine is confusingly different. Made either from pastry or a firm, butter-rich cake mixture such as Genoese sponge, French Madeleines are baked in shallow, shell-shaped moulds. They are served undecorated or lightly dusted with icing sugar.

TUTTI FRUTTI CAKE

MAKES 10 SLICES

200 g (7 oz) soft tub margarine
175 g (6 oz) caster sugar
finely grated rind of 1 orange
finely grated rind and juice of 1 lemon
2 eggs
175 g (6 oz) self-raising flour
50 g (2 oz) ground almonds
25 g (1 oz) green glacé cherries, chopped
50 g (2 oz) glacé pineapple pieces
50 g (2 oz) glacé papaya pieces
ICING AND DECORATION
75 g (3 oz) icing sugar
juice of 1 orange
pineapple or papaya pieces
toasted flaked almonds

/ 1 / Grease a deep 20.5 cm (8 inch) round cake dish and line the base with greaseproof paper.

/ 2 / Put the margarine, sugar, orange rind, lemon rind and juice, eggs, flour and almonds in a bowl and beat together until smooth.

/ 3 / Stir in the cherries, pineapple and papaya. Pour the mixture into the prepared dish and level the surface. Stand the dish on the wire rack and cook on combination at 200°C/LOW for 22-30 minutes or until well risen and firm to the touch.

/ 4 / Turn the cake out on a wire rack, remove the lining paper and leave to cool.

/ 5 / When the cake is cold, make the icing. Sieve the icing sugar into a bowl, then beat in enough of the orange juice to make a mixture thick enough just to coat the back of a spoon.

/ 6 / Pour the icing over the cake and sprinkle with a few pineapple or papaya pieces and toasted flaked almonds. Leave until the icing has set before slicing.

ENGLISH MADELEINES

SERVES 8

100 g (4 oz) softened butter or soft tub margarine
100 g (4 oz) caster sugar
2 eggs
100 g (4 oz) self-raising flour
75 ml (5 tbsp) red jam
40 g (1½ oz) desiccated coconut
4 glacé cherries, halved, and angelica pieces, to decorate

/ 1 / Line the bases of 8 paper drinking cups with rounds of greaseproof paper.

/ 2 / Put the butter or margarine, sugar, eggs and flour in a bowl and beat until smooth. Alternatively, put the ingredients in a food processor or mixer and mix until smooth.

/ 3 / Divide the mixture evenly between the prepared cups. Place the cups on 2 flat plates, 4 on each plate.

/ 4 / Microwave 1 plate at a time on HIGH for 1½-2 minutes or until risen, but still slightly moist on the surface. Leave to stand for 1-2 minutes, then turn out and leave to cool on a wire rack.

/ 5 / When the cakes are cold, trim the bases, if necessary, so that they stand firmly and are about the same height.

/ 6 / Put the jam in a small bowl and microwave on HIGH for 1-2 minutes until melted. Stir well.

/ 7 / Spread the coconut out on a large plate. Spear a cake on a skewer or a fork, brush with the jam and then roll in the coconut until evenly coated. Repeat with the remaining cakes, then stand them on a plate.

/ 8 / Top each cake with half a glacé cherry and small pieces of angelica. These cakes are best eaten on the day of making.

BATTENBURG CAKE

SERVES 8-10

175 g (6 oz) softened butter or soft tub margarine
175 g (6 oz) caster sugar
a few drops of vanilla flavouring
3 eggs, beaten
175 g (6 oz) self-raising flour
30-60 ml (2-4 tbsp) milk
30 ml (2 tbsp) cocoa powder
120 ml (8 tbsp) apricot jam
225 g (8 oz) marzipan
caster sugar, for dredging

/ 1 / Grease a shallow 18×23 cm (7×9 inch) dish. Divide the dish in half lengthways with a 'wall' of greaseproof paper. To make a wall of greaseproof paper, take a piece about 7.5 cm (3 inches) wider than the cake dish and make a 4 cm (1½ inch) pleat in the centre. Place this greaseproof paper in the dish.

/ 2 / Put the butter or margarine, caster sugar, vanilla flavouring, eggs, flour and 30 ml (2 tbsp) milk in a bowl and beat until smooth. Alternatively, put the ingredients in a food processor or mixer and mix until smooth.

/ 3 / Spoon half the mixture into 1 side of the prepared dish and level the surface.

/ 4 / Add the cocoa powder and a little more milk, if necessary, to the remaining mixture to make a very soft dropping consistency. Spoon this into the other side of the prepared dish and level the surface. Microwave on HIGH for 5-6 minutes or until the cake is well risen, but still looks slightly moist on the surface.

/ 5 / Leave to stand for 5 minutes, then carefully turn out and leave to cool on a wire rack.

/ 6 / Trim the 2 sponges to an equal size and cut each in half lengthways.

/ 7 / Put the apricot jam in a small bowl and microwave on HIGH for 1½-2 minutes or until hot, stirring frequently. Spread 1 side of 1 piece of the vanilla sponge with apricot jam and then place a piece of the chocolate sponge next to it and press them firmly together.

/ 8 / Spread more jam on top of the 2 halves and place the remaining 2 sponges on top, alternating the colours.

/ 9 / Roll out the marzipan to an oblong long enough to go around the sponge cakes. Brush the marzipan with apricot jam and place the sponge cakes in the centre. Bring the marzipan up over the sides to enclose the sponges, then turn the cake over so the join is underneath.

/ 10 / Press the marzipan firmly around the sponges to seal. Trim each end neatly. Use a small knife to decorate the top of the cake with a criss-cross pattern. Pinch the top side edges between thumb and forefinger to give a fluted edge. Dredge lightly with caster sugar and place on a serving dish.

Battenburg Cake; English Madeleines

QUEEN CAKES

MAKES 18

100 g (4 oz) softened butter or soft tub margarine
100 g (4 oz) caster sugar
2 eggs
100 g (4 oz) self-raising flour
50 g (2 oz) sultanas
30 ml (2 tbsp) milk

/ 1 / Put the butter or margarine, sugar, eggs and flour in a large bowl and beat until smooth. Alternatively, put the ingredients in a food processor or mixer and mix until smooth. Mix in the sultanas and add the milk to make a soft dropping consistency.

/ 2 / Arrange 6 double layers of paper cases in a microwave muffin tray. Fill the prepared paper cases half-full and microwave on HIGH for 1 minute until risen, but still slightly moist on the surface. Transfer to a wire rack to cool. Repeat twice with the remaining mixture.

VARIATIONS

Replace the sultanas with one of the following:
50 g (2 oz) chopped dates; 50 g (2 oz) chopped red glacé cherries; 50 g (2 oz) chocolate chips; 50 g (2 oz) chopped crystallized ginger.

CHOCOLATE PRALINE CAKE

SERVES 8

175 g (6 oz) blanched almonds
275 g (10 oz) caster sugar
100 g (4 oz) softened butter or soft tub margarine
2 eggs
45 ml (3 tbsp) clear honey
150 ml (¼ pint) soured cream
100 g (4 oz) self-raising flour
40 g (1½ oz) cocoa powder
50 g (2 oz) ground almonds
300 ml (½ pint) whipping cream

/ 1 / Make the praline: grease a baking sheet and set aside. Spread out the almonds on a large ovenproof plate and microwave on HIGH for 4-5 minutes until lightly browned, stirring frequently during cooking.

/ 2 / Put 175 g (6 oz) of the sugar in a large heat-proof bowl with 60 ml (4 tbsp) water and microwave on HIGH for 3 minutes. Stir until the sugar has dissolved, then continue to microwave on HIGH for 5-7 minutes until the sugar is golden brown. Turn the bowl occasionally but do not stir. Add the nuts and stir until they are all coated.

/ 3 / Pour the praline on to the baking sheet and leave for 10-15 minutes for the praline to cool and harden.

/ 4 / Meanwhile, make the cake. Grease a 1.6 litre (2¾ pint) ring mould and set aside.

/ 5 / Put the butter or margarine and remaining sugar in a bowl and beat together until pale and fluffy. Gradually beat in the eggs, honey and soured cream. Fold in the flour, cocoa and ground almonds.

/ 6 / Spoon the cake mixture into the prepared dish. Stand on a roasting rack and microwave on HIGH for 10 minutes until risen but still slightly moist on the surface. Leave to stand for 5 minutes, then turn the cake out on to a wire rack to cool.

/ 7 / While the cake is cooling, coarsely crush half the praline with a rolling pin in a strong polythene bag. Finely crush the remaining praline in a coffee grinder or food processor.

/ 8 / Whip the cream until stiff, then gradually fold in the finely crushed praline. Spread the cream on to the cake to coat it completely. Sprinkle with the coarsely crushed praline.

QUEEN CAKES
If you want to add some colour to these pale cakes, ice them with glacé icing and decorate appropriately.

CHOCOLATE PRALINE CAKE

Coarsely crush half the praline with a rolling pin in a strong polythene bag. Finely crush the remaining praline in a coffee grinder or food processor.

When making the praline, it is important to dissolve the sugar completely before cooking to a light golden colour, to prevent it crystallizing. Likewise, once the sugar has dissolved, do not stir but turn the bowl, in case your cooker has a hot spot.

Picture opposite:
Chocolate Praline Cake

CHOCOLATE FUDGE CAKE

This is a favourite with chocaholics everywhere! It is a deep moist cake sandwiched together and iced with a rich sticky icing. The icing is a proper fudge icing made on the hob using a sugar thermometer. Do not attempt to do this in the microwave. If preferred, make a simple chocolate butter cream icing using 275 g (10 oz) softened butter, 150 g (5 oz) icing sugar, 50 g (2 oz) melted chocolate and 15 ml (1 tbsp) cocoa powder dissolved in a little hot water. Simply beat all the ingredients together.

CHOCOLATE FUDGE CAKE

◨ M A K E S   1 0 - 1 2   S L I C E S

| 100 g (4 oz) plain chocolate, broken into pieces |
| 225 g (8 oz) dark soft brown sugar |
| 175 g (6 oz) self-raising flour |
| 25 g (1 oz) cocoa powder |
| 2.5 ml (½ tsp) baking powder |
| 225 g (8 oz) butter or margarine |
| 50 g (2 oz) ground almonds |
| 3 eggs |
| 60 ml (4 tbsp) milk |
| FUDGE ICING |
| 225 g (8 oz) granulated sugar |
| 75 g (3 oz) butter |
| 196 g (7 oz) can condensed milk |
| 25 g (1 oz) plain chocolate, broken into pieces |
| 50 g (2 oz) cocoa powder |

/ 1 / Grease a deep 18 cm (7 inch) round cake dish and line the base with greaseproof paper.

/ 2 / Put the chocolate and sugar in a large bowl and microwave on HIGH for 2 minutes or until melted, stirring frequently. Add the flour, cocoa, baking powder, butter or margarine, almonds, eggs and milk and beat until the mixture is smooth and glossy.

/ 3 / Pour the mixture into the prepared dish and level the surface. Stand on the wire rack and cook on combination at 200°C/MEDIUM LOW for 15-20 minutes or until well risen and firm to the touch.

/ 4 / Leave to stand for 5 minutes, then turn the cake out on to a wire rack, remove the lining paper and leave to cool.

/ 5 / Make the icing: put all the ingredients in a large, heavy non-stick saucepan with 45 ml (3 tbsp) water. Heat very gently until the sugar dissolves, then bring to the boil and continue boiling until the temperature reaches 110°C (225°F). Stir frequently to prevent the mixture from sticking. Remove from the heat and leave to cool for about 20 minutes or until just thick enough to coat the cake.

/ 6 / Split the cake horizontally in half, then sandwich together again with some of the icing. Place on a wire rack standing on a baking sheet and pour over the remaining icing.

/ 7 / Let it trickle down the sides and, using a palette knife, spread it over the cake to give a smooth top and sides. Leave to set in a cool place, not the refrigerator.

GENOESE APPLE CAKE

◨ M A K E S   8 - 1 0   S L I C E S

| 30 ml (2 tbsp) dried breadcrumbs |
| 75 g (3 oz) butter |
| 3 eggs |
| 100 g (4 oz) caster sugar |
| 100 g (4 oz) self-raising flour |
| finely grated rind of 1 lemon |
| 450 g (1 lb) Golden Delicious apples, peeled, cored and thinly sliced |
| icing sugar |

/ 1 / Grease a 20.5 cm (8 inch) round cake dish and sprinkle with the breadcrumbs to coat the base and sides of the dish. Sprinkle any excess in the base.

/ 2 / Cut the butter into small pieces, put in a small bowl and microwave on HIGH for 1½ minutes or until just melted. Leave to cool slightly while making the cake.

/ 3 / Put the eggs and sugar in a large bowl and whisk, using an electric whisk, until pale and very thick. The mixture should be thick enough to leave a trail on the surface when the whisk is lifted.

/ 4 / Sift the flour over the surface of the whisked mixture, then carefully fold in, using a large metal spoon. Slowly trickle the melted butter into the mixture and carefully fold in. Finally, fold in the lemon rind and then the thinly sliced apples.

/ 5 / Pour the mixture into the prepared dish and level the surface. Stand the dish on the wire rack and cook on combination at 180°C/ MEDIUM LOW for 10-15 minutes or until risen and golden brown.

/ 6 / Leave to stand for 5 minutes, then turn out and leave to cool on a wire rack. Dredge the cake with icing sugar before serving.

GENOESE APPLE CAKE

Grease a 20.5 cm (8 inch) round cake dish and sprinkle with the breadcrumbs to coat the base and sides of the dish.

This recipe for a Genoese sponge, packed with sweet apples, is made in the classic way by whisking together eggs and sugar until thick and mousse-like, then folding in sifted flour and finally trickling in melted butter. This method of cake making gives a light, airy result. If the cake is slightly undercooked on the bottom once turned out, simply place it on a plate and microwave on HIGH for 2 minutes. Serve plain with coffee or afternoon tea, or with cream as a dessert.

Genoese Apple Cake

Sticky Ginger Cake

STICKY GINGER CAKE

C MAKES 8-10 SLICES

275 g (10 oz) plain flour
7.5 ml (1½ tsp) bicarbonate of soda
2.5 ml (½ tsp) salt
10 ml (2 tsp) ground cinnamon
10 ml (2 tsp) ground ginger
125 g (4 oz) butter or margarine
125 g (4 oz) caster sugar
1 egg
100 g (4 oz) golden syrup
100 g (4 oz) black treacle

/ 1 / Grease a 2.3 litre (4 pint) rectangular dish and line the base with greaseproof paper. Sift together the flour, bicarbonate of soda, salt, cinnamon and ginger into a bowl.

/ 2 / Place the butter or margarine and sugar in a bowl and cream together until pale and fluffy. Beat in the egg, followed by the sifted flour mixture, until well combined.

/ 3 / Put the syrup, treacle and 225 ml (8 fl oz) water in a saucepan and bring to the boil. Pour into the cake mixture, beating all the time to make a smooth batter.

/ 4 / Pour the batter into the prepared dish, stand on the wire rack and cook on combination at 180°C/MEDIUM LOW for 12-15 minutes or until firm to the touch and a skewer inserted in the centre comes out clean.

/ 5 / Leave the cake to stand for 5 minutes, then turn out on to a wire rack, remove the lining paper and leave to cool. When the cake is cold, wrap in greaseproof paper and foil and store for 2-3 days to allow the flavour to mature before cutting.

CHOCOLATE HAZELNUT BROWNIES

C MAKES 16

75 g (3 oz) hazelnuts
125 g (4 oz) plain chocolate
125 g (4 oz) butter or margarine
75 g (3 oz) self-raising flour
225 g (8 oz) dark soft brown sugar
3 eggs
2.5 ml (½ tsp) vanilla essence

/ 1 / Grease a 16×22 cm (6½×8½ inch) deep rectangular dish and line the base with greaseproof paper.

/ 2 / Put the hazelnuts in a large ovenproof dish and cook on convection at 250°C for about 10 minutes or until lightly browned. Tip the nuts out on to a clean tea-towel and use the tea-towel to rub the loose skins off the hazelnuts. Roughly chop the nuts.

/ 3 / Break the chocolate into small pieces and put in a small bowl with the butter or margarine. Microwave on MEDIUM LOW for 4 minutes or until melted, stirring occasionally.

/ 4 / Meanwhile, put the hazelnuts, flour, sugar, eggs and vanilla essence in a large bowl. Add the melted chocolate mixture and beat thoroughly together. Pour into the prepared dish, stand on the wire rack and cook on combination at 200°C/MEDIUM LOW for 9-12 minutes or until risen and just firm to the touch. Leave to cool in the dish.

/ 5 / Turn out on to a wire rack, remove the lining paper and leave the brownies to cool. Cut into 16 pieces.

CHOCOLATE HAZELNUT BROWNIES
Chocolate brownies should be rich, gooey and very chocolaty. To achieve the right texture, it is necessary to add lots of sugar to a brownie mixture. As foods with a high sugar content burn easily when cooked in the microwave, it is important to remove any large lumps of sugar before cooking, so beat the mixture thoroughly, or sieve the sugar first.

STICKY GINGER CAKE
This cake really lives up to its name – if you don't like sticky fingers, eat it with a fork!

PEANUT BUTTER BISCUITS

MAKES 16

60 ml (4 tbsp) crunchy peanut butter
75 g (3 oz) dark soft brown sugar
50 g (2 oz) butter or margarine
1 egg, size 2
100 g (4 oz) self-raising wholemeal flour

/ 1 / Cream the peanut butter, sugar and butter or margarine together until they are very soft and fluffy. Beat in the egg and then stir in the flour to make a firm dough.

/ 2 / Roll the dough into 16 walnut-sized smooth balls. Place them on large, flat, greased ovenproof plates, about 4 to a plate, spacing them well apart in a circle.

/ 3 / Press criss-cross lines on each ball of dough with a fork to flatten slightly.

/ 4 / Microwave on HIGH for 2 minutes, a plate at a time. Allow the biscuits to cool slightly on the plates, then remove them to a rack to cool completely.

OATY APRICOT SLICES

C   MAKES 12 SLICES

350 g (12 oz) no-soak dried apricots
175 g (6 oz) butter or margarine, cut into small pieces
225 g (8 oz) plain wholemeal flour
100 g (4 oz) porridge oats
75 g (3 oz) light soft brown sugar

/ 1 / Grease a shallow 23 cm (9 inch) round dish and line the base with greaseproof paper.

/ 2 / Put the apricots in a bowl with 225 ml (8 fl oz) water, cover and microwave on HIGH for 5-7 minutes or until the apricots are softened, stirring occasionally. Cool slightly, then transfer to a blender or food processor and purée until smooth.

/ 3 / Put the butter or margarine in a bowl and microwave on HIGH for 1-2 minutes or until melted. Mix in the flour, porridge oats and sugar and stir until coated.

/ 4 / Spoon half of the oat mixture into the pre-pared dish and press down evenly over the base. Spread the apricot purée evenly over the oat mixture, and sprinkle the remaining oat mixture on top. Press down gently.

/ 5 / Stand the dish on the wire rack and cook on combination at 200°C/MEDIUM LOW for 15-20 minutes or until the mixture feels just firm. Leave to cool in the dish, then mark into wedge-shaped portions.

JUMBLES

MAKES 20

150 g (5 oz) butter or margarine
150 g (5 oz) caster sugar
1 egg, size 2, beaten
275 g (10 oz) self-raising flour
5 ml (1 tsp) grated lemon rind
50 g (2 oz) ground almonds
20 whole almonds

/ 1 / Put the butter or margarine into an oven-proof glass bowl and microwave on LOW for about 1 minute to soften it slightly, add the sugar and beat well until the butter becomes soft and fluffy.

/ 2 / Beat half of the egg into the creamed mix-ture, then mix in the flour, lemon rind, ground almonds and the rest of the egg.

/ 3 / Form the mixture into 20 walnut-sized balls and place them on large, greased, flat ovenproof plates, about 4 to a plate, spacing them well apart in a circle. Press out with a fork to a thickness of about 0.5 cm (¼ inch). Place an almond on top of each biscuit.

/ 4 / Microwave on HIGH, a plate at a time, for about 2 minutes until the jumbles are cooked and a wooden cocktail stick or skewer inserted into the centre comes out clean.

/ 5 / Leave to stand for 1 minute, then transfer to a rack to cool.

PEANUT BUTTER BISCUITS
Crunchy peanut butter gives these biscuits a good texture, but the smooth variety can be used – the flavour will not be affected.

JUMBLES
These biscuits are very pale in colour – as they would be if made conventionally.

OATY APRICOT SLICES
A favourite wholefood treat, these slices are to be found in every vegetarian takeaway. Use dried dates, figs, apples, peaches or pears in place of the apricots and add a few chopped nuts to the oat mixture once you tire of the basic recipe.

Picture opposite:
Oaty Apricot Slices

210

COOK

3:00

POWER
LEVEL   TIME   CLOCK

1   2   3

4   5   6

MENU SUGGESTIONS

TRADITIONAL SUNDAY LUNCH

Roast Beef with Yorkshire
Puddings
(see page 58)

Roast Potatoes

Vegetables

Gingered Apple Pie and
Cream
(see page 187)

No more than 3 hours before serving, make up the Gingered Apple Pie to the end of step 4.

About 1 hour before serving, peel about 1.1 kg (2½ lb) potatoes and cut into chunks. Place in a shallow dish with 25 g (1 oz) lard, stand on the wire rack and cook on combination 250°C/HIGH for 10-15 minutes or until the potatoes are soft and beginning to brown; stir once.

Meanwhile, prepare the beef as instructed, weigh and calculate the cooking time. Push the potatoes to one side of the dish and add the beef. Cook on combination at 200°C/MEDIUM LOW for the calculated time. Halfway through cooking, drain off any excess fat and stir the potatoes. When cooked, transfer to a hot serving dish and keep warm.

Meanwhile, make the Yorkshire Pudding batter. Pour into the prepared dishes and stand on the wire rack and cook on combination at 250°C/MEDIUM LOW for 10-15 minutes until risen and golden.

Cook the vegetables conventionally.

Meanwhile, make the gravy; transfer the beef cooking juices to a saucepan with 300 ml (½ pint) beef stock; season to taste. Boil and simmer gently until ready to serve.

Serve the meat with the potatoes, Yorkshire Puddings, gravy and vegetables.

Meanwhile, stand the Gingered Apple Pie on the wire rack and cook on combination at 200°C/MEDIUM LOW for 18-22 minutes until golden. Stand until ready to serve.

VEGETARIAN LUNCH FOR FOUR

Mushroom and Spinach Pâté
(see page 21)

Wholemeal Toast

Cheese Potato Pie
(see page 155)

Salad

Fresh Date Clafouti
(see page 183)

Make the pâté at least 1 hour before serving. Make the Cheese Potato Pie to the end of step 4 and set aside.

Make the Clafouti to the end of step 1. Then about 10 minutes before serving the meal, put the fat in the dish, stand on the rack and cook on convection at 250°C for 10 minutes.

Meanwhile, toast some wholemeal bread to go with the pâté. Add the dates to the fat and pour over the batter. Place the dish under the

rack (or on the lowest rack or shelf) and stand the Cheese Potato Pie on a plate on the wire rack. Cook on combination at 200°C/MEDIUM LOW for 18-23 minutes or until the pie is hot.

Meanwhile, serve the pâté and toast.

Serve the Cheese Potato Pie with a mixed salad. Meanwhile, continue to cook the clafouti on the wire rack on convection at 250°C for 5-7 minutes until lightly browned, leave in oven to keep warm until ready to serve.

SUMMER DINNER PARTY FOR FOUR

Potted Shrimps
(see page 37)

Sesame Drumsticks
(see page 78)

Mixed Salad

Tomatoes with Pine Nut and
Basil Dressing
(see page 132)

Almond-Stuffed Peaches
(see page 179)

Make the Potted Shrimps and chill in the refrigerator until ready to serve.

Prepared the Almond-Stuffed Peaches to the end of step 5, cover and set aside. Prepare the Tomatoes with Pine Nut and Basil Dressing, to the end of step 2. Add the tomatoes.

Prepare the Sesame Drumsticks from Step 2 and set aside. Preheat the oven for 10 minutes on convection at 250°C. Place the drumsticks on the wire rack and cook on combination at 200°C/MEDIUM LOW for 15-18 minutes.

Meanwhile, serve the potted shrimps straight from the pots with brown bread and

lemon wedges.

Two minutes before the end of cooking, place the salad beneath the wire rack (or on the lowest rack or shelf) and continue cooking until the tomatoes are just warm and the drumsticks are golden and the juices run clear when pierced with a knife. Remove from the oven.

Cover the prepared peaches and microwave on HIGH for 3-5 minutes or until tender. Leave to stand, whilst serving the drumsticks and the salad and tomatoes.

Serve the peaches warm with the juices spooned over, and decorated with mint.

CHINESE-STYLE BANQUET

Barbecued Spare Ribs
(see page 47)

Sweet and Sour Duck Breasts
with Peppers,
make double quantity
(see page 83)

Okra with Coconut
(see page 128)

Egg Noodles

If possible, prepare the duck the previous day and marinate overnight or for 3 hours.

The following day, prepare the Barbecued Spare Ribs to the end of step 3. Cook on the wire rack for 35-45 minutes until the ribs are crisp and the sauce is thick and sticky.

About 20 minutes before the end of their cooking time, place the drained duck breasts on an ovenproof plate and cook underneath the wire rack (or on the lowest rack or shelf) for 18-20 minutes or until the duck is cooked but still pink in the middle. Meanwhile, cut the pepper into very thin strips and put in a bowl with 30 ml (2 tbsp) water. Then prepare the Okra with Coconut, remove the duck and ribs from the oven and cook the okra.

Keep the duck and okra warm and serve the spare ribs, garnished with spring onions.

Cook the noodles conventionally. Microwave the peppers on HIGH for 5-6 minutes or until tender. Microwave the marinade on HIGH for 3-4 minutes or until boiling. Drain the peppers and slice the duck, spoon over the marinade. Serve with the okra and noodles.

SUMMER LUNCH FOR FOUR

Trout Pâté
(see page 19)

Lamb Cutlets en Croûte
(see page 64)

Carrot and Courgette
Timbales
(see page 137)

Baked Egg Custards with
Passion Fruit
(see page 175)

At least 1 hour before serving, making the Trout Pâté as instructed and chill until required.

Prepare the Lamb Cutlets en Croûte to the end of step 4 and chill.

Meanwhile, prepare the Carrot and Courgettes Timbales to the end of step 3. Preheat the oven on convection at 250°C for 10 minutes whilst serving the pâté.

Place the timbales underneath the rack (or on the lowest rack or shelf) and stand the lamb cutlets on the rack (or highest rack or shelf). Cook on combination at 200°C/MEDIUM LOW for 12-15 minutes or until the pastry is golden brown. Serve with the timbales.

Make the Baked Egg Custards with Passion Fruit when ready to serve the dessert.

SLIMMER'S SUPPER

Turkish Aubergines with
Tomatoes
(see page 22)

Lime and Hake Kebabs with
Tabouleh
(see page 113)

Cucumber with Onion and
Tarragon
(see page 143)

Blackcurrant Jelly with Fresh
Fruit
(see page 183)

At least 4 hours before serving, prepare the blackcurrant jelly to the end of step 3.

Prepare the Turkish aubergines and chill for at least 2 hours. Prepare the Cucumber with Onion and Tarragon to the end of step 1 and leave for 20 minutes, as instructed, then drain.

Meanwhile, prepare the Lime and Hake Kebabs with Tabouleh to the end of step 3.

Continue with the cucumber from step 2 and keep warm. Serve the Turkish Aubergines with Tomatoes.

Complete the lime and hake kebabs from step 4. Serve the kebabs and cucumber together.

Just before serving, turn out the jellies and decorate with fruit.

HEARTY WINTER LUNCH FOR SIX

Shepherd's Pie
(see page 59)

Cauliflower Cheese
(see page 94)

Blackberry and Apple Lattice
(see page 187)

Prepare the Blackberry and Apple Lattice up to step 5 and set aside. Make the Shepherd's Pie to step 5 and set aside. Make the Cauliflower Cheese to the end of step 2.

About 30 minutes before serving, preheat the oven on convection at 250°C for 10 minutes. Put the Shepherd's Pie underneath the rack (or on the lowest rack or shelf) and stand the Cauliflower Cheese on the rack (or the highest rack or shelf). Cook on convection at 250°C for 15-20 minutes or until potato and cheese are golden brown. Serve immediately.

Meanwhile, cook the Blackberry and Apple Lattice in the hot oven on combination at 200°C/MEDIUM LOW for 20-25 minutes or until golden brown. Serve warm with cream.

MIDDLE EASTERN MEAL FOR SIX

Feta Cheese and Spinach
Puffs
(see page 34)

Spiced Vegetables with
Couscous
(see page 151)

Hot Stuffed Dates,
make triple quantity
(see page 179)

Prepare the Feta Cheese and Spinach Puffs and
serve warm or cold. Meanwhile, prepare the
Spiced Vegetables with Couscous to the end of
step 4 and serve.

Meanwhile, prepare the Hot Stuffed Dates
to the end of step 2, microwaving for 6-8

minutes in step 1. After removing the vegetables from the oven, cover and microwave the
dates on HIGH for 2-3 minutes and leave to
stand until ready to serve. Just before serving,
complete the date recipe from step 4, microwaving on HIGH for 10-12 minutes.

MEDITERRANEAN MEAL

Pastina & Summer
Vegetable Soup
(see page 14)

Crusty Bread

Italian Lamb
(see page 67)

Courgettes à la Provençale
(see page 132)

New Potatoes

Fruit and Polenta Pudding
(see page 180)

At least 3 hours before serving, make the pudding and refrigerate. Prepare the soup to the
end of step 2 and set aside. Prepare the courgettes to the end of step 1. Add the courgettes,
tomatoes and herbs and season. Set aside.

Prepare the lamb to the end of step 3. About
40 minutes before the end of the calculated
cooking time, stir the mint and lettuce into the
soup, season with salt and pepper and place
underneath the wire rack (or on the lowest
rack or shelf). Cook for 1-2 minutes or until
piping hot and the lettuce is wilted.

About 20 minutes before the end of the calculated time, cook the new potatoes conventionally. Place the prepared courgettes underneath the lamb on the wire rack (or on the
lowest rack or shelf) and cook on combination
at 200°C/MEDIUM LOW or until the courgettes
are done. Drain the potatoes.

Transfer the lamb to a serving plate, cover
with foil and keep warm with the vegetables.
Meanwhile, complete step 5 to make the gravy
and then serve with the lamb.

WEEKEND BREAKFAST FOR FOUR

Dried Fruit Compote
(see page 176)

Scrambled Egg with Smoked
Salmon
(see page 37)

Bran Muffins
(see page 191)

If possible make the Dried Fruit Compote the
previous day and leave to chill overnight. If
this is not possible make at least 1 hour in
advance. Serve before the eggs and muffins.

About 15 minutes before serving, make the
muffins to step 3. Leave to stand whilst you
make the eggs. Complete step 1, then microwave on HIGH for 1-2 minutes or until the mix-

ture just begins to set around the edge of the
bowl. Whisk vigorously to incorporate the egg
mixture. Add the smoked salmon and microwave on HIGH for 2-3 minutes, whisking every
30 seconds, taking care not to break up the salmon, until the eggs are just set but still very
soft. Check seasoning, then serve with the
muffins, split and spread with butter.

VEGETARIAN DINNER FOR FOUR

Parmesan Mushrooms with
Garlic Sauce,
make double quantity
(see page 21)

Spinach and Ricotta Filo Pie
(see page 00)

Mixed Salad

Apple and Pear Meringue
(see page 171)

Make up the Spinach and Ricotta Filo Pie to
the end of step 5. Make the Parmesan Mushrooms to the end of step 3 and set aside to chill.

Prepare the Apple and Pear Meringue to the
end of step 2; do not make the meringue.

Preheat the oven on convection at 250°C
for 10 minutes. Stand the dish of mushrooms
on the wire rack and cook on combination at
200°C/MEDIUM LOW for 5 minutes. Drizzle with
the oil and cook for a further 6-8 minutes or
until lightly browned. Serve as in step 4.

Meanwhile, cut the remaining filo sheet
into 2.5 cm (1 inch) strips, scatter on top of the
Spinach Pie and brush with any remaining butter or margarine; sprinkle with the sesame
seeds. Remove the mushrooms from the oven
and immediately place the pie on the wire rack
and cook on combination 200°C/MEDIUM LOW
for 10 minutes or until lightly browned. Serve
warm with a mixed salad.

About 15 minutes before serving the dessert,
complete from step 3 and cook as instructed.

INDEX